Professional Chef

LEVEL 1

Neil Rippington

DELMAR
CENGAGE Learning™

Australia ... Spain • United Kingdom • United States

Professional Chef Level 1 Diploma, 2nd Edition
Neil Rippington

Publishing Director: Linden Harris
Commissioning Editor: Lucy Mills
Development Editor: Carol Usher
Editorial Assistant: Claire Napoli
Project Editor: Alison Cooke
Production Controller: Eyvett Davis
Marketing Manager: Lauren Redwood
Typesetter: MPS Limited, a Macmillan Company
Cover design: HCT Creative
Text design: Design Deluxe, Bath

This work is adapted from *Professional Chef Level 1 Diploma* by *Neil Rippington* published by Delmar a division of Cengage Learning, Inc. © 2008.

British Library Cataloguing-in-Publication Data
A catalogue record for this book is available from the British Library.

ISBN: 978-1-4080-3908-3

Cengage Learning EMEA

Cheriton House, North Way, Andover, Hampshire, SP10 5BE

United Kingdom

Cengage Learning products are represented in Canada by Nelson Education, Ltd.

For your lifelong learning solutions, visit **www.cengage.co.uk**

Purchase your next print book, e-book or e-chapter at **www.cengagebrain.com**

Printed in Malta by Melita Press
1 2 3 4 5 6 7 8 9 10 – 13 12 11

Contents

About the author

Neil Rippington grew up in Bournemouth and got a taste for the catering industry at an early age by working in hotels while at school and college. Following a chefs' programme at The Bournemouth and Poole College, Neil went on to work in a Michelin starred restaurant in France and in London's Capital Hotel in Knightsbridge. Neil then went to work in the USA for two years before returning to the UK as a head chef in a country house hotel in the New Forest.

In 1994, Neil was presented with the opportunity to return to education as a chef lecturer at South East Essex College. After five years, he moved on to Redbridge College as a Programme Manager for Hospitality and Catering, later taking up the post as Quality Manager for the College.

In 2003, Neil joined Colchester Institute as Head of Centre for Hospitality and Food Studies where the Centre was awarded Grade 1 for outstanding provision, the first in the history of the college. In August 2010, Neil took the position as Dean of the College of Food at University College Birmingham.

Neil's purpose for writing the book was because he believes that learners entering Colleges or the industry need a foundation of skills and knowledge before they can progress to more technical work. With proficient knife skills and the ability to apply the fundamental cookery processes across a range of foods, learners will have the foundations to build a successful career in the industry.

Neil is married to Amanda and they have three children, Joseph, Luke and Freya. Neil is a keen sportsman and, although it is four years since the publication of the 1st edition of Professional Chef, Level 1 Diploma, he is still managing to play football for his club on Saturdays.

Acknowledgements

The Author would like to thank the following:

Nathan Allan for the excellent photography.

Tony Wright for his help in producing the videos for the online resource.

Phil Dobson for his assistance preparing the food throughout the photo shoot. Thanks also to chef lecturers Lewis Walker and Alan Oliver for donating time to help and also to graduating Level 3 student, Daniel Jeavons, for giving up his day off to join us.

Amanda, my wife, for putting up with me, following me wherever I go, and providing constant support.

Andreas Antona for writing the inspirational foreword and the chefs from the various colleges for providing examples of their regional specialities.

Steve Thorpe of City College, Norwich, Shyam Patiar of Coleg Llandrillo and Raj Mandal of Bedford College for their detailed reviews of the manuscript.

Professor Ray Linforth, Principal of University College Birmingham, for the use of the kitchens at University College Birmingham for the photo shoot and videos.

The Publisher wishes to thank the following:

For granting permission to use images: istockphoto; Shutterstock; Dreamstime Photos; Russums; Nisbetts.

Nathan Allan and Laura Pinnell of Nathan Allan Photography for providing commissioned photography.

Web address: **www.nathanallanphotography.com**

Video content provided by Ken Franklin and Video 4 Ltd.

Web address: **www.video4.co.uk**

Photo research and video/photo project management was provided by Jason Newman, Annalisa de Hassek, Bradley Hearn and Alexander Goldberg of Media Selectors Ltd. Web address: **www.mediaselectors.com**

For endorsing the book:

Craft Guild of Chefs
Web address: **www.craftguildofchefs.org**
The Master Chefs of Great Britain
Web address: **www.masterchefs.co.uk**
Email: masterchefs@msn.com
British Culinary Federation
Web address: **www.britishculinaryfederation.co.uk**
Email: secretary@britishculinaryfederation.co.uk

This book is endorsed by:

BRITISH CULINARY FEDERATION
National Member of the World Association of Chefs' Societies

British Culinary Federation

Craft Guild of Chefs

The Master Chefs of Great Britain

For providing the Nutritional Information for the Recipes:

KitMan

Olympus Associates specialises in providing consultancy and management services to the catering industry. With a unique kitchen management system called The KitMan System the company is able to assist operations in controlling food costs and managing their food service operations more effectively.

The KitMan System is a food cost control and kitchen management system used by many leading catering establishments throughout the UK in hospitality, healthcare and education markets.

The company has a specialist version for the education sector, and has working partnerships with many catering colleges and universities throughout the United Kingdom and Ireland using the program, including the authors of this book, not only for controlling their own food costs, but also as a teaching tool for the catering and hospitality students.

KitMan provides valuable detailed analysis of costs per class, per student and is ideal for use for the commercial activities of a college including refectory and restaurant services.

We are pleased to be associated with Cengage Learning and to continue our relationships with the Hospitality & Catering departments of colleges.

For more information please visit **www.kitman.com**

Notes on Nutritional Information and recipe processing

Please note the Nutritional Information is for guidance only and may not necessarily match the final result. The sample ingredients are based on average contents. The Nutritional Information is calculated **per portion**.

The final nutritional content can be effected by any of the following factors: seasonality; storage method; storage time; brand, breed, variety; cooking method; cooking time; regeneration method. Wastage and yield may also result in the final nutritional content being lower than the results shown.

Where two alternative ingredients have been listed, the first has been used wherever possible.

If an ingredient is listed as optional it has been included if it appears in the main ingredient listing, where possible, but has not if it appears in the method or Chef's Tips part of the original recipe.

Foreword

My journey started in 1974 by attending Ealing Technical College where I achieved a qualification in the City & Guilds Professional Cookery Examination.

One of the first books I used was similar to the one you are learning from today. The basics have never changed and it is so important for young people coming into this industry to understand the basics.

Even today, I still pick up my old cookery book and check upon recipes. I hope this book will be a guiding light in your future career as a chef by teaching you the fundamentals.

I have found this book to be invaluable for tomorrow's chef as it is well illustrated, informative and has some great recipes and photos to help you in your studies. Future chefs are introduced to all the skills and primary cooking processes and many other essential tips and secrets.

The beauty of this book is that it gives you a sound knowledge of good practices, an understanding of how professional kitchens operate and informs you of your responsibilities to be compliant in law.

Since my days at Ealing I have gone on to achieve many notable highlights. I am the proud owner of my own Michelin starred restaurant and my Beef concept restaurant, a fellow of the Academy of Culinary Arts and Master Chefs of Great Britain, a long standing member of the governing body of the University College Birmingham and Vice President of the British Culinary Federation. This would never have happened without the sound knowledge of the basics.

I wish you a happy, long and successful career and hope you fulfil your dreams and aspirations as much as I have.

Andreas Antona

Quick reference guide to the Diploma units

The following 12 units make up the Diploma in Introduction to Professional Cookery:

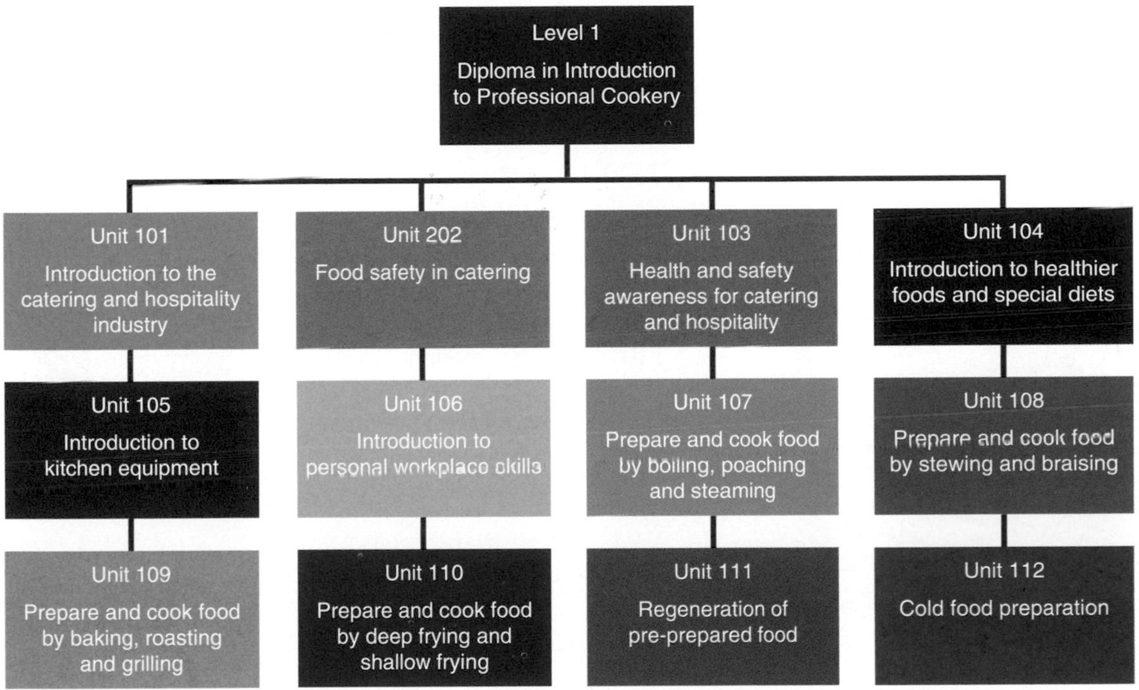

The textbook chapters are structured in a standard format and comprise of the following:

Unit reference and title – e.g. Chapter 8; Unit 108 - Prepare and cook food by stewing and braising

Learning Objectives – explaining what you will be able to do at the end of each chapter

Chef's Tips – providing snippets of key information relevant to the subject

Tasks – small research activities and tasks to widen your subject knowledge

Health & Safety tips – to highlight key points regarding safe practices

Signposted Video Clips – for online video demonstrations relevant to the subject

Step-by-step sequences – to demonstrate key processes and skills

Test Yourself sections – to review your learning at the end of each chapter

Web-links – providing interesting links to further information and resources

Recipes – from each of the cookery process featured throughout the book

About the book

The philosophy behind the Diplomas in Professional Cookery, particularly at Level 1, is that a chef needs to have a sound foundation of high quality skills and to be able to apply these skills across a range of processes and commodities.

The qualification has been designed for delivery in a college environment or similar. It intends to provide learners with a broad range of skills and knowledge and to prepare them to meet the needs of industry.

The Diplomas in Professional Cookery are the qualifications of choice for college-based delivery and are supported by People 1st, the sector skills council for Hospitality and Catering, and also by the National Skills Academy for Hospitality.

All candidates enrolled on a Diploma in Professional Cookery will follow a specific programme, completing a range of theoretical and practical tasks and activities. Individuals will receive a final grade for each of the different components of work to highlight areas of high achievement.

In 2010, the suite of Diplomas in Professional Cookery was placed on the Qualifications and Credit Framework at which time the units were revised to update them to meet the needs of today's industry requirements. This book reflects the revisions to the curriculum and, together with the online resources, provides an invaluable resource for candidates following this qualification.

Recipes

Apple tart 143
Bread rolls 144
Caramel creams 145
Plain scones 146
Roast chicken with bread sauce and roast gravy 147
Salmon and courgette kebab with tomato vinaigrette 148
Yorkshire pudding 148
Roasting beef 149
Sardines with tomato sauce 149
Ricotta and spinach cannelloni with tomato and basil sauce 150
Baked cod with a cheese and herb crust 150
Cottage pie 151
Roast loin of pork and apple sauce 151
Roast potatoes 152
Apple and blackberry crumble 152

RECIPE ONLINE:

LEARNER SUPPORT Gary Rhodes' bread and butter pudding

9 Baking, roasting and grilling

Unit 109 Baking, roasting and grilling

Mapped to the qualification each chapter addresses a specific unit of the Level 1 Diploma in Professional Cookery

VIDEO CLIP Roasting a chicken.

Video Clips If your college adopts Coursemate Professional Chef Level 1 you will be able to view video demonstrations of key processes online

TASK Think of the potential causes of fire in the kitchen. How could each of these be prevented?

Task boxes provide additional tasks for you to try out

CHEF'S TIP Some items, such as sweet steamed puddings, will rise during the steaming process. Do not fill the mould to the top, fill to about two-thirds of the way up the mould to allow space for the sponge to rise.

Chef's Tip boxes share author's experience in the catering industry, with helpful suggestions for how you can improve your skills

> **HEALTH & SAFETY** Food should never be thrown into hot oil or fat or dropped from a height.

Health & Safety tip boxes draw your attention to important health and safety information

Step-by-step: Chicken stir-fry

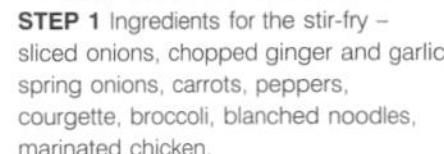

STEP 1 Ingredients for the stir-fry – sliced onions, chopped ginger and garlic, spring onions, carrots, peppers, courgette, broccoli, blanched noodles, marinated chicken.

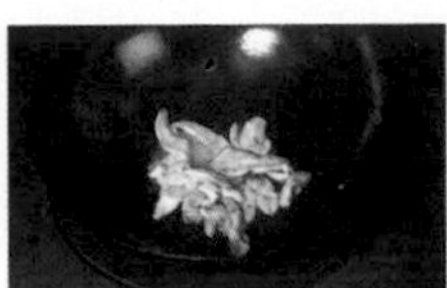

STEP 2 Heat oil in a wok or frying pan and stir-fry the chicken.

STEP 3 Add the onions, carrots, spring onion and the chopped garlic and ginger.

Step-by-step sequences illustrate each process and provide an easy-to-follow guide

LEARNING OBJECTIVES

On completion of this chapter you will be able to:

- Identify foods used in cold preparation.
- Identify the quality points when preparing cold foods.
- Describe a range of hors d'œuvres, salads and sandwiches.
- List the techniques used to present cold foods.
- List the general safety points to follow when preparing and presenting foods for cold presentation.

Learning Objectives at the start of each chapter explain key skills and knowledge you need to understand by the end of the chapter

TEST YOURSELF

1 What is the difference between a simple salad and a composite salad?

2 Why is it important to cut foods into regular shapes and sizes for cold presentation?

3 List four sauces that are regularly used with cold dishes.
i) ______
ii) ______
iii) ______
iv) ______

4 What size should a canapé be served and why?

5 Name four possible bases for a canapé.
i) ______
ii) ______
iii) ______
iv) ______

6 What factors would you take into consideration when producing an assortment of hors d'œuvres (hors d'œuvres variés).

7 Name four items that could be used as single hors d'œuvres.
i) ______
ii) ______
iii) ______
iv) ______

8 What is the purpose of seasoning and dressing cold food items?

9 Name four types of lettuce.
i) ______
ii) ______
iii) ______
iv) ______

10 What is the difference between shredding and chopping?

11 Why should you dress a salad just before it is served?

12 Name three pieces of equipment that could be used to serve an assortment of buffet items.
i) ______
ii) ______
iii) ______
iv) ______

13 Why is it important to have the correct proportions of mixed cold food items when binding them together?

Test Yourself questions are provided at the end of each chapter. You can you use questions to test your learning and prepare for assessments

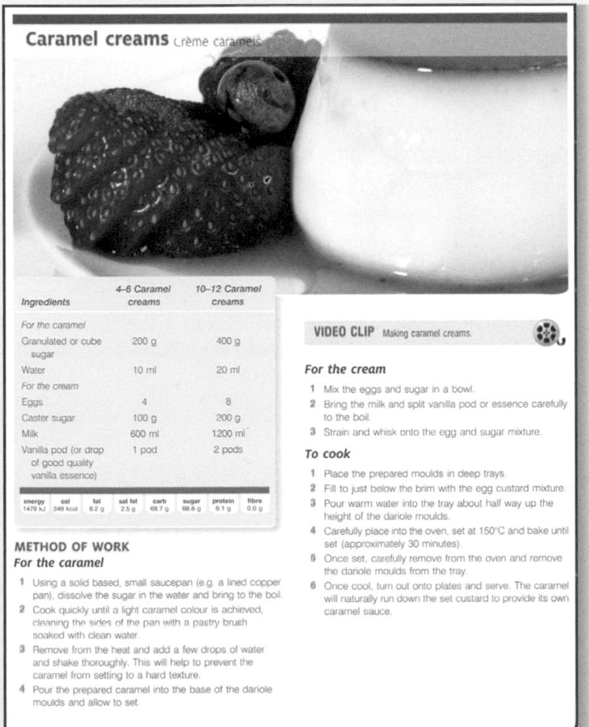

Caramel creams crème caramels

Ingredients	4–6 Caramel creams	10–12 Caramel creams
For the caramel		
Granulated or cube sugar	200 g	400 g
Water	10 ml	20 ml
For the cream		
Eggs	4	8
Caster sugar	100 g	200 g
Milk	600 ml	1200 ml
Vanilla pod (or drop of good quality vanilla essence)	1 pod	2 pods

energy	cal	fat	sat fat	carb	sugar	protein	fibre
1479 kJ	349 kcal	6.2 g	2.5 g	68.7 g	68.6 g	9.1 g	0.0 g

METHOD OF WORK

For the caramel

1 Using a solid based, small saucepan (e.g. a lined copper pan), dissolve the sugar in the water and bring to the boil.
2 Cook quickly until a light caramel colour is achieved, cleaning the sides of the pan with a pastry brush soaked with clean water.
3 Remove from the heat and add a few drops of water and shake thoroughly. This will help to prevent the caramel from setting to a hard texture.
4 Pour the prepared caramel into the base of the dariole moulds and allow to set.

VIDEO CLIP Making caramel creams.

For the cream

1 Mix the eggs and sugar in a bowl.
2 Bring the milk and split vanilla pod or essence carefully to the boil.
3 Strain and whisk onto the egg and sugar mixture.

To cook

1 Place the prepared moulds in deep trays.
2 Fill to just below the brim with the egg custard mixture.
3 Pour warm water into the tray about half way up the height of the dariole moulds.
4 Carefully place into the oven, set at 150°C and bake until set (approximately 30 minutes).
5 Once set, carefully remove from the oven and remove the dariole moulds from the tray.
6 Once cool, turn out onto plates and serve. The caramel will naturally run down the set custard to provide its own caramel sauce.

Recipes provide examples of the different cooking processes for you to try out.
Nutritional Information is provided for guidance and is calculated per portion.

Guest Chef

Chicken breast with ham and cheese sauce

Chef *Robert Strachan*
Centre *Eastleigh College, Hampshire*

A slightly different take on the classic 'chicken *cordon bleu*' dish found on many menus in the 1970s and 1980s. Juicy chicken together with succulent cured ham and a full-flavoured cheddar cheese sauce.

Ingredients	4 portions
Chicken breasts trimmed	4 and skin removed
Wiltshire ham	4 slices
Mornay sauce	500 ml (made with cheddar)
Fresh breadcrumbs	160 g
Seasoned flour	
Grated parmesan cheese	40 g
knob of butter	
Olive oil	

METHOD OF WORK

1 Heat oven to 180°C.
2 Lightly batten the chicken breasts and cut each into three even-sized pieces.
3 Cut the ham slices into three pieces.
4 Heat a frying pan with a little olive oil.
5 Pass the chicken through seasoned flour, dust off any excess.
6 Add a knob of butter to the pan and when frothing slowly place in the chicken breasts and lightly colour on both sides.
7 Remove from the pan.
8 Place one piece of chicken onto a clean non-stick tray and place a piece of ham on top. (a cutter or ring can be used to give a more precise shape) and spoon over some of the cheese sauce.
9 Repeat this process three times, finishing with a layer of cheese sauce and top with breadcrumbs and Parmesan.
10 Bake in oven for 10 minutes until piping hot.
11 Gently using a step palette knife or slice to place onto a hot serving plate.

Guest Chef Recipes provide examples of different cooking processes and dishes using local ingredients from around the British Isles college lecturers from different regions of the UK.

CourseMate

CourseMate is unique blended learning solution. Watch student comprehension soar as your class works with the printed textbook and the textbook-specific website. CourseMate includes: an interactive eBook; interactive teaching and learning tools including videos, games and quizzes and Engagement Tracker, a first-of-its-kind tool that monitors student engagement in the course.

Engaging, Trackable, Affordable

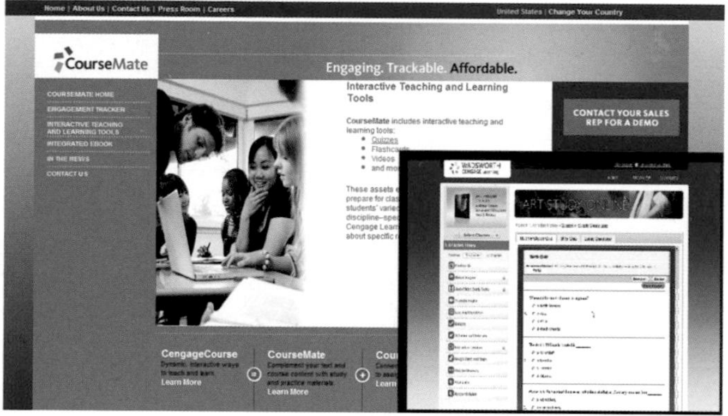

Professional Chef Level 1 CourseMate

Professional Chef Level 1 CourseMate brings course concepts to life with interactive learning and study tools that support the printed textbook. Professional Chef Level 1 CourseMate goes beyond the book to deliver what you need!

INTERACTIVE LEARNING TOOLS

The Professional Chef Level 1 CourseMate interactive learning tools include:

- Quizzes
- Games
- Videos demonstrations of recipes
- Flashcards
- Bonus recipes
- Interactive Food Map of the British Isles

PowerPoints, Lesson Plans, the Learner Engagement Tracker and other teaching resources are included in the Coursemate package for the instructor.

INTERACTIVE EBOOK

In addition to interactive learning tools, Professional Chef Level 1 CourseMate includes an interactive eBook. You can take notes, highlight, search and interact with embedded media specific to your book. Use it as a supplement to the printed text, or as a substitute – the choice is up to you with CourseMate.

To purchase access to CourseMate as a learner go to: www.cengagebrain.co.uk/shop/isbn/9781408048184

To purchase access to CourseMate as an instructor or institution please contact emea.fesales@cengage.com **for more information.**

1

Introduction to the catering and hospitality industry

Unit 101 Introduction to the catering and hospitality industry

LEARNING OBJECTIVES

At the end of this chapter you will be able to:

- **Define the terms 'hospitality' and 'catering'.**
- **Compare the sectors and different types of operations in the industry.**
- **Describe the main features of establishments within the different sectors.**
- **Identify staffing structures and job roles in different establishments.**
- **Identify training opportunities, related qualifications and employment rights and responsibilities.**
- **List some of the associations related to professional cookery.**

Hospitality and catering

The hospitality and catering, leisure, travel and tourism **sector** covers many industries, the following 14 are the main ones:

- hotels
- restaurants
- pubs
- bars and nightclubs
- contract food service providers
- hospitality services
- membership clubs
- events
- gambling
- travel services
- tourist services
- visitor attractions
- hostels
- holiday centres and self-catering **accommodation**.

Hospitality is the art of being hospitable. Hospitality is the professional service or offer of food, drink and/or accommodation. These aspects can be provided individually, for example when buying a coffee in a coffee shop or a drink in a pub, or collectively as you might experience if staying in a hotel.

Catering refers specifically to providing food. There are a huge variety of examples. For example, the food supplied at an outside event would usually be supplied by caterers. Obviously, drinks are also served to accompany food as part of the enjoyment of eating and socializing. A number of organizations, small and large, specialize in the provision of catering. This might be through fixed term contracts or individual events such as weddings and parties.

CHEF'S TIP The hospitality sector employs in the region of 1.9 million people across the UK. It is one of the largest employers in the UK and looks set to continue to grow despite a difficult time for the national **economy**.

Each hospitality operation is unique, but they all provide food and drink and/or accommodation. A large number of people are employed in core hospitality occupations, such as chefs, kitchen assistants, reception staff, food service and bar staff. The main industries employing the majority of these people are as follows:

- travel
- retail
- business
- education
- healthcare
- corporate and executive dining
- government and local authority provision
- leisure venues and events (concerts, sporting events, parties)
- restaurants
- hotels.

The dining area of a cruise ship

The different types of operations within the industry

The scope for employment in the hospitality and catering industry is huge with many career pathways available. As leisure time increases, so have the many venues people can visit. Some examples are theme parks, family friendly pubs, coffee shops, restaurants, major sporting events and hotels.

The industry is broken down into two main sectors according to the main purpose and aim of the business. They are the commercial sector and the catering services sector.

The commercial sector – In this case, the provision of hospitality and catering is the main purpose of the organization. It aims to make a profit in return for the supply of their products and services. Examples include restaurants and hotels.

The catering services sector – In this case, the provision of hospitality and catering is a secondary purpose of the organization. However, the organization may still aim to make a profit in return for the supply of their products and services. Examples include the catering supplied to employees working in a large bank or factory. In these examples, banking and production are the main purposes of the organizations and catering is supplied as a secondary feature. It is a 'service' to the staff employed in either of these organizations. Such functions were previously labelled as the public service sector, where catering in outlets such as hospitals, army barracks, prisons, schools, colleges and residential homes were provided through state managed services. However, few such facilities are now under the management of local councils or the state and are mostly provided by commercial contract companies.

CHEF'S TIP Some catering services may be subsidized by the company. A 'subsidy' is a payment by the company to keep the selling price at a low rate to individual employees.

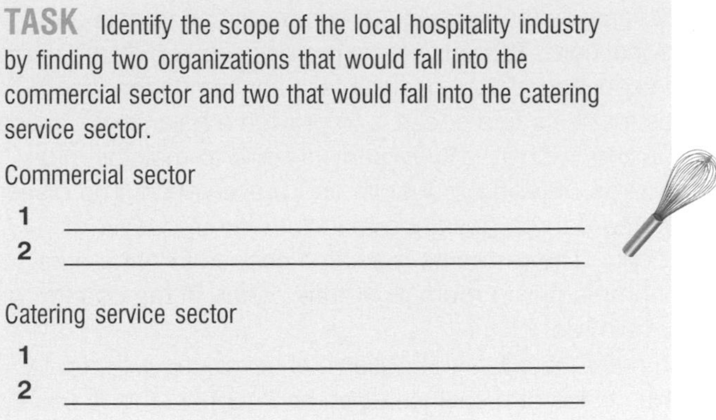

TASK Identify the scope of the local hospitality industry by finding two organizations that would fall into the commercial sector and two that would fall into the catering service sector.

Commercial sector

1 __________
2 __________

Catering service sector

1 __________
2 __________

The main features of establishments within the different sectors

Contract food service

Contract food service providers support a number of wider industries from hotels and restaurants to schools and airlines. Traditionally the sector has provided a food and drinks service, but it is developing products and services in other areas such as retail, facilities management, fine dining restaurants, vending, healthcare, school meals provision and prison catering.

CHEF'S TIP Hospital catering is sometimes classified as 'welfare catering'. The object is to assist the medical staff to get a patient back to health as soon as possible.

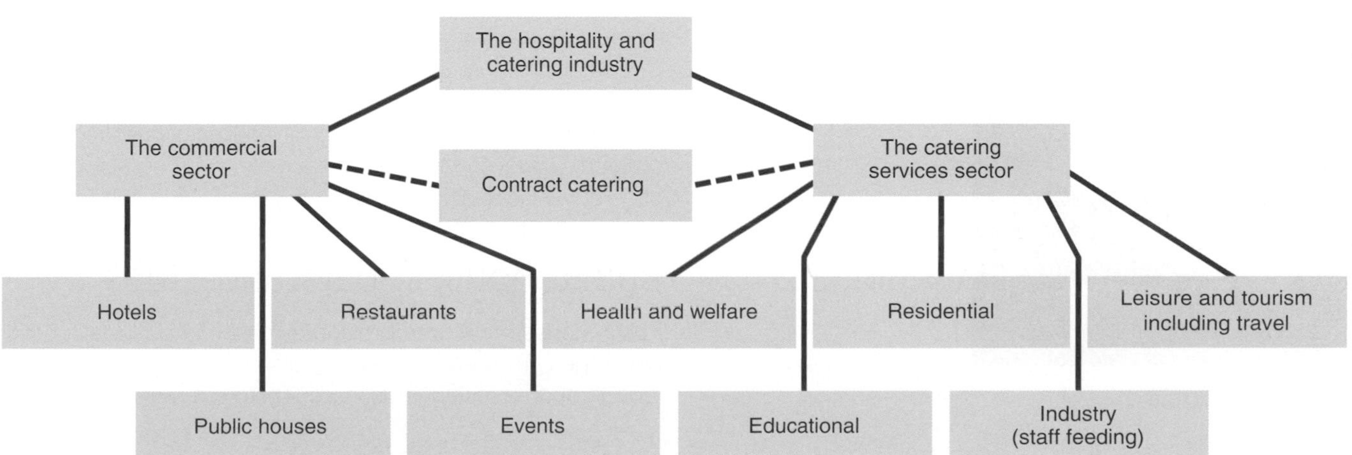

An overview of the sectors within the hospitality and catering industry

Healthcare and hospitals

Healthcare homes provide accommodation, meals and personal care. They also have professional registered nurses and experienced care assistants in constant attendance. The focus for chefs and cooks is to provide a balanced nutritious diet using fresh, quality ingredients and to maintain high standards of food production and presentation. The dishes prepared can be designed to include the requests of residents. The residents may also choose to eat a meal in the home's dining room or, if they prefer, in the comfort of their own room.

In many hospitals the patients are provided with a daily **menu** choice of breakfast, lunch and supper. This is usually ordered a day in advance. **Dieticians** are employed to liaise with the head chef or catering manager to help plan each menu. They design specialized diets for individual patients and help introduce diet conscious recipes and advice to patients.

Hospitals also cater for staff, visitors and guests. In addition, they might provide hospitality for meetings, seminars and conferences.

Hotels

It is estimated that there are over 12 000 individual hotels in the UK. With the addition of smaller hotels and guest houses the total is probably nearer 30 000. There are the following categories of hotels.

- budget hotels
- bed and breakfast accommodation (guest houses)
- one star
- two star
- three star
- four star
- five star (luxury).

Large hotel chains generally have the market share of business found across the world today. The food and drink service departments need chefs, kitchen assistants and service staff. Hotels also employ staff for the accommodation and leisure facilities. These areas are:

- reception
- housekeeping
- front office management
- porter service
- leisure management
- events and banquet management
- business services.

Because hotels are residential, they will usually provide breakfast, lunch, tea, dinner and snacks (sometimes for 24 hours a day). Banquets and functions also play an important role in the business.

Location, opening times, staffing, menu pricing, furnishings and facilities vary massively from one hotel to another. What a hotel provides depends on where it sits in terms of the market they are serving, i.e. the budget market, middle market or luxury market. However, hotels should strive to meet the needs and expectations of their guests, provide good value for money and a safe, comfortable and hygienic environment.

Dining area at the Ritz hotel

Restaurants

The restaurant sector is the largest area in the hospitality and catering industry. This has had a steady increase of turnover and it is estimated that there are over 65 000 restaurants in the UK.

Restaurants can be classified by their origin of **cuisine**, for example, European, North American, Asian, Oriental, Central and South American. The restaurant industry can be broken down into four different segments:

- fast food establishments
- cafes and coffee shops
- mainstream restaurants
- fine dining restaurants.

Restaurants are also focussed on different markets. For example, fine dining restaurants would not normally promote themselves to attract teenagers or families with young children. However, fast food restaurants, such as McDonalds, often advertise specifically with these markets in mind.

Public houses, bars and clubs

Public houses and bars provide alcoholic and non-alcoholic beverages. They are increasingly also providing snacks or food through a restaurant service. There are many similarities between a bar and a public house. The most obvious factor is the style and ambience. One way to segment the sector has been to look at ownership:

- **Managed houses** – Include those which are owned by a brewery who employ salaried staff to manage and work in the outlet.
- **Tenanted or leased pubs** – Are owned by a brewery but are occupied by licensees who pay rent to the brewery and are usually contracted to take their supply of beer and other alcoholic drinks directly from the brewery.
- **Freehouses** – Are owned and managed by the licensee with the choice to purchase from a number of different suppliers and brewers.

Nightclubs are establishments where the primary offer is dancing to music. Drink and sometimes, food are offered as a secondary service (or where there is a legal requirement to do so).

Bars can be found in other sectors, such as hotels and restaurants and other areas, such as sports grounds.

The opening hours for pubs, bars and clubs are more relaxed than it was in the past. **Licences** are now granted by individual application. Many factors are considered, such as late-night disturbance to local residents or the extra policing that might be required.

Tourist attractions

Food signs at a theme park

Popular tourist attractions attract high numbers of visitors and are vital to local economies.

- theme parks and gardens
- sporting locations (e.g. football stadia)
- museums
- other attractions – e.g. theatres and cinemas.

Usually the attraction provides some form of food and drink from vending facilities to restaurants, some of which may be sub-contracted to the catering services industry.

TASK Provide examples of menus in the following catering/hospitality operations:

- healthcare home
- guesthouse
- chain restaurant
- large city bank.

Explain the differences between them.

Employment within the industry

A high proportion of the industry's workforce is employed on a part-time basis. In this sector custom tends to be concentrated into a short number of hours (evenings and weekends), so the amount of staff needed in peak hours is considerably higher than at quieter times. A relatively high proportion of this workforce is described as casual employment, many of whom may be working in the industry while studying.

Staffing structures and job roles

Organizations, regardless of their size, will have a staffing structure. Members of staff perform different job roles that contribute to the overall aims of the organization. Organizations range from individuals working by themselves to very large companies with thousands of employees.

In smaller organizations, it is likely that individuals will have to perform a wide variety of roles. All operational (and management) requirements have to be completed by a few people. In larger organizations, job roles are likely to be more specific. Many people are working towards the aims of the organization and the breakdown of roles can be more detailed.

Staffing structures can be divided into three main categories. These are as follows:

Operational staff – Operational staff are the employees who perform the everyday practical operations. They are the staff who cook the food and serve the customers, clean the bedrooms and public areas and generally provide the services that customers expect from the organization.

Supervisory staff – Supervisory staff are generally more experienced than operational staff. They will oversee the work and performance of operational staff and deal with any day-to-day issues as they arise. Supervisory staff should also provide a first point of call for operational staff if they have a problem that they need help with.

Management staff – Managers have responsibility for ensuring that the organization is performing well, that suitably trained staff are employed and customers receive the products and services they expect. Managers have many other responsibilities including planning for the future, managing finance and ensuring health and safety policies and employment laws are followed.

CHEF'S TIP Depending on the size of the organization, managers often perform supervisory and operational roles. As organizations become larger then managers perform these operational tasks on a less frequent basis, or perhaps never at all.

Examples of staff in a medium to large kitchen operation would be:

Manager–Head chef (In larger organizations, sometimes referred to as the executive head chef).

Supervisor(s) – Sous chef (second chef); chef de partie (section chefs – have a supervisory function to monitor the work of the commis chefs within their section but also have an operational role to perform to cover the required tasks).

Operational – Commis chefs; apprentices.

TASK Other than the examples provided above, think of two additional roles that operational, supervisory and management staff perform as part of their job role.

Operational	Supervisory	Management

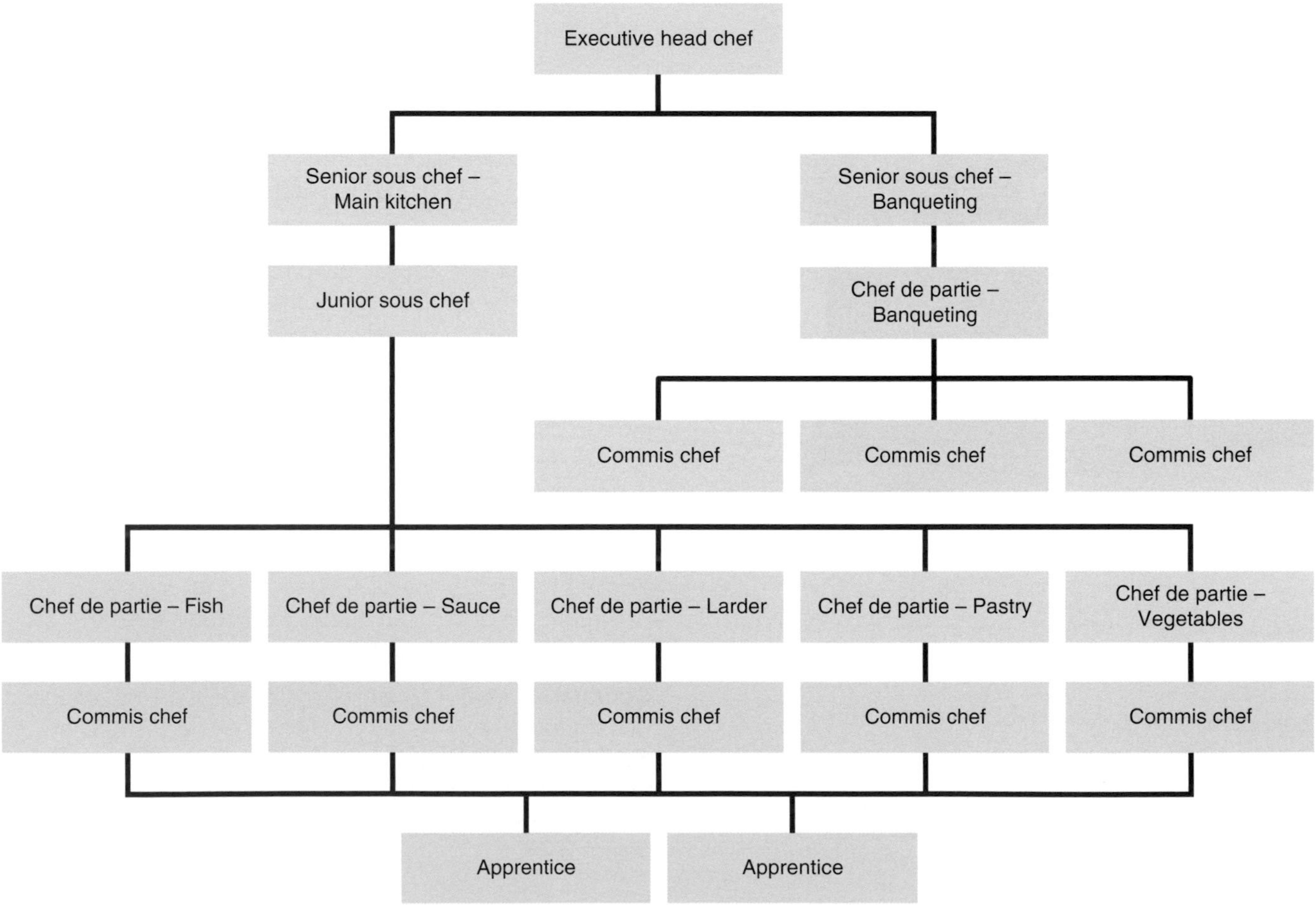

- Executive head chef
  - Senior sous chef – Main kitchen
    - Junior sous chef
      - Chef de partie – Fish
        - Commis chef
      - Chef de partie – Sauce
        - Commis chef
      - Chef de partie – Larder
        - Commis chef
      - Chef de partie – Pastry
        - Commis chef
      - Chef de partie – Vegetables
        - Commis chef
          - Apprentice
          - Apprentice
  - Senior sous chef – Banqueting
    - Chef de partie – Banqueting
      - Commis chef
      - Commis chef
      - Commis chef

Example of a possible kitchen structure for a city centre hotel

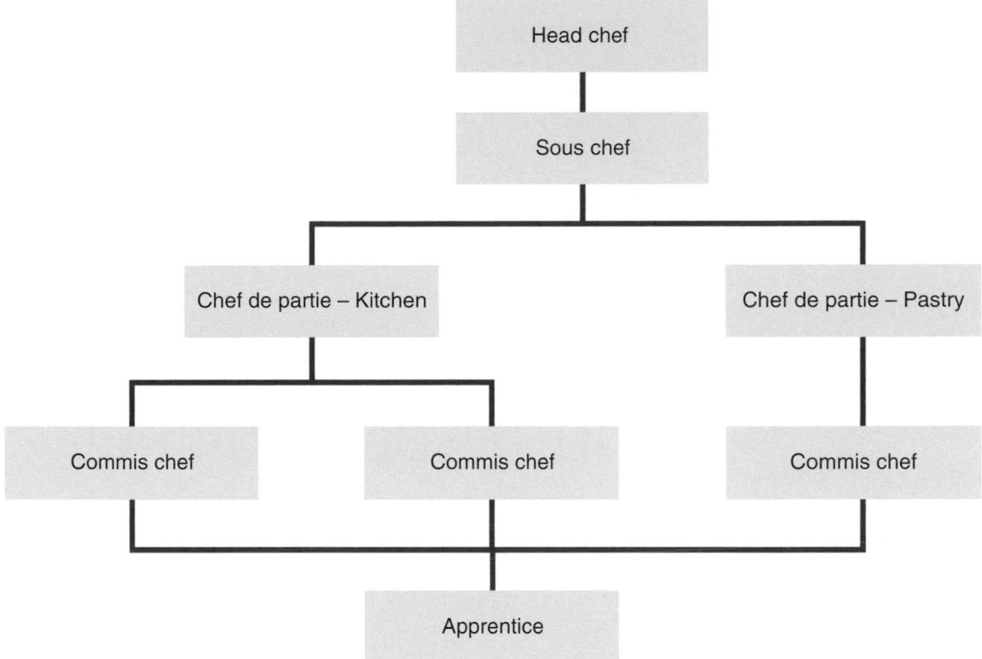

Example of a possible kitchen structure for a 50 cover restaurant

In a larger organisation (like that shown on the bottom of page 6) the executive head chef is the most senior ranking manager and may undertake more managerial type roles, such as purchasing, planning and budgeting. The senior sous chefs will also undertake management responsibilities and supervise the various kitchens. The junior sous chef will support the senior sous-chef but with less managerial responsibility and more hands-on supervision of the chef de parties. The chef de parties are responsible for their own sections and supervise the commis chefs beneath them. They have a supervisory role but undertake the majority of food preparation and cooking required to produce the menus planned by the executive head chef. Commis chefs have an operational role and will be fully engaged with the preparation and cooking of food, following the instructions and direction from the chefs above them. Apprentices are employees who are learning as they work. They are likely to work in all sections over time to gain the experience they require to complete their qualification.

In a smaller organisation (such as the one above) the structure is much smaller. Staff at the various levels will have to cover more tasks, although the output from tasks will also be much smaller than that in a large city centre hotel. The head chef, as the manager, will perform managerial tasks but is likely to work alongside the chefs in the kitchen much more than the executive chef in the previous example. The sous chef is likely to have first-line management of the brigade and will supervise and direct all the chefs under their supervision. At the chef de partie level, this is broken into two, one for savoury work, such as meat, fish, sauce and vegetable dishes and the other is for pastry work, which includes desserts, pastries and breads.

Training opportunities, related qualifications and employment rights and responsibilities

Working in the hospitality industry and particularly as a chef is a never-ending learning opportunity. There is always more to learn with constant **innovation** from very talented chefs from around the world. There are always new and different ways to work with new commodities and different approaches and techniques. This makes working in the industry, an interesting and rewarding experience.

As someone entering the industry, needing to gain experience, the training opportunities are vast and varied. The following describes some of the ways in which training is provided:

On the job – This refers to bite size, regular chunks, of training that is provided whilst at work. Occasionally, short courses (e.g. 1 or 2 days) may be provided to learn about specific aspects of the job – health and safety and food hygiene, for example.

College based – Most colleges in the UK offer courses and qualifications in hospitality and catering. Students can learn about the industry and develop skills in an educational environment. There are also opportunities to learn other subjects and improve skills, such as the use of language, number and IT.

Training providers – These organizations often work in conjunction with employers and perform the **assessment** of skills for apprentices in the workplace.

e-Learning – IT based resources enhance training. Modern materials are very interactive and have a personalized approach. The streaming of video-based material also makes it possible for learners to review material at their own pace.

Work placement – A placement provides a controlled period of time when there is a great opportunity to observe the way in which an organization operates and performs tasks.

Qualifications

There are many qualifications designed for people working or aspiring to work in the catering and hospitality industry. For trainee chefs, there are vocational (career based) qualifications that are designed to meet the current needs of the industry. The two main routes, although there are others, are the NVQ (National Vocational Qualification – designed to be delivered in the workplace, usually as part of an apprenticeship framework) and the Diplomas in Professional Cookery (usually delivered on a full-time basis in further education colleges).

There are many short courses that people working in the industry may take to increase their knowledge in specific areas. Examples include short courses in health and safety, food safety, communication and the certificate for personal licence holders.

Qualifications are also written at different levels to enable individuals to build on their existing skills and knowledge.

NVQs and Vocational Related Qualifications (VRQs) in Food Preparation and Cooking/Professional Cookery are written at Levels 1, 2 and 3. This intends to develop skills and knowledge from a broad and sound base to a refinement of skills, as candidates move from one level to the next.

There are also academic (more scholarly/less practical) qualifications written for the hospitality and catering industry. Such qualifications usually take a broader view of the industry from a more business perspective, focussing on the wider operations within hospitality organisations, e.g. food service, marketing, finance, front-office operations, accommodation. Qualifications and courses along this route range from Level 1 through to Foundation, Bachelors and Masters Degrees.

TASK Research the types of qualifications and experience you might need for the following job roles:

- head chef in a large city centre hotel
- commis chef in a Miichelin star restaurant
- station waiter aboard a cruise ship
- bar manager in a night club.

Employment rights and responsibilities

Employers and employees have certain rights and responsibilities.

Employers must supply a job description and contract of employment, detailing the following:

- contracted working hours, and
- holiday entitlement.

They must also provide a healthy and safe working environment and pay at least the minimum wage.

Employees must:

- Work to the conditions in their job description and contract of employment and follow organizational policies.
- They must also follow health and safety **working practices**, including food safety.

Visit the following website **www.hse.gov.uk/catering/** to find out more about health and safety in the hospitality and catering industry.

Some of the associations related to professional cookery

- The Academy of Culinary Arts
- The Association Culinaire Française

- The Craft Guild of Chefs
- Euro Toques
- PACE (Professional Association of Catering Education)
- The Institute of Hospitality
- People 1st – The Sector Skills Council for the Hospitality Industry
- The National Skills Academy for Hospitality.
- Springboard UK
- The Savoy Educational Trust

TASK These are just some of the associations that can help you in your career. Research these and other organizations that support sectors, such as pubs, bars and clubs. Create a table of organizations and their contact details that might help you in your future career.

TEST YOURSELF

You have now learned about the different sectors of the industry. You have now learned about the different sectors in the hospitality and catering industry. The industry is important in terms of its contribution to employment and economic output. In most locations it is seen as a priority sector.

To test your level of knowledge and understanding, answer the following short questions.

Hospitality and catering

1 Describe the term 'hospitality'.

2 Describe the term 'catering'.

3 Explain the difference between 'commercial' and the 'service' sectors.

4 List five different establishments from each sector.

5 Choose one establishment from each sector and describe three job roles from each establishement.

6 Describe how some staff restaurants are subsidized by the employer.

7 Other than price, list three differences between budget hotels and five-star hotels.

8 What is the difference between a leased public house and a freehouse?

9 List three benefits that a tourist attraction can have within the region.

10 List four things you would expect to find in a contract of employment.

2

Food safety in catering

Unit 202 Food safety in catering

LEARNING OBJECTIVES

At the end of this chapter you will be able to:

- **Understand how you can take personal responsibility for food safety.**
- **Understand the importance of keeping yourself clean and hygienic.**
- **Understand the importance of keeping the work areas clean and hygienic.**
- **Understand the importance of keeping food safe.**

Introduction

Food hygiene is more than just the sanitation of work areas. It includes all practices, precautions and legal responsibilities involved in the following:

1 Protecting food from risk of contamination.

2 Prevention of **organisms** from multiplying to an extent which would pose a health risk to customers and employees.

3 Destroying any harmful bacteria in food by thorough heat treatment or other techniques.

4 Prevention against potential to harm customers, colleagues and any others.

5 Protection against potential legal action against the business or self.

The aim of food hygiene is to protect the customer from food poisonoing of any kind. It is defined as all conditions and measures necessary to ensure the safety and suitability of food to be consumed.

What is food poisoning?

Food poisoning is a group of medical conditions that result from eating food that is contaminated with harmful bacteria or toxic poisons from bacteria. Food poisoning can also be caused from other sources such as metals, viruses and poisonous plants. Bacteria are a part of all living things and are found on all raw agricultural products. Harmful bacteria can be transferred from food to people, from people to food, or from one food to another.

Food Safety Hazards can be summarized in the following terms:

- physical (e.g. broken glass, packaging, bits of equipment, fingernails, plasters, insects, bits of clothing, flaking paint)
- biological (e.g. mould, yeasts, bacteria, toxins, viruses, **spores**, parasites)
- chemical (e.g. cleaning materials, pesticides, disinfectants)
- allergenic (e.g. from nuts, wheat products, dairy products, shellfish, green sprouting potatoes).

Hazard analysis

The hazards to food (listed above) should be assessed and measures put in place to prevent them happening.

CHEF'S TIP Chemicals, such as degreasers, polishes, detergents and sanitizers, **must** be stored in a designated area away from food production.

Hazard controls

This is achieved in the following ways:

- Regular **servicing of equipment**
- Use of a temperature probe to check on food to be stored
- Use of a temperature probe to check on food storage equipment
- Investigation of all complaints of suspected food-borne illnesses
- Regular inspections by an environmental health practitioner
- Frequent self-inspections
- Comprehensive cleaning programmes in place
- Adequate staff training in food handling and hygiene practices.

(Please see page 215 for a table of where hazards might occur.)

Personal hygiene

Good hygiene systems are required to be followed by all food handlers.

Regular hand washing is a fundamental requirement for a chef. The following procedures should apply:

1 An approved hand washing detergent should be provided by the employer, preferably in liquid form and from a dispenser.
2 Hot water and an approved drying system should be in place.
3 The application of an alcohol-based hand disinfectant allows for maximum disinfection, although it is not a substitute for correct hand washing.

Hand washing must be undertaken:

- before commencing work (to wash away general bacteria)
- after using the toilet or being in contact with faeces
- after breaks
- between touching raw food and cooked food
- before handling raw food
- after disposing of waste
- after cleaning the work space
- after any first aid or dressing changes
- after touching face, nose, mouth or blowing your nose.

Note: Food businesses should provide staff with access to a separate sink for hand washing only.

Cuts, boils and septic wounds

Food handlers should always cover cuts, grazes, boils and **septic** wounds with the appropriate dressing or with brightly coloured (blue) waterproof plasters. Cuts on fingers may need extra protection with waterproof fingerstalls or disposable latex gloves.

Smoking

This is **prohibited** where food is being prepared due to the following issues:

- The danger of contaminating food by *Staphylococcus aureus* from the fingers which may touch the lips and from saliva from the cigarette end.
- Smoking encourages coughing.

Jewellery and cosmetics

Food handlers and chefs should not wear earrings, watches, rings or other piercings because they can harbour dirt and bacteria. Plain wedding bands are sometimes permitted for compassionate reasons, but these can still harbour significant levels of bacteria. Strong smelling perfume may cause food to be tainted and make-up should be used minimally.

Reporting procedures

It is essential that sickness or injuries causing cuts and/or wounds are reported as soon as possible to avoid any further developments.

Examples of common illnesses that should be reported include:

- diarrhoea
- vomiting
- colds
- sore throats
- congested eyes
- skin infections
- stomach upsets
- suspected food poisoning.

Any close or prolonged contact with people who have suffered from any of the above symptoms should also be reported, for example, a family member family or close friend that you have spent a lot of time with.

A clean and hygienic work area

The use of **premises** which are clean and can be correctly maintained is essential for the preparation, cooking and service of food. Cross-contamination risks should be minimized by the provision of separate preparation areas for the various raw and cooked foods. The table on page 13 describes the various fittings and fixtures that need to be considered in a kitchen before other equipment is thought of.

An example of an dirty, cluttered kitchen

An exemplary kitchen

Equipment

Work surfaces and equipment for the preparation, cooking and service of food should not allow anything to pass through (impervious) and easy to clean. Equipment should be constructed from materials which are non-toxic, **corrosion** resistant, smooth and free from cracks. Surface should also be easy to clean even when hot. A **bain-marie** is designed to store hot food and liquids for up to 2 hours at a temperature of 63°C or above, although regular temperature checks should be recorded and documented.

CHEF'S TIP A dishwasher is a very effective way to clean plastic chopping boards. Dishwashers can wash at very high temperatures, which kills bacteria. Otherwise, wash chopping boards thoroughly with hot water and washing-up liquid.

Worktops and chopping boards

It is very important to keep all worktops and chopping boards clean because they come into direct contact with the food your customers are going to eat. If they are not cleaned properly, bacteria could spread to food and make your customers ill.

- Always wash worktops before you start preparing food.
- Wipe up any spilt food straight away.
- Always wash worktops thoroughly after they have been touched by raw meat, including poultry, or raw eggs.
- Never put ready-to-eat food, such as tomatoes or fruit, on a worktop or chopping board that has been touched by raw meat, unless you have washed it thoroughly first.
- It is good practice to have different boards for use with different foods e.g. fish, raw meat, cooked meat, vegetables, dairy produce, etc. This will help to prevent cross-contamination.

Cleaning products

Different cleaning products are designed to perform different tasks. The following describes the purpose of the main categories of cleaning products.

Detergent – A detergent is defined as a compound, or a combination of compounds, that is put to use for cleaning purposes. Detergents need to be diluted with water for cleaning.

Sanitizer – A sanitizer is a chemical that cleans and disinfects. A sanitizer is a chemical that reduces the number of microorganisms, such as bacteria and viruses, to safe levels.

Disinfectant – A substance that destroys micro-organisms with the potential of spreading disease, such as bacteria. Before disinfectant is used, the area concerned must be thoroughly cleaned.

Sterilization – A sterilizing product is used after cleaning to make a surface sterile (germ-free).

FIXTURES AND FITTINGS	RECOMMENDATIONS
Ceilings	White in colour to reflect the light. Smooth textured, without cracks or peeled paint/plaster. Usually panelled to hide **ventilation** systems.
Floors	Should be durable, non-slip and made of non-permeable materials.
Lighting	Good lighting is essential to provide clear vision and avoid eye strain.
Ventilation	A high performance kitchen ventilation system is a requirement for a modern kitchen. The extracted air should be free from grease and odours. A canopy system should be built around the existing structure of the kitchen to cover at least all cookery areas, particularly gas appliances.
Walls	In the past, ceramic wall tiles were considered the best surface for areas where liquids splash a wall surface, potentially overcoming a damp or hygiene problem. Modern alternatives to ceramic wall tiles include PVC wall cladding systems, resin wall coatings and screed mortars. They offer a hygienic finish capable of withstanding heavy impact. Stainless steel walls provide an excellent non-porous and easy-clean surface.

It is important to note that cleaning chemicals can be dangerous and harmful to humans if ingested. The Control of Substances Hazardous to Health Regulations 2002 (COSHH) specifies the general requirements for employers to protect employees and other persons from the hazards of substances used at work by risk assessment, control of **exposure**, health surveillance and incident planning.

Web Link Further details can be found at the Health and Safety Executive website: **http://www.hse.gov.uk/coshh/**

Careful handling of such chemicals is vital to ensure that the products are used in the way that they were designed to be used. Labels on cleaning materials should never be tampered with and the **manufacturer**'s instructions should be read very carefully and understood before use and also before disposal (throwing away).

Prevention of cross-contamination

It is standard practice to have separate chopping boards for raw meat and for other foods. A system of coloured boards and knife handles that can help to minimize cross-contamination are widely available.

A typical system is:

- Red Raw meat and poultry
- Yellow Cooked meat and poultry
- Blue Raw fish (in this book, white and wooden backgrounds may be used for photographic purposes)
- Brown Vegetables
- Green Fruit and salads
- White Bakery and dairy items

Chart to show colour codes for chopping boards

All boards must be cleaned between use, ideally with a sanitizer. Storage of such boards must be in racks and not touching each other. If boards become damaged they should be discarded because bacteria can multiply in cracks and blemishes. This can lead to contamination.

TASK Look at the recipe for **escalope** of pork cordon blue on page 173.

Identify the hygiene considerations when producing this dish and list the potential dangers of cross-contamination.

The importance of keeping work areas clean and hygienic

It is good practice to clean as you go rather than allowing areas to becoming unclean, cluttered and untidy. Cleaning processes and procedures should also be put into place to prevent contamination. Cleaning processes need to consider the working methods of the business and analyze the areas for their level of risk, for example, if foods items or equipment are coming into contact with hands on a regular basis.

Processes for cleaning can change according to **circumstances**. For example, it is common practice that crockery and cutlery are cleaned using an automatic dishwasher. A dishwasher is **programmed** to follow a number of processes that should also be followed when using a manual washing system, for example, when using a double sink to wash items.

Pre-clean to remove as much food/debris as possible

↓

Main clean using a detergent (1st sink)

↓

Rinse in disinfected water above 82°C (2nd sink)

↓

Drain and air dry

Cleaning large equipment is also a very important task to maximize food safety and this should be done on a regular and planned basis. Where possible, larger equipment should be moved to ensure that is can be cleaned from all angles. This will also allow access to the areas, such as walls, behind larger equipment so that they can be cleaned at the same time.

Protective clothing

It is important to note that clothing is an essential part of personal safety (e.g. to avoid burns and scalds) and personal hygiene. To keep clothing as clean and hygienic as possible, it should not be worn outside of the workplace.

Additional items such as disposable gloves and hairnets are designed to provide further protection from bacteria being passed through direct contact with the hands and to prevent loose hair from falling into food.

Kitchen cloths

Dirty, damp cloths are the perfect breeding ground for bacteria. Therefore, it is very important to wash all cleaning cloths and sponges regularly.

Ideally, try to keep different cloths for different jobs. For example, use one cloth to wipe worktops and another to wash dishes and small equipment. This helps to stop bacteria spreading.

The safest option is the use of disposable single-use cloths or kitchen towels to wipe worktops and chopping boards. This is because you throw the kitchen towel away after using it once, so it is less likely to spread bacteria than cloths you use repeatedly. Tea towels can spread bacteria, so it's important to wash them regularly and be careful how you use them.

Knives, spoons and other utensils

It is important to keep knives, wooden spoons, spatulas, tongs and other utensils clean to help stop bacteria spreading to food. It is especially important to wash utensils thoroughly after using them with raw meat, as otherwise they could spread bacteria to other food.

Waste disposal

Waste should be disposed of on a regular basis and should not be left in food preparation areas overnight. Bins should be lined with good quality bin bags that can be tied securely and placed in secure external waste disposal areas until collection. With the current environmental concerns there is also the consideration of recycling and it is good practice that waste items are separated into their specific categories, such as:

- food waste
- plastics
- tins
- paper / cardboard
- glass.

Prevention of pests

Undomesticated animals, like all living creatures, require food, water, shelter and warmth to feel comfortable. A kitchen or food store with easy access to food, including waste food, provides all of these comfort factors, so it is important that everything possible is done to prevent pests from gaining entry. The reason it is so important is due to the infestation that pests bring with them, which can easily lead to contamination and disease. The law also states that food premises cannot operate if there is an infestation and upon finding such problems, an environmental health practitioner would have little choice other than to stop the business from trading.

The signs that pests leave behind

Pests usually visit when they feel safest, which is normally when there are no signs that people are present. This is often at night when the business is not operating and the staff have left to go home. However, pests leave a number of signs revealing their visit.

TASK Complete the following table. The first row has been completed to demonstrate the type of signs left behind.

Type of pest	Signs of their visit
Mice/rats	Droppings Gnawed cables/wires Gnawed boxes Gnawed food items Paw prints Unpleasant smell
Flies and insects	
Domestic pets (cats / dogs)	
Birds	
Weevils	
Cockroaches	
Other examples	

HEALTH & SAFETY Remember, if you wipe your hands on a tea towel after you have touched raw meat, this will spread bacteria to the towel. Then, if you use the tea towel to dry a plate, the bacteria will spread to the plate.

Risk assessment

HACCP stands for 'Hazard Analysis and Critical Control Points'. It is an internationally recognized and recommended system of food safety management. It focuses on identifying the 'critical points' in a process where food safety problems (or 'hazards') could arise and putting steps in place to prevent things going wrong. This is sometimes referred to as 'controlling hazards'. Keeping records is also an important part of HACCP systems.

HACCP involves the following seven steps:

1. Identify what could go wrong (the hazards).
2. Identify the most important points where things can go wrong (the critical control points – CCPs).

3 Set critical limits at each CCP (e.g. cooking temperature/time).

4 Set up checks at CCPs to prevent problems occurring (monitoring).

5 Decide what to do if something goes wrong (corrective action).

6 Prove that your HACCP plan is working (verification).

7 Keep records of all of the above (documentation).

Your HACCP plan must be kept up-to-date. You will need to review it from time to time, especially whenever something in your food operation changes. You may also wish to ask your local environmental health practitioner for advice.

Remember that, even with a HACCP plan in place, you must still comply with all requirements of current food safety **legislation**.

Legal responsibilities

Food handlers have a legal as well as ethical responsibility to ensure that the food they produce is safe for human **consumption**. As part of this responsibility, it is a requirement that personal hygiene is kept at the highest possible standard and any illness is reported and an appropriate amount of time is spent before returning to work (usually 48 hours after the last symptoms).

A food related business has an obligation to ensure that staff are adequately trained in food safety and that appropriate procedures are put in place to minimize the potential for a food safety related issue. Food related businesses are also required to register their business with the local authority, which will then be routinely inspected by environmental health practitioners/enforcement officers.

The Food Standards Agency (FSA) (**www.food.gov.uk**) provides guidance for businesses to operate safe food practices. This is a set of procedures known as 'Safer Food, Better Business' and provides a system for food related businesses to conform to in order to ensure that the food sold or served to customers is safe to eat.

Scores on the doors

'Scores on the doors' is another strategy put into place by the FSA to improve food safety standards. The process involves an inspection from an environmental health practitioner. On completion of the inspection a rating of zero to five stars is awarded dependent on the food safety standards and procedures that are evident at the time of the visit. A certificate is provided which is placed in a public area of the business so that customers can see the score the business has achieved, zero being the lowest grade and five the highest. The score can also be seen by visiting the local authority website.

Food safety legislation

The Food Hygiene (England) Regulations 2006 provide the framework for the EU legislation to be enforced in England. The main new requirement is to have 'food safety management procedures' and keep up-to-date records of these procedures.

Disposal of waste is another HACCP matter, as bacteria and **pathogens** can multiply at an alarming rate in waste disposal areas. For example, waste bins in the kitchen should be emptied at regular and short intervals and be kept clean. Food waste can be safely disposed of in a waste disposal unit. Oil can only be disposed of by a specialist oil disposal company and must not be placed in a sink or waste disposal unit.

Reporting maintenance issues

Food for cookery must be prepared on surfaces that are hygienic and suitable for use. Work surfaces, walls and floors can become damaged, and they too can be a source of contamination and danger to customers and staff alike. Damaged areas should be reported to your line manager. A maintenance reporting system can be easily designed to suit each establishment and each section of the kitchen. Areas for attention are:

- cracks in walls
- damage to tables and work benches
- cooking equipment such as pots, pans and utensils
- windows, sanitary systems and lights
- flooring and any other structural issues
- electrical equipment relating to that particular operation.

Food safety procedures

The HACCP food management system will also examine the point of food storage. It should cover the receiving of goods where the core temperatures and condition of the delivery is thoroughly checked. Fresh meat that has been delivered should have a core temperature of a maximum of 8°C. All fresh produce should be delivered in unbroken, clean packaging and in clean delivery vehicles that are refrigerated. If you suspect a delivery has not met the requirements of your HACCP it should not be accepted and it should be returned immediately to the supplier.

A well laid out storeroom

After a commodity has been received it needs to be correctly stored. Raw meat and fish should be stored, covered, in separate refrigerators at 1°C to 4°C. However if there is not enough capacity for two separate refrigeration systems, **cooked products must be stored above fresh meat**. Fish should be stored as low in the refrigerator as possible. This is the coolest part of the refrigerator and a layer of crushed ice will help to keep the temperature down. This method will help to prevent cross-contamination from storage and optimizes quality. All foods should be labelled with the date of delivery or production, a description of the contents and the recommended use-by date.

Dealing with food spoilage

It is important that chefs know how to deal with food spoilage. Recognition of a problem is a natural and very fast way to detect a problem. This can be visual through signs of mould, decay or a change from a foods natural colour. A food's smell is also a natural warning that the food has past its best, as can its feel and texture.

Food is a significant cost to the business, so it is important that it is handled well and used as it was originally planned. However, occasionally, it may become necessary to dispose of food as it has become unsafe to eat or past its best in terms of its eating qualities. It is essential that disposal of food is reported to supervisors and/or line managers so that they are made aware.

Disposal of food should be clearly labelled 'Not for human consumption' and separated from general waste. It should also be disposed of away from food storage areas/kitchen.

Maintenance report sheet

Date ________

Name ________________

Production area ________________

Nature of problem

Action taken

Reported to

Follow-up action taken

Weekly maintenance checklist ✓		
	Date	Comments
Sinks		
Freezers		
Refrigerators		
Tables		
Food processors		
Mincers		
Ovens		
Stoves		
Windows		
Evidence of pests		
Other equipment		

Signature ________________________

Example of a maintenance report sheet

Chef's name ______________

Production area ________________

Goods received checklist

Date	Time	Supplier	Order correct	Delivery note/ invoice number	Fault (identify product)	Action	Temperature reading

Example of a goods received checklist

SATURDAY
Sabado - Samedi
MM

Item: ____________________

Prep Date: ________ Time: ________ ☐ AM ☐ PM

Shelf Life: ________________ ☐ Shifts ☐ Fresh Daily

Use By: ________ ☐ 4 PM ☐ Close Emp: ________

A food label to record details of when food was made and when it should be used by.

Bacteria and food poisoning

SALMONELLA

There are over 2000 types of *salmonella*. The commonest types are *salmonella enteriditis* and *salmonella typhimurium*.

These organisms survive in the intestine and can cause food poisoning by releasing a toxin on the death of the cell. The primary source of *salmonella* is the intestinal tract of animals and poultry and will therefore be found in:

a. human and animal **excreta**
b. excreta from rats, mice, flies and cockroaches
c. raw meat and poultry
d. some animal feed.

STAPHYLOCOCCUS AUREUS

If present in food, *Staphylococcus aureus* will produce a toxin which may survive boiling for 30 minutes or more. The majority of outbreaks are caused by poor hygiene practices which result in direct contamination of the food by people from sneezing or through uncovered septic cuts and **abrasions**. Common outbreaks occur when cooked food is handled whilst still slightly warm. This encourages the organism to produce its toxin, leading to food poisoning.

HEALTH & SAFETY About 40–50 per cent of adults carry *staphylococcus aureus* in their nose, mouth, throat, ears and hands. Make sure you wash your hands and do not sneeze over food.

CLOSTRIDIUM PERFRINGENS

This is commonly found in human and animal faeces and is present in raw meat and poultry. This organism forms spores which may survive boiling temperatures for several hours. Outbreaks are common in stews and large joints of meat which have been allowed to cool down slowly in a warm kitchen and either eaten cold or inadequately reheated the following day.

CLOSTRIDIUM BOTULINUM

This is commonly found in soil, fish, meat and vegetables. Symptoms include difficulties in swallowing, talking and breathing, double vision and paralysis of the cranial nerves. Fatalities (deaths) are common and the recovery period for survivors can take several months.

BACILLUS CEREUS

This is a spore forming organism. The spores survive normal cooking and rapid growth will occur if the food has not been cooled quickly and refrigerated. This bacteria will induce **nausea** and vomiting within 5 hours of **ingestion**.

CAMPYLOBACTER ENTERITIS

Campylobacter is the most common cause of diarrhoea from bacteria. It is found in raw poultry, meat and milk, as well as farm animals, pets, birds, sewage and untreated water. As well as diarrhoea, symptoms also include abdominal pain, nausea and fever.

E-COLI (0157)

Escherichia coli is often fatal if contracted by the elderly or young children. It is present in the intestines of people and animals as well as in sewage and untreated water. Symptoms include nausea, diarrhoea, abdominal cramps and kidney failure, especially in children.

LISTERIA

Listeria multiplies in refrigerated foods, even foods stored below 3°C. It is found in soil, sewage, water, vegetation, people, animals and birds. Symptoms include flu-like conditions, vomiting, diarrhoea and fever.

NOROVIRUS

This is commonly found in people who are ill as well as in the environment and sewage. Norovirus only multiplies within the body but is airborne and can easily be spread from person to person. Symptoms include projectile vomiting, diarrhoea, abdominal pain and fever.

TYPHOID

Typhoid is caused by salmonella enterica. It is present in sewage, manure and water as well as carriers. Typical symptoms include fever, nausea, malaise, headaches, a slow pulse, anorexia, constipation and sometimes diarrhoea.

Bacterial multiplication

Bacteria multiply by dividing into two. If conditions are ideal this can occur every 10 to 20 minutes. Therfore, one bacterium (single form of bacteria) is capable of reproducing over 2 million more bacteria in just 7 hours.

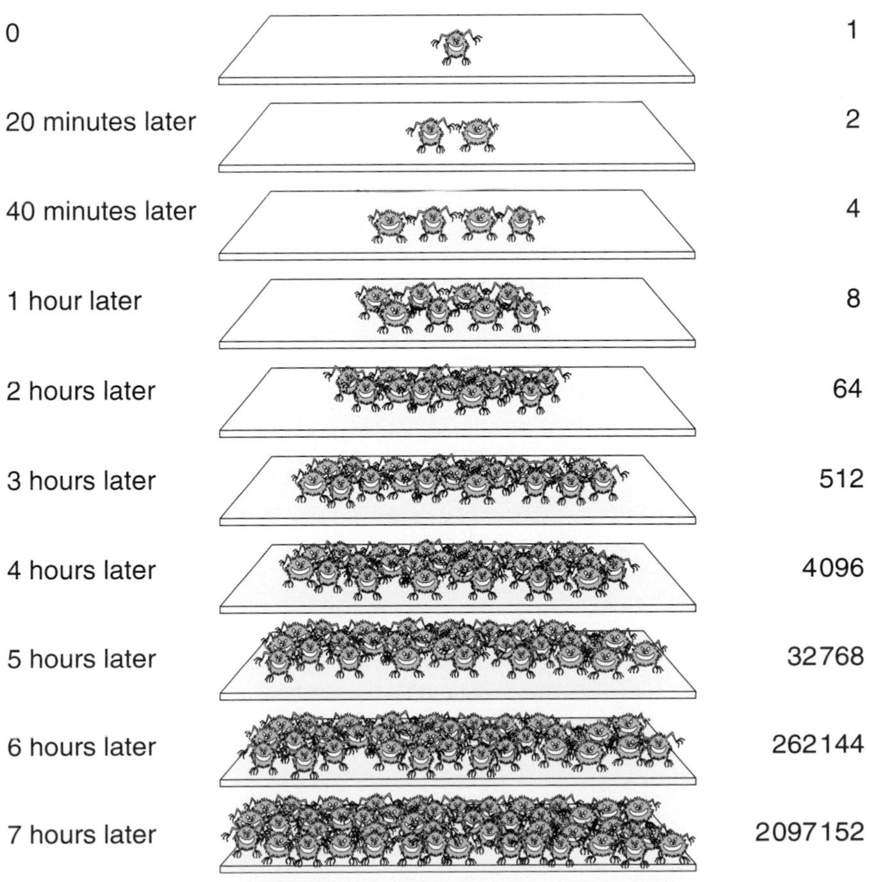

Bacterial multiplication timeline

High risk groups

Some people are more vulnerable to contamination than others depending on their physical state and/or period of life. Particularly vulnerable are pregnant women, the young, the elderly and people who are sick. This is largely due to them having a weakened or developing **immune system**.

Food storage and temperatures

Freezers, whether upright or chest freezers, should be maintained at a temperature range of –18°C to –22°C. All food should be covered to prevent freezer burn and labelled with the date of production and a use-by date.

Ambient stores should be clean and well ventilated, with mesh over windows and doors to help with pest control. All foodstuffs must be stored away from the floor and be rotated on a first in and first out basis.

Preparing, cooking and storing food safely

Frozen food should be defrosted in a refrigerator and treated as fresh food with the same use by date. All root vegetables must be washed prior to peeling and then re-washed after peeling. Leaf vegetables such as cabbage and spinach

• Raw meat, poultry and game *2°C to 4°C*	*Store away from cooked meat and cooked meat products to avoid any risk of cross-contamination.*
• Cooked meat *2°C to 4°C*	*Keep away from raw meat and raw meat products.*
• Uncooked fish *1°C to 2°C*	*Keep in separate compartments or in plastic fish trays with lids if possible and away from other foods which may become tainted.*
• Frozen food *–18°C to –22°C*	*Thaw only immediately prior to using the commodity.*
• Fish (**smoked** or cured) *5°C*	*Keep in chilled storage away from other foods, which may become tainted.*
• Fruit (fresh and dried)	*Store in a cool, dry and well-ventilated area away from other food, at least 15 cm from the ground. Discard at the first sign of mould growth. Do not overstock.*
• Pasta, rice and cereals	*Store in self-closing tightly lidded containers in dry cool storeroom or cupboard.*
• Eggs *4°C to 8°C*	*Use strictly in rotation and ensure the shells are clean and undamaged.*
• Fats, butter, dairy and non-dairy spreads *1°C to 5°C*	*Keep covered and away from highly flavoured food, which may taint.*
• Milk and cream *1°C to 5°C*	*Ideally in a separate refrigerator, or at least in a separate section.*
• Prepared desserts *1°C to 4°C*	*Ideally prepared on the day of use.*
• Sauces and soups *1°C to 5°C*	*Should be prepared only on day of use and stored in plastic containers with a tight fitting lid.*
• Salads and fresh herbs *2°C to 5°C or below*	*Always wash before use.*
• Tinned and bottled goods	*In a cool, dry and well-ventilated storage area. Blown, rusty or split tins must not be used.*
• Root vegetables	*Store in sacks or nets as delivered in a cool, well-ventilated area.*
• Leaf and green vegetables *1°C to 5°C*	Use as quickly as possible, ideally on the day of delivery.

should be washed in several changes of cold water to allow soil and grit to go to the bottom of the sink. A separate preparation area should be used ideally to help prevent cross-contamination.

CHEF'S TIP Some restaurants will ask customers to sign a disclaimer if they ask for foods to be served raw or undercooked, e.g. steak tartare (raw) or a rare fillet steak..

When cooking in large scale catering operations such as hospitals and schools, a core temperature of 75°C is usually maintained for 2 minutes as a core temperature of 75°C will kill pathogens. However, a consequence of this is that all foods will be well done. In Scotland, best practice is to reheat above 82°C core temperature for 2 minutes. Food should be reheated once only. In restaurants and hotels the core temperature is sometimes dependent on the requirements of the customer. For example, customers often request steaks to be served rare, in which case the core temperature cannot reach 63°C. At a core temperature of 63°C or above, the meat would be well done.

The holding and serving temperature for cold food should be below 5°C and above 63°C for hot food.

Chilling food not for immediate use should ideally be achieved in blast chillers where the core temperature is brought down from 70°C to 4°C in 90 minutes or less. With these temperature ranges both pathogenic and bacterial growth is inhibited although not completely stopped.

If food that has been cooked is not for immediate consumption, or is to be frozen, it should be well covered with cling film or ideally vacuum packed to create an airtight barrier and prevent freezer burn. Storage times should be appropriate to the product or within manufacturer's guidelines and all foods must be clearly labelled.

CHEF'S TIP For information regarding allergies, refer to pages 43 in Chapter 4 (unit 104) – Introduction to healthier foods and special diets.

VIDEO CLIP Using a probe thermometer.

HEALTH & SAFETY

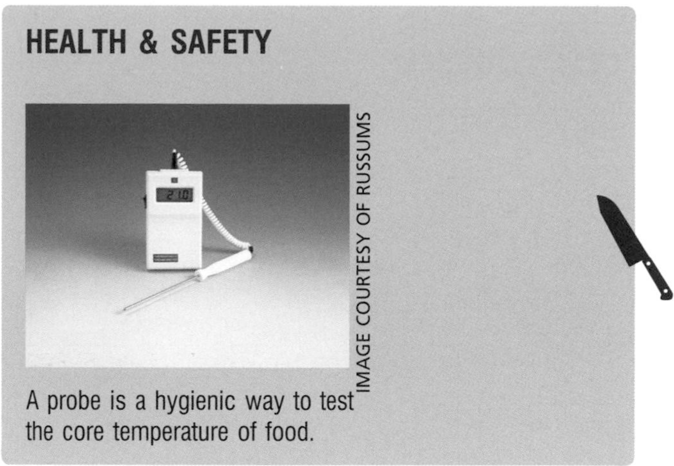

A probe is a hygienic way to test the core temperature of food.

Food safety temperature guide

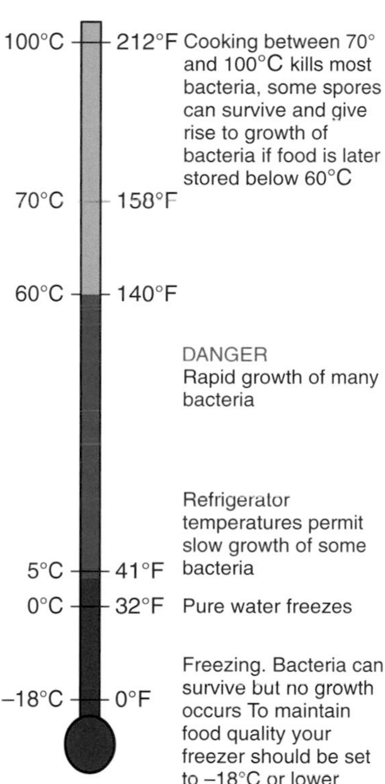

TEST YOURSELF

1 Explain what food poisoning is.

____

____

2 Give three examples of times when you should wash your hands.

i) ______________________________
ii) ______________________________
iii) ______________________________

3 Explain why different coloured chopping boards should be used.

____

____

4 By drawing a line, match up the colour chopping board with the food items it should be used to prepare.

Red	Vegetables
Yellow	Dairy and pastry items
Blue	Raw meat and poultry
Brown	Fruits and salads
Green	Raw fish
White	Cooked meat and poultry

5 What does HACCP stand for?

____

____

____

6 Give the correct food storage temperature for the food items listed below.

Raw meat	________	°C or below
Cooked meat	________	°C or below
Uncooked fish	________	°C or below
Milk	________	°C or below

7 Give three ways in which you can help to control food safety hazards in the workplace.

i) ______________________________
ii) ______________________________
iii) ______________________________

8 What is the name of the scheme used by environmental health practitioners to inform the public of food safety conditions following an inspection?

____

____

9 Name four food poisoning bacteria.

i) ______________________________
ii) ______________________________
iii) ______________________________
iv) ______________________________

10 Describe the term 'cross-contamination'.

____

____

____

3

Health and safety awareness for catering and hospitality

Unit 103 Health and safety awareness for catering and hospitality

LEARNING OBJECTIVES

At the end of this chapter you will be able to:

- **Understand the need for health and safety practices in the workplace.**
- **Identify hazards in the workplace.**
- **Understand the importance of following health and safety procedures.**
- **Describe the types and use of safety signs and the types of hazards and incidents that require reporting.**

Introduction

Health is described as an individual's physical and mental well-being. If a person is in good health, they will feel well, stable in their mind and not be suffering from any illness or disease.

Safety refers to the absence of risks that could potentially damage someone's health. Whatever function you have in the hospitality industry, everyone is required to behave safely and professionally. Reasonable care must be taken for the health and safety of yourself and others who may be affected by what you do. Everyone has the right to feel safe at work.

Health and safety in the work place

Factors that affect health and safety

There are a number of factors that affect health and safety in the workplace. These can be broken down into the following three areas.

OCCUPATIONAL FACTORS

'Occupational' refers to issues that are specific to the type of work being undertaken. For example:

- *The type of equipment being used* – Kitchens have many pieces of equipment that could cause harm if used incorrectly, e.g. gravity food slicers, electric mixers, blenders, etc.
- *The chemicals used for cleaning* – It is essential that the manufacturer's instructions are followed carefully and that personal protective equipment is used as required to prevent injury through direct contact or inhalation.
- *The processes being used to produce food* – Food preparation and cookery processes have risks attached. For example, when smoking foods there is the risk of inhaling smoke.
- *The food itself* – Certain foods can present a natural risk without any of the above. For example, the tiny particles in flour can cause respiratory problems if someone is exposed to working in an environment using a lot of flour for a long period of time. It is recommended that a flour mask is worn in such cases to reduce inhalation.

ENVIRONMENTAL FACTORS

The 'environment' refers to the surroundings in which a person works and the conditions to which they may be exposed. For example:

- *High levels of noise* – High levels of noise can cause damage to a person's ears, especially if the exposure is over a long period of time.
- *Poor lighting* – Poor lighting reduces vision and increases the possibility of an accident.
- *Temperature* – For example, if we get overheated, this can make us feel dizzy, faint and even nauseous (sick).
- *Facilities* – Facilities should be clean, safe and fit for purpose. A variety of welfare facilities should also be provided for employees, including:
  - toilets
  - changing areas
  - drinking water
  - washing facilities
  - personal protective equipment (PPE) storage facilities
  - rest facilities.

HUMAN FACTORS

The way in which we behave at work has a massive impact on the health and safety of ourselves, those working near us and any customers we serve. For example:

- *Carelessness* – A lack of concentration or a carefree approach could result in something going wrong with the task in hand.

- *Inexperience or a lack of training* – A lack of experience and/or training may expose the person performing the task to danger and a risk to their personal health and safety as well as the health and safety of others. It is essential that inexperienced staff are properly supervised and provided with the required training to perform tasks safely.
- *Physical and/or mental state* – The physical and mental state of a person can be critical in the way that they perform at work. The way in which a task is approached can change due to stress and anxiety. It can be difficult to focus and concentrate when suffering from stress.
- *Drugs and alcohol* – Someone who is under the influence of alcohol or drugs is obviously a danger to themselves and others and should be prevented from working immediately.

The benefits of following good health and safety practices?

To reduce accidents and illness

Health and safety practices are intended to protect people from any form of harm, injury or illness. If such practices are well planned and monitored with regular training and updating for all staff concerned, the likelihood of accidents and illness is reduced significantly.

Preserves and promotes a good reputation

The benefits of reducing accidents and potential ill-health include the prospect of a contented and motivated workforce. Such a workforce is much more likely to achieve increased **productivity**, an **enhanced** reputation and may potentially increase profitability.

On the contrary, a damaged reputation to a business can lead to eventual closure due to insufficient trade.

Prevents legal action and associated costs

People have the right to seek legal action if their health and safety have been put at risk or harmed as a result of another's actions. An employer has a responsibility to protect staff, visitors and customers from any form of risk to their health and safety.

CHEF'S TIP If good practices are developed and there is regular training and monitoring of health and safety, it is much less likely that anyone will become subject to harm.

Helps to control costs

Any accident or illness related directly or indirectly to the workplace could have a cost implication. This could be from increased sick leave, poor performance or staff turnover. There is also the possibility that a case could lead to prosecution, fines, high legal costs and **compensation** claims.

The personal costs can be equally damaging. An accident can be particularly painful and may affect the rest of a person's life. Someone's life is the ultimate cost. In the most serious cases, people can die from poor health and safety practices.

WEB LINK Discover more about health and safety issues and tips for making your workplace safer by visiting the following website **www.hse.gov.uk/catering/**

Responsibilities for health and safety and the consequences of non-compliance

EVERYONE HAS A RESPONSIBILITY FOR HEALTH AND SAFETY

Employers have a duty to provide and maintain a working environment which is safe and healthy. This includes regular checking and servicing of equipment and also ensuring that chemical substances are handled safely and with due care and attention. An employer has a responsibility to train all employees in health and safety on a regular basis. They must also ensure that the work environment is in good repair with sufficient lighting, ventilation, temperature control and that safety equipment and clothing are provided. An employer should provide employees with a health and safety policy statement.

Employees have a responsibility to take care of their own health and safety as well as the health and safety of those around them. Employees should co-operate with their employers in the good practices and promotion of health and safety at work.

Failure to comply with such recommendations or acts of a serious nature is likely to result in the loss of employment. Employees also face the possibility of prosecution following any unsafe actions!

Identifying hazards in the workplace

Hazards and risks

The Health and Safety at Work Act (1974) covers all full-time and part-time employees and unpaid workers (such as students on work placements).

The Health and Safety Executive (HSE) is the body appointed to support and enforce health and safety in the workplace. They defined the two concepts for hazards and risk as described on page 26.

THE MOST COMMONLY USED TERMS IN HEALTH AND SAFETY

TERM	DEFINITION
Workplace	Place of work.
Accident	An unintended incident.
Hazard	Something with the potential to cause harm.
Risk	The likelihood of the hazard actually causing harm.
Control measure	A measure to control the risk.
EHP/EHO	Environmental Health Practitioner (formerly Environmental Health Officer).
PPE	Personal Protective Equipment.
PAT	Portable Appliance Testing (portable electrical products).
Electric shock	The shock received if the body comes into direct contact with an electricity source.
Evacuation route	A planned route to leave a building or premises in the case of emergency (e.g. fire).
Occupational health	Health at work.
Manual handling	Lifting procedures – very important to protect the back.
Noise	The volume and type of sound that people may be exposed to.
Report	Usually a written document e.g. a record of an incident or situation/recommendations for improvements.
Harassment	Unwanted behaviour which makes the receiver feel uncomfortable or threatened. Harassment can be of a verbal (including written), physical or sexual nature.

1. A hazard is something with the potential to cause harm.
2. A risk is the likelihood of the hazard's potential being realized.

Two examples of this are as follows:

1. A light bulb that requires replacing is a potential hazard. If it is one out of several, it presents a very small risk. However, if it is the only light within a 'walk-in' cold room, it poses a high risk.
2. A stockpot full of hot stock being moved from one kitchen to another using a trolley presents a potential hazard. The pot could fall off completely or could spill over during transit causing spillage onto clothes, **scalding** and creating a wet and slippery floor surface. Therefore it is high in risk.

TASK Identify three hazards in the kitchen. This could be through the use of equipment or a process.

1. What are the risks?
2. Measure the risk as high, medium or low
3. How can they be managed? What steps can be put into place to minimize the risk?
4. Measure the risk as high, medium or low.

The main causes of slips, trips and falls

The likelihood of someone slipping, tripping or falling in the workplace is increased by a number of factors. Poor design can lead to such problems. For example, an unexpected step, whether up or down, could lead to a loss of balance and a fall. The risk of this happening is further increased if there is no signage to warn people of this unexpected hazard or if the signage is not obvious or unclear.

WEB LINK To find out about slips and trips in the catering industry and other health issues, have a look at the following website **www.mb-hs.com** and click on Restaurants and Catering. At the bottom of the page click on 'Health and safety in the catering industry'.

HEALTH & SAFETY A clean and tidy environment without obstructions and clear signage helps to minimize accidents caused by slips, trips and falls.

Other examples include:

Lighting and ventilation – Poor lighting restricts vision and as such potential hazards will not be as obvious. Poor ventilation can lead to someone overheating, causing dizziness and even fainting.

Dangerous working practices – For example, not drying wet floors after a spillage or leaving items in areas that are inappropriate and therefore unsafe (poor storage practices).

Distraction or lack of attention – For example, not looking where you are going increases the likelihood of a collision, trip or fall.

Working too quickly – During a busy service, chefs and front-of-house staff often work at a much faster pace than usual. With everyone working at greater speed, the likelihood of a collision, trip or fall increases. In such situations, concentration and communication are vitally important.

Ignoring rules and working practices – Many restaurants operate a workflow system between the restaurant and kitchen. This includes a route into the kitchen from the restaurant and another route from the kitchen back to the restaurant. If everyone follows this system, there will be a good workflow and it is unlikely that there will be a collision as staff will always be walking in the same direction and never across each other. If this working practice is broken and someone chooses to walk in the opposite direction, the likelihood of an accident is increased significantly.

Not wearing the correct 'PPE' – For example, the employer must provide:

- protective gloves when washing pots and pans
- masks and goggles when cleaning stoves and ovens with **hazardous substances**
- provide staff changing and correct storage facilities.

Employees have a responsibility to comply with the policy of wearing PPE at all necessary times and to report any defects in the PPE to the employer.

Physical/mental state – We are less likely to slip, trip or fall when we are fresh in our minds and concentrating on the tasks ahead.

Manual handling

Working in hospitality and catering, and particularly in kitchens, often involves manual handling to some degree. In kitchens, items come in many shapes and sizes, various temperatures from frozen to boiling, and different weights. All have the potential to cause injury if not handled correctly. The main injury, and perhaps the most severe, is the damage that poor manual handling techniques can have on the back and spine. Other injuries associated with manual handling include:

- muscular injuries
- fractures
- sprains
- cuts and bruises.

MAXIMUM LOAD

The maximum load a person can handle will depend upon individual strength at the time. If in any doubt, do not attempt the task and seek advice from your supervisor. Always take into account your size, general health, and in particular any unnatural movement needed such as twisting or reaching.

Where there is any possibility of risk, break a load into smaller items, e.g. liquids and loose items can be put into smaller containers. This is particularly the case when using trolleys to transport multiple items, e.g. make trolleys lighter by increasing the number of journeys.

THE DO'S AND DO NOT'S WHEN LIFTING

- Do not handle any load if the floor or the item is damp or slippery.
- Do not store anything other than light loads above shoulder height.
- Do not store liquids or sharp items or anything remotely heavy above eye level.
- Make maximum use of legs, keep the back as straight as possible and avoid twisting or bending forward.

HEALTH CONSIDERATIONS

- Report any medical condition (high blood pressure, osteoporosis, etc.) to your supervisor before handling heavy loads.

SEQUENCE OF LIFTING BOXES

Stand with your feet apart

Your weight should be evenly spread over both feet

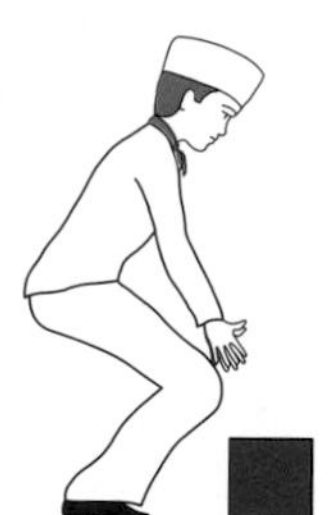

Bend your knees slowly keeping your back straight

Stand with your feet apart

Tuck your chin in towards your chest

Get a good grip on the base of the item

Bring the item to your waist height keeping the lift as smooth as possible

Keep the item close to your body

Proceed carefully making sure that you can see where you are going

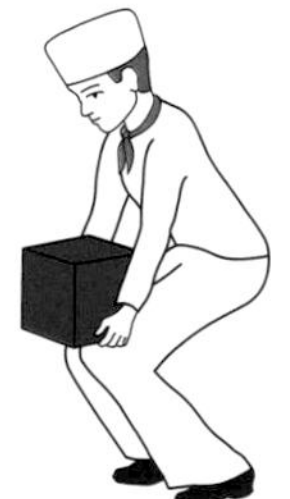

Lower the item, reversing the lifting procedure

PROTECT YOURSELF

- Wear the protective clothing provided. Wear sturdy footwear.
- If you feel that you require protective clothing and footwear then raise this with your supervisor.
- Spillages are your responsibility. If you spill anything, or come across a spillage or wet floor, you must either clean it up yourself or arrange for someone else to clean it. Ensure that warning notices are posted in the interim.

The main ways in which equipment can cause injury and the control measures to avoid injury

Injuries can happen in many ways. For example:

By entanglement or entrapment – This could happen by getting clothing or a limb caught up in a mixing machine while it is in operation. People sometimes get tempted to move something or push a piece of food that may have been displaced back towards the centre of the mix. If such actions were to take place whist the machine is switched on, the consequences can be extremely unpleasant.

By impact – The safe storage of items is essential in the kitchen environment. Equipment is regularly stored on racks, shelves and even hooks. This can often be at quite a height. If items are not stored properly and become unbalanced, there is significant potential for them to fall causing injury to anyone in their path.

Ejection – Ejection refers to items flying out unexpectedly. For example, items of food or pieces of broken or loose equipment, for example, a loose blade or screw in a mixing machine could fly out when switched on.

Faulty equipment – Faulty equipment presents a serious risk of injury. If equipment is not in good condition, its performance will suffer and it will not function as it should. Damaged electrical equipment is particularly dangerous and should not be used.

Improper use of equipment – All equipment is designed to be used in a certain way. Manufacturers of equipment should provide user guidelines to demonstrate how a piece of equipment should be used. If guidelines or training in the safe use of equipment are ignored, the likelihood of an accident is increased significantly.

CHEF'S TIP Any equipment that is faulty should be reported immediately and removed to avoid potential injuries.

Hazardous substances

There are many hazardous substances used in the kitchen environment. Such substances include cleaning chemicals, cooking liquids and gas as well as the gels and spirits that are sometimes used to maintain the temperature in hot **buffet** containers.

THE CONTROL OF SUBSTANCES HAZARDOUS TO HEALTH (COSHH) REGULATIONS (1999)

COSHH is a workplace policy that is relevant to everyday working practices. Chemicals that are toxic such as detergents are hazardous and present a high risk. They must be stored, handled, used and disposed of correctly in accordance with COSHH regulations.

Any substance in the workplace that is hazardous to health must be identified on the packaging and stored and handled correctly.

Hazardous substances can enter the body via:

- the skin
- the eyes
- the mouth (ingestion)
- the nose (inhalation).

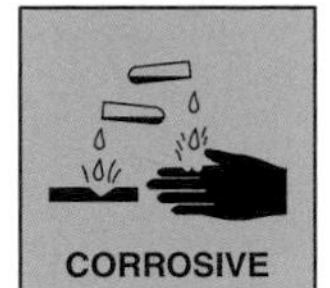

Hazardous substances are usually shown through use of symbols

The COSHH regulations were **consolidated** in 2002 and they state that employers are held responsible for assessing the risks from hazardous substances and for controlling the exposure to them to prevent ill-health. Any hazardous substances identified should be formally recorded in writing and given a risk rating. Safety precaution procedures should then be implemented and training given to employees to ensure that the procedures are understood and followed correctly.

The main causes of fire and explosions

Fire can be started from a number of sources. However, fire needs three separate elements to survive.

1. Fuel
2. Air (oxygen)
3. Heat

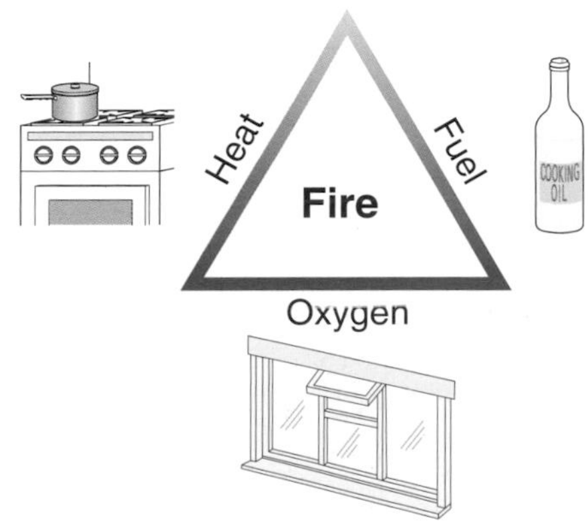

Should any one of these elements be removed, ignition cannot take place.

The main causes of fire in kitchens arise through the following:

- electricity and electrical faults
- gas leaks or a build-up of gas
- the ignition of oils, liquids and other **flammable substances**
- misuse of tools and equipment with a naked flame.

With this in mind, it is essential that flammable materials are stored safely and securely in a locked fireproof cupboard. Gas canisters should be kept stored away from direct sunlight or any other direct heat source.

TASK Think of the potential causes of fire in the kitchen. How could each of these be prevented?

In the event of a fire it is essential that no-one is placed at risk and that the emergency alarm is operated as soon as possible to alert others. The **emergency services** should also be contacted as quickly as possible. Fires can spread quickly and easily, so it is important to leave the building at once, closing doors to slow down the spread of fire and report to the identified fire assembly point.

A relatively new fire law came into force on 1 October 2006. The law is called the Regulatory Reform (Fire safety) Order 2005. It replaces all the previous legislation relating to fire, including fire certificates which no longer have any validity. This law is applicable to England and Wales only. Northern Ireland and Scotland have their own similar legislation.

This new legislation puts the responsibility for fire safety onto the employer being the 'responsible person'. The 'responsible person' has a duty to ensure the safety of everyone who uses their premises and those in the immediate vicinity who may be at risk if there is a fire. Anyone responsible for premises must carry out a fire safety risk assessment. The fire and rescue service will carry out inspections and failure to comply could lead to enforcement action or even prosecution.

Fire risk assessments will include:

- Identifying and removing any obstacles that may hinder fire evacuation.
- Ensuring that suitable **fire detection equipment** is in place.
- Making sure that all escape routes are clearly marked and free from obstacles.
- Testing fire alarm systems regularly to ensure they are in full operational condition.

All staff must be trained in fire and emergency evacuation procedures for their workplace. The emergency exit route will be the easiest route by which all staff, customers and visitors can leave the building safely. Fire action plans should be prominently displayed to show the emergency exit route.

Fire extinguishers should be available to tackle different types of fire. It is important that these are checked and maintained as required.

FIRE EXTINGUISHERS

Fire can be caused and started by many factors. Different portable fire extinguishers are used to fight small fires, but remember you should only use these if you have received training. Fire extinguishers are predominantly red with a colour label or band around the top identifying their contents. Also found on the fire extinguishers is a symbol and letter indicating the type of fire the extinguisher can be used for.

Fire blankets may be used to smother small localized fires such as a frying pan or burnt sugar pan. Fire blankets are also used to wrap people in if their clothes catch fire. The blanket smothers the oxygen and will put out the flames.

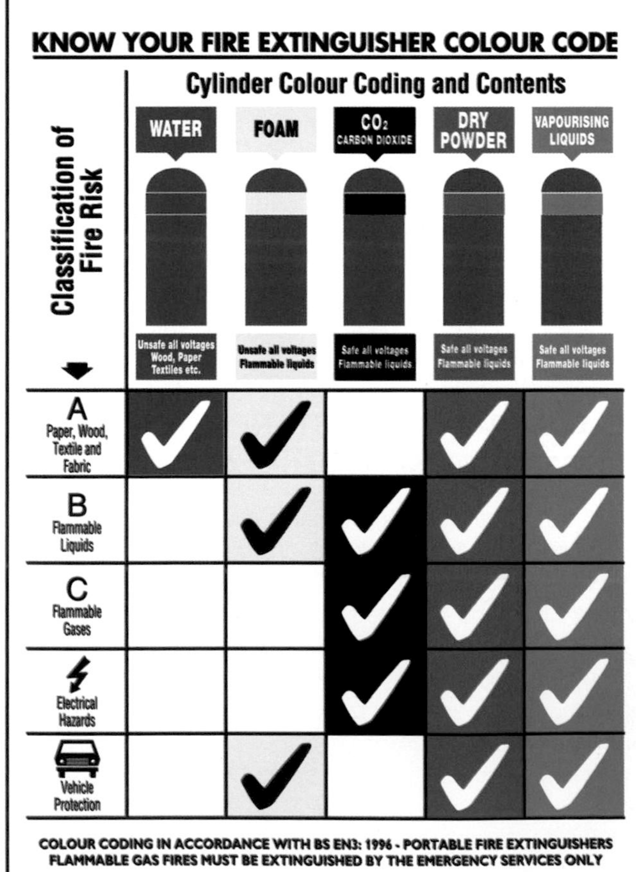

The dangers associated with electricity

If a person comes into direct contact with electricity, the consequences can be severe. Direct contact is referred to as an electric shock and the severity of an electric shock ranges from a short, sharp jolt to death!

It is also recommended that certain staff within an organization are trained to check cables, flex and plugs to ensure that the basic principles or electric circuitry in **portable appliances** are safe. This is referred to as Portable Appliance Testing – abbreviated as PAT.

Emergency procedure

In a case of fire or emergency, the following sequence must be followed:

- raise the alarm
- switch off any source of power (if safe and possible to do so!)
- call for help (first aid, emergency services)
- evacuate.

Following health and safety procedures

Health and safety is critical to our well-being. It can literally mean the difference between life and death and all that comes between.

The main reasons for working in a healthy and safe manner are to:

- prevent accidents and injuries
- maintain health
- increase productivity.

CHEF'S TIP Productivity refers to the amount of (good quality) work that a person can do in a specific time. For example, a highly skilled chef will be able to produce good quality results in the preparation and cooking of food in the same time that someone with low skill level may produce lower quality results and in, possibly, lower quantity.

Personal Protective Equipment (PPE)

PPE should be issued as a last resort. This may sound strange, but before issuing equipment to protect, all other possible solutions for carrying out the task in a way that does not require such equipment should be explored. For example, if using a cleaning chemical that requires a mask to be worn, is there another product available that will do the job but does not require the use of a mask?

HEALTH & SAFETY Examples of PPE include:

- gloves to protect hands from cleaning chemicals
- goggles to protect eyes from substances that will cause damage to eyesight.

RESPONSIBILITIES FOR THE USE OF PERSONAL PROTECTIVE EQUIPMENT

This is quite simple – employers must provide staff with PPE, when their role involves working in situations or with substances where PPE is deemed necessary.

Employees must use the PPE provided and comply with policy covering this issue. An employee must also report any faults or defects of the PPE to the employer.

Hazards and incidents that require reporting

To promote health and safety, it is important that any health and safety related issues or problems are reported to the appropriate person (e.g. supervisor or manager) so that remedial action can be taken.

Hazards can originate from a number of sources. For example:

- problems with buildings or equipment (e.g. through damage or misuse)
- ill-health (e.g. dermatitis, infectious diseases)
- environmental issues (e.g. excess noise or heat)
- abuse (e.g. mental or physical).

Signage in the kitchen environment

Safety signs are used in the kitchen and surrounding areas to help identify hazards, **obligatory** actions and prohibited actions for all staff, customers and visitors.

Yellow – Warning signs to alert people to various dangers such as slippery floors and hot water. Yellow signs also provide a warning of hazards, e.g. corrosive substances.

Warning
Hot fat

Blue – Mandatory signs to inform everyone what they must do in order to progress safely through a certain area or process. Usually this would indicate the need to wear protective clothing.

Red – Prohibition signs are designed to stop people from certain processes or actions in a hazardous area, such as no smoking or no access. Red signs also represent fire-fighting equipment, such as a fire hose.

Green – These are escape route signs, designed to show fire and emergency exits to staff, visitors and customers. Green is also the colour used to identify first aid equipment.

TEST YOURSELF

1 Describe three reasons for working safely.

i) ______
ii) ______
iii) ______

2 List four potential causes of slips, trips and/or falls.

i) ______
ii) ______
iii) ______
iv) ______

3 List four potential benefits of following good health and safety practices.

i) ______
ii) ______
iii) ______
iv) ______

4 Describe the terms 'hazard' and 'risk'.

______
______

5 What is meant by the abbreviation 'PAT' as used in the context of health and safety?

______
______

6 Describe four points to be considered when lifting an item from the floor and taking it into a different section of the kitchen.

i) ______
ii) ______
iii) ______
iv) ______

7 Name the three elements of fire.

i) ______
ii) ______
iii) ______

8 Identify the type of extinguisher that should be used in the following types of fire.

TYPE/CAUSE OF FIRE	EXTINGUISHER	LABEL COLOUR
Electrical fire		
Flammable liquids (e.g. oils)		
Solid material fire (e.g. wood)		
Vaporising liquids (e.g. gas)		

9 What is meant by the abbreviation 'PPE' as used in the context of health and safety?

______
______

10 What is the procedure when dealing with electrical accidents and dangers?

______
______

4

Introduction to healthier foods and special diets

Unit 104 Introduction to healthier foods and special diets

LEARNING OBJECTIVES

At the end of this chapter you will be able to:

- **State the benefits of healthier ingredients.**
- **Identify the types of ingredients that contribute to a healthier diet.**
- **Describe the consequences of a poor diet.**
- **Describe why it is important for catering establishments to offer healthier choices.**
- **Identify sources of current government nutritional guidelines and outline them.**
- **Describe the changes that can be made to dishes to make them healthier choices.**
- **Identify dietary/nutritional requirements groups of people who have special dietary needs.**

Introduction

There is the balance of different foods that determines whether a person's diet is healthy or not. For example, a diet high in fats, such as chips, burgers, chocolate and doughnuts would not be healthy over a long period of time. However, the odd treat is not going to cause problems, if eaten as part of a balanced diet.

The types of food and drink that we eat are very important. They are linked to our general health and well-being. For example, a healthy diet can help you to live a longer and healthier life. It can also reduce the likelihood of disease and illnesses, such as heart problems, diabetes, certain cancers and strokes. The food and drink we consume contributes to the amount of energy we have, our appearance as well as how we feel generally. It is therefore vital to our enjoyment of life. On this basis, we should be very conscious of the variety and quantities of the foods we eat. From a chef's perspective, it is important to be aware of health issues relating to food consumption. As people become more aware of the links between food consumption and health, they are likely to become increasingly demanding in terms of healthier food options.

The types of ingredients that contribute to a healthier diet

The FSA provides simple advice on eating a healthy diet called 'eight tips for eating well':

1 Base your meals on starchy foods.

HEALTH & SAFETY Many foods are processed or refined to make them more appealing and some people find them easier to eat. An example is wholemeal flour, which is refined to white flour to make items such as white bread and pasta. This removes much of the fibre content.

2 Eat lots of fruit and vegetables.

3 Eat more fish – including a portion of oily fish each week.

4 Cut down on saturated fat and sugar.

HEALTH & SAFETY You can cut down on saturated fat by eating lean meats. Use oils that are low in saturated fats and high in polyunsaturated or monounsaturated fats, such as sunflower oil and olive oil.

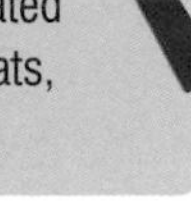

5 Try to eat less salt – no more than 6g a day.

6 Get active and try to maintain a healthy weight.

7 Drink plenty of water.

8 Don't skip breakfast.

Chefs should have a good understanding of ingredients. Then, when they choose menus, they can select healthier ingredients for the benefit of their customers. The FSA provides very simple guidance on the recommended **proportions** we should eat from each of the five following categories of food. This forms the basis of a well-balanced and healthy diet.

1 Fruit and Vegetables.
2 Bread, rice, potatoes, pasta and other starchy foods.
3 Meat, fish, eggs, beans and other non-dairy sources of protein.
4 Milk and dairy foods.
5 Foods and drinks high in fat and/or sugar.

This is shown as 'The eatwell plate'.

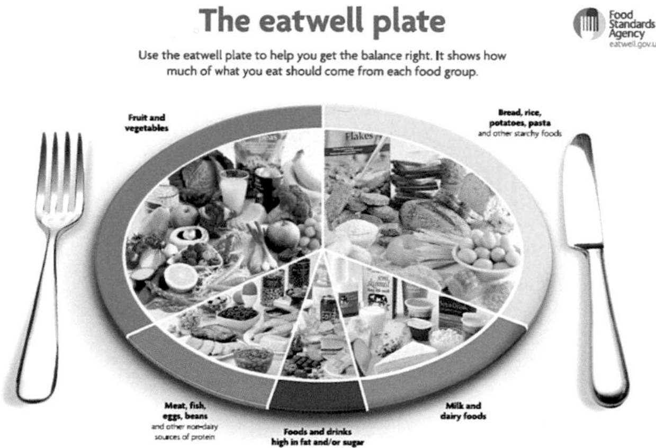

Why catering establishments should offer healthier choices

The government is very aware of the issues that are caused by unhealthy diets. There are campaigns to promote the benefits of healthy eating as well as the harm that a prolonged period of unhealthy eating can cause. There is also the increase in costs attributed to healthcare to consider. Most people are aware of the benefits of eating a healthy diet and this provides a sales opportunity for catering establishments. As a result, demand for healthier products and dishes is increasing. Establishments that do not offer healthier options are likely to face a drop in sales and therefore profit. Therefore, they should ensure that they have at least some food items and/or dishes to offer that will make a healthy **contribution** to the diet. Catering establishments form part of the healthy eating scene and, as chefs and practitioners, an awareness of this subject is essential.

A good example is the case of school meals. After much recent pressure, school caterers are monitored to ensure that children consume foods that match those seen on the eatwell plate. In 2005, the famous chef, Jamie Oliver, became extremely concerned with the highly processed foods eaten by children at school. Jamie ran a TV campaign to publicize the scale of the problem. He put pressure on the government to start to tackle the problem and asked for money to train staff to prepare meals from fresh and healthier ingredients. Another issue is that fresh foods can cost more to produce and take longer to prepare and cook. Highly processed foods are manufactured on a large scale and are often made from low quality ingredients, making them cheap to produce. This makes such foods appear cheap and convenient compared to producing fresh foods.

Making dishes healthier according to current nutritional guidelines

Every change can help. Caterers can look at the food they produce and see how it can be made healthier. They can ask the following questions:

- Are there any ingredients that could be changed for a healthier alternative? For example, could the chef substitute cream for yoghurt without impacting the dish too much?
- Can the fat or sugar content of the food be reduced without affecting the eating quality of the dish?
- When garnishing or thinking about the accompaniments for dishes, is it possible to add extra vegetables to add vitamins, minerals and fibre?
- Can the amount of salt be reduced or even removed?

HEALTH & SAFETY Too much salt in the diet can lead to the development of high blood pressure, which can cause heart attacks and strokes.

TASK Once per week, a school canteen traditionally offers children chicken Kiev and chips. The chicken Kiev is made from processed chicken and is bought in frozen. The chips are also bought in frozen and both items are deep-fried to serve. This dish is very popular with the students, although the canteen manager knows that it is not particularly healthy.

What could be done to produce a similar dish but in a healthier way?

Nutrients and their importance

Nutrients are the parts of foods that help the body to perform and maintain **bodily functions**. This includes our movement, sight, growth and repair. Nutrients are broken down into five main categories: carbohydrates, fats, proteins, vitamins and minerals.

Carbohydrates

Carbohydrates provide our greatest source of energy. They can be split into three sub-groups. These groups are sugars, starches and dietary fibre.

SUGARS

There are many different types of sugar, the most obvious being the sugar that we use to sweeten tea and coffee or when making cakes and biscuits, etc. This is sucrose.

Sucrose

It is found in fruits and vegetables. Sugar cane and beet contain high quantities of sucrose.

Other forms of sugar include:

Maltose – The sugar that is found in cereal grains and used in beer making. Maltose is not as sweet as sucrose.

Lactose – The type of sugar that is present in milk. The amount of sugar present depends on the type and source of the milk.

STARCHES

Starches are made up of simple sugars. Starches do not dissolve in water like sugars do, but become much easier to digest once cooked. Starches are present in many types of food, but are particularly high in cereals, rice and root vegetables. If you leave peeled and cut potatoes in water for a while, some of the starch from the potatoes will leak and fall to the bottom of the bowl. It appears as a smooth, silky and waxy white substance.

Other products that are high in starch include flour and products made from flour, such as pasta and bread.

TASK Diet can influence how children behave and concentrate. Some schools are trying to achieve this by providing healthier foods. Find out what changes the schools are making and why.

HEALTH & SAFETY It is better for your carbohydrates to come from eating starchy foods rarther than sugary foods. Energy is released more slowly, so you avoid mood swings.

DIETARY FIBRE

Unlike sugars and starches, dietary fibre cannot be digested. It does not provide the body with energy. However, dietary fibre is a very important part of a balanced diet for the following reasons;

- It aids **digestion** and promotes bowel action, removing waste products from the body.
- It helps to control the digestion of nutrients and the way nutrients are processed.
- It adds bulk to the diet, reducing the feeling of hunger and the desire to eat.

Fats

Fats have many functions in the human body and are naturally present in many of the foods we eat.

Fats come from animals, fish, vegetables or cereals, seeds and nuts. They are referred to as saturated or unsaturated. Saturated fats are usually found in animal products whereas unsaturated fats are usually associated with oily fish, vegetables, seeds and nuts.

CHEF'S TIP We use fats and oils in many cooking processes and as an ingredient within recipes. The main difference between fats and oils is that at room temperature, fats are solid whereas oils are liquid. This is an easy way to tell them apart.

HEALTH & SAFETY Saturated fats, for such as butter and lard, increase cholesterol in the blood. Too much cholesterol can lead to heart disease.

Fats are important in the body for a number of reasons:

- The body can produce energy from fats in greater quantities than carbohydrates (sugars and starches).
- Fat provides protection for the vital organs. Our vital organs are mostly within the chest and stomach area. Some of our organs, in particular the kidneys, have a thick layer of fat surrounding them to protect them from impact and other potential damage.
- Fats help to keep our body temperature stable.

HEALTH & SAFETY Although we need fats in our diet, there is a great deal of concern about eating too much. Too much fat in our diet can cause **obesity** (being overweight) as well as other health issues, such as heart disease.

Proteins

Proteins are very important to the body as they are the major part of the cells that actually form the body. It is essential that we have a good supply of proteins in our diet.

The following points describe the main functions of proteins.

GROWTH

Cells make up our bodies. As we grow from birth into adulthood, our bodies change and develop. To make new cells we need proteins.

REPAIR

The life span of cells ranges from about a week to a few months. Throughout our lives, our bodies need to replace cells as they die. Cells also become damaged if we get injured and we need proteins to replace the dead cells with new ones.

TO CARRY OUT BODILY FUNCTIONS

Throughout life our bodies perform millions of tasks. This is happening every second of our lives in our thoughts, actions and in the functions required to stay alive. These are controlled by types of protein called enzymes and hormones.

A SECONDARY SOURCE OF ENERGY

Any excess protein in our diet is converted into carbohydrate or fat. It cannot be stored for use at a later time. Protein is referred to as a secondary source of energy because its main function is not as a source of energy.

Vitamins

As far as we are aware, the body requires 13 vitamins to function properly. In comparison to carbohydrates, fats and proteins, vitamins form a much smaller structural part within the foods we eat. Vitamins are essential for the body to perform two major functions:

- growth and repair of the body
- control of the functions of our body cells.

Minerals

Currently we know that the body needs 19 minerals to function properly. Minerals are present in a vast range of foods and form a tiny structural part within the foods we eat. Minerals have many functions in the body:

MINERALS AND BONES AND TEETH

Minerals found in our bones and teeth include calcium, magnesium, phosphorus and fluorine.

MINERALS AND BODILY FUNCTIONS

We need minerals to help control actions like energy release, digestion, excretion and circulation in the body.

MINERALS AND THE LEVELS OF FLUIDS HELD IN THE BODY

The body is approximately 60–65 per cent water. Minerals are very important for controlling the level of fluids in the body.

HEALTH & SAFETY Without water a human can only survive for a few days.

A balanced diet

It is important that our diet includes the full range of nutrients in the right quantities for us to enjoy a healthy life. One way to look at the balance in our diet is to place foods into groups, linked to the nutrients contained within those foods. It is then easier to make sure each of the groups is included in the diet to create a balanced diet.

The majority of nutrients are found in the groups of fruit and vegetables, breads and cereals, milk and dairy products and meat and fish. The table on page 39 shows how the main food groups are classified.

Drinks are also a form of nutritional intake and should be considered in the same way as food. Alcoholic drinks, in particular, have an impact on our bodies if consumed on a regular basis. As well as the health implications and potential organ damage from regular and excessive consumption of alcohol, there is also the impact from the levels of carbohydrate consumed. The body converts excess levels of carbohydrate to fat and may contribute to becoming overweight.

FOOD GROUP	EXAMPLES OF FOODS	NUTRIENTS PRESENT
Fruits and vegetables	Fruits Fruit juices Vegetables **Pulses** (peas, beans, lentils)	Carbohydrate Dietary fibre Vitamins – C group Minerals Carotene – orange pigment converted to Vitamin A in the body Protein (from pulses)
Breads and cereals	Breads Cereals (e.g. rice, couscous) Breakfast cereals and porridge Pasta Flour and associated products	Carbohydrate Dietary fibre Vitamins – B group Minerals Protein
Milk and dairy products	Milk Cheese Cream Yoghurt Butter Eggs	Protein Carbohydrate Fat Vitamins – A and D Minerals – calcium
Meat and fish	Meat Poultry **Offal** Fish Shellfish	Protein Fat Vitamins – A, B group, D Minerals – iron
Fatty foods (non-dairy)	Foods containing animal fats (suet, lard, dripping) Vegetable oils Vegetable suet Many convenience foods – Fast foods (burgers, fried foods)	Fat Vitamins A and D
Sugary foods	Confectionery – sweets, chocolate, biscuits, cakes, soft drinks, carbonated sweetened drinks Preserves and jams	Carbohydrate Fat

Water and fibre in the diet

Water is one of the most important substances in life and without it we would not survive for very long. A large part of our bodies, approximately 60–65 per cent, is water. Without water, a human being can only survive for 1 or 2 days, whereas without food, we can survive for a number of weeks.

We need to replace water regularly due to going to the toilet, breathing and sweating. We also lose large quantities of water when we are ill through sickness and diarrhoea. It is extremely important that we drink water regularly to keep our bodies hydrated and provide the organs with enough water

to function properly. It is recommended that we drink eight glasses of water throughout the day.

Water performs many functions in the body. The following points describe these functions.

TO ASSIST THE BODY IN REMOVING WASTE PRODUCTS

It is very important that waste is removed from the body. If waste is not removed, it could start to release toxins (poisons) which could cause organ damage and/or sickness.

TO CONTROL BODY TEMPERATURE

Water helps to control our body temperature through sweating. When our bodies get hot or overheat, water is released through our pores. This brings our temperature down to a more comfortable level.

TO TRANSPORT OXYGEN AND NUTRIENTS AROUND THE BODY

Nutrients, enzymes and hormones are dissolved in water, allowing nutrients to be transported to the many cells around the body.

TO SUPPLY MINERALS DIRECTLY TO THE BODY

Water contains minerals naturally, although the amounts of minerals can differ according to the origin of the water.

TO ACT AS A LUBRICANT

Water helps to **lubricate** certain areas of the body, particularly the eyes and eyelids. Water also helps to ensure that our joints are flexible, allowing free and easy movement.

Dietary fibre

We cannot digest dietary fibre like other foods, although it will soften through cooking. When eaten, it is broken down mechanically by our teeth and swallowed but it is not broken down any further beyond this stage.

Dietary fibre promotes the removal of waste from the body and provides a feeling of being 'full'. It satisfies our hunger and reduces the likelihood of overeating. Many recent findings recommend that we should aim to reduce the amounts of sugar, fat and salt in our diets and increase the quantities of dietary fibre. All dietary fibre comes from vegetables, fruits and cereals. Animal products contain no dietary fibre.

To increase the amount of dietary fibre in our diet, we can:

- eat wholemeal or granary bread
- use wholemeal flour in place of white flour
- eat wholegrain cereal products or bran enriched cereals
- eat wholemeal pasta and wholegrain rice
- eat plenty of fruit or vegetables
- eat plenty of pulses and lentils.

TASK Using the advice and information from this chapter, create a healthy menu for your family for a weekend, which will help to provide a balanced diet.

Special diets

Vulnerable groups

Each person is different and the nutritional needs of each of us depends on a whole range of factors. These include age, height, size, lifestyle and occupation, as well as hereditary factors.

However, at key stages and under certain circumstances, our nutritional needs will change. The following points highlight the **vulnerable groups** that have particular nutritional needs.

BABIES AND YOUNG CHILDREN

In the first 6 months of life, babies survive on milk to provide all of their **nutritional requirements**. Although this is an extremely important time for development, a baby will not use vast amounts of energy at this stage. In fact, a great deal of time is spent sleeping and eating!

As children continue to develop and grow, their nutritional requirements grow as well. By the time children start school, their nutritional needs increase rapidly, particularly the need for

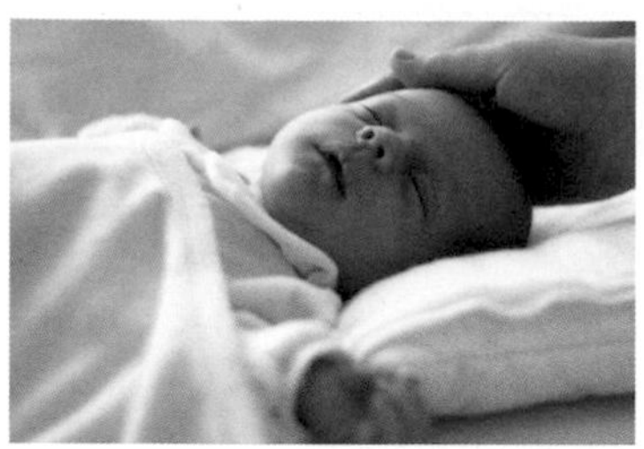

calcium, protein and iron. Children are also very active during this time, demanding lots of nutrients to keep the body functioning. As they are not fully grown at this stage, they will not eat the quantities of an adult. They should, however, eat smaller amounts regularly throughout the day to keep up their energy levels.

TEENAGERS

As children move into their teenage years, the body is subject to a great deal of physical change and growth. This can also be an emotional time for young people, so it is important that they have a well balanced diet. The diet should supply the body with all the nutrients it needs.

PREGNANCY

During pregnancy, a woman is supporting the growth and development of her baby. It is vitally important that her nutritional intake is enough for the higher levels of energy and nutrients required at this time.

Once the baby is born, the mother may breast-feed the baby during the first months of its life and this will be the main source of food for the baby. With this extra demand, the mother will again need higher levels of nutrients to support the baby's growth as well as her own well-being.

Expectant mothers require a diet with a high nutritional value. It should contain the range of vitamins and nutrients and, in particular, folic acid. However, vitamin A, which is found in liver, is one vitamin which should be avoided. Pregnant women should not eat foods that have a high risk of food poisoning, such as raw egg products, pates and unpasteurised cheese.

THE ELDERLY

During the later years of life, the body generally starts to slow down and requires less energy. Appetite also tends to get smaller as we get older. Despite these facts, the elderly still need a diet with a high nutrient content to support good health and well-being. As with children, it is recommended that smaller meals are eaten regularly throughout the day to ensure adequate levels of nutrients, particularly calcium and iron. The elderly should eat foods high in vitamin D, which is found in a small number of foods. Good food sources are oily fish and eggs. Other food sources include fortified foods such as margarine, breakfast cereals and powdered milk.

Most vitamin D intake is absorbed from sunlight on our skin. This is because the vitamin forms under the skin in reaction to sunlight. The best source is summer sunlight although people must take care not to burn.

PEOPLE SUFFERING FROM ILL-HEALTH

People suffering from ill-health can often lose their appetite. Their immune system and energy levels are likely to be lower than usual. For this reason, it is important that the body gets the nutrients it requires to function and to make its recovery to health. This group need foods that are easy to digest, contain all the nutrients the body needs and are tempting to eat.

TASK One of your friends, Tom, has been very ill with glandular fever. Tom is still very weak and needs cheering up. You decide to make him dinner. Design a menu that would be suitable for his needs.

People with special dietary requirements

In modern times we live in a society of many cultures. People are becoming more aware and concerned about the nutritional content of food and its **origin**. Some people may follow a particular diet for a specific reason. This may be due to their religion, personal preference, moral stance, or for health reasons, such as allergies or intolerances.

For example, there are several reasons why some groups do not eat meat.

VEGETARIAN

Vegetarians do not eat meat, meat products or fish. Some vegetarians eat dairy products. These are called lacto-vegetarians. Vegetarians who do not eat dairy products are known as vegans.

RELIGION

In many religions, eating meat is forbidden. Many of the religions in India and the Eastern world are vegetarian. As more people travel and relocate around the world, religions, such as Hinduism and Buddhism, are becoming more widespread throughout the western world.

PERSONAL PREFERENCE

Some people simply dislike the texture or flavour of meat and fish. On this basis, they choose not to include meat in their diet.

HEALTH

There has been a great amount of research into diets containing meat and meat products. The main focus is on the levels of saturated fat in meat and the impact this has on obesity, the high levels of cholesterol and heart related illnesses. Many people in poorer countries do not have access to meat in the quantities that we are used to in the Western world. Scientists have compared western diets with those in poorer countries. Findings suggest that a largely vegetarian diet, high in dietary fibre and nutrients, is healthier than a diet high in saturated fats. It is for this reason that some people may have opted to follow a vegetarian diet.

ALLERGIES AND INTOLERANCES

Some people may be allergic to eating meat or fish or it may cause them discomfort or unpleasant side-effects. In this situation, the removal of meat and fish from the diet is more of a necessity than a preference.

The effects of a lack or excess of nutrients

A lack of food and the nutrients within food is called 'malnutrition' in the form of 'under-nutrition'. An excess of food consumption and nutritional intake is called 'over-nutrition'.

The major concern is that both under-nutrition and over-nutrition have clear links to health problems. The tables on page 43 provide a summary of some of the health problems related to a lack or excess of certain nutrients.

UNDER-NUTRITION

NUTRIENT UNDERSUPPLIED	CONSEQUENCES WITH REGARD TO HEALTH
Protein	Water retention, muscle wastage, ulcers, hair loss.
Carbohydrate	Weight loss, lack of energy, low immune system.
Fat	Weight loss, lack of energy, low immune system.
Dietary fibre	Constipation, bowel disorders, bowel cancer.
Vitamin A	Potential blindness, hydration problems.
Vitamin B1	Nervous disorders.
Vitamin B2	Growth, irritable skin, cracks in skin.
Vitamin B6	Sickness and depression, eczema, irritability.
Vitamin B12	Mental problems, anaemia, blood disorders.
Vitamin C	Scurvy, depression, fatigue, blood loss, bruising.
Vitamin D	Rickets.
Niacin	Cuts in the skin, mental problems, depression, diarrhoea.
Iron	Fatigue, lack of strength, lack of energy.
Calcium	Rickets.
Trace elements	Associated with poor health and development.

OVER-NUTRITION

NUTRIENT OVERSUPPLIED	CONSEQUENCES WITH REGARD TO HEALTH
Carbohydrate	Tooth decay caused by eating sugar. Overweight. Diabetes caused by eating too many sugary foods over a long time.
Fat	Overweight. Heart disease, heart attack, high blood pressure, angina, all are linked to a diet high in fat, particularly saturated (animal) fats.
Salt (sodium chloride)	High blood pressure and heart problems.

Health and safety

Allergies can cause 'anaphylactic shock'. This is the way the body reacts to foods it rejects. A major concern with anaphylactic shock is that the reaction gets stronger and more severe each time the body is exposed to the food concerned. In extreme cases the throat closes leaving the person unable to breath.

Foods that may cause allergies or intolerances

Food labelling law states that packaged food must be labelled if it contains any of 14 identified allergens. It is good practice for caterers to identify allergens in dishes. They should train their staff to respond to customer questions on the subject. It is essential that front-line service staff know the ingredients contained in a dish. Menus must also accurately identify ingredients that commonly cause reactions when eaten.

THE 14 MOST COMMON CAUSES OF REACTIONS TO FOOD

1 Molluscs (e.g. mussels and clams).
2 Crustaceans (e.g. lobster and prawns).
3 Gluten (products made from wheat, rye, barley and oats, such as biscuits and bread).
4 Nuts (e.g. hazelnuts, almonds, walnuts, Brazil, etc.).
5 Peanuts.
6 Fish.
7 Eggs.
8 Lactose in milk and milk products (e.g. yoghurt and cheese).
9 Celery and celeriac.
10 Mustard and associated products (e.g. mustard seeds, leaves and oil).
11 Sesame seeds and associated products (e.g. sesame oil, some types of biscuits and breads).
12 Soybeans (e.g. tofu, textured vegetable protein – TVP and soy sauce).
13 Lupin (found in common garden plants, related to legumes such as peanuts, peas, lentils and beans. The seeds from some types of lupin can be used in foods such as seeded bread and can also be ground to make lupin flour, sometimes used in foods such as pastries).
14 Sulphites – over ten parts per million (commonly found in wine, the chemicals known as sulphites are naturally present in a few foods but generally are added as preservatives to a wide range of foods, drinks, medicines and cosmetics. Sulphur dioxide is found in the air as a result of the burning of fossil fuels).

It is possible for any food to cause an allergic reaction or intolerance in an individual as we are all unique in our bodily make-up. However, there are certain foods that more commonly cause allergies. The most frequent food causing an allergic reaction is the peanut and peanut products. It is advised that young children are not introduced to peanuts, partly due to the risk of allergy but also to avoid choking.

People who are aware of allergies are provided with medicine to counteract the effects of the shock. Depending on the severity of the shock, the time in which a person needs to receive the antidote will shorten. It is essential that foods associated with allergies and intolerances are clearly labelled so that people know what ingredients they contain. Other foods that commonly cause food allergies include alcohol, seafood, fish, fruit, flour, cow's milk and cereals.

CHEF'S TIP People with specific allergies often carry an 'EpiPen'. These auto-injectors are intended for immediate self administration in the emergency treatment of allergic anaphylactic reactions.

Intolerance may not be as immediately dangerous as an allergy but can cause significant discomfort and potential illness through repeated exposure.

Coeliac disease

Gluten is a substance formed from proteins found in wheat and rye. Gluten causes damage to the small intestine in some people. This causes a condition called **coeliac** disease.

Coeliac UK - www.coeliac.org.uk/

Diabetes

Diabetes is a condition where the body cannot produce insulin, does not produce enough insulin or the insulin produced does not work. Insulin is the hormone that controls the level of sugar in the blood. Diabetes can be due to the long-term eating of foods that are high in sugar. Diabetes can be fatal if it is not managed. It is controlled by insulin injections, diet and exercise.

TASK Your mother is a diabetic and you want to make her a birthday cake. Find or create a recipe for a cake that will be suitable and safe for your mother to eat.

Current government guidelines

Current guidelines and further information can be sourced from the following websites.

- *The British Nutrition Foundation* – **www.nutrition.org.uk**
- *Department of Health* – **www.dh.gov.uk**
- *The Department for Environment, Food and Rural Affairs (DEFRA)* – **http://ww2.defra.gov.uk/**
- *The Food Standards Agency (FSA)* – **www.fsa.gov.uk**
- *The National Advisory Committee on Nutritional Education – NACNE*
  A committee of experts examining the links between health and diet.
- *The Committee on Nutrition – (SACN)*
  The Scientific Advisory Committee on Nutrition is a UK-wide Advisory Committee set up to replace the Committee on Medical Aspects of Food and Nutrition Policy (COMA). It advises the UK health departments as well as the Food Standards Agency.

TEST YOURSELF

1 What are the benefits of eating a low fat diet? Give two ways that a chef could reduce fat in their menus.

____

2 List the main two functions of the following nutrients.

CARBOHYDRATES	
1.	2.

FAT	
1.	2.

PROTEINS	
1.	2.

VITAMINS	
1.	2.

MINERALS	
1.	2.

3 Provide two reasons why dietary fibre is so important in the diet.

i) ____________________
ii) ____________________

4 What is meant by the term 'balanced diet'?

____

5 Why is water so important in the diet?

____

6 Provide three reasons why it is advisable to reduce the amount of sugar we eat in the diet?

i) ____________________
ii) ____________________
iii) ____________________

7 List two reasons why someone might choose to follow a vegetarian diet.

i) ____________________
ii) ____________________

8 Which of the following foods would a person suffering from coeliac disease have to avoid?

- Milk
- Bread
- Seafood
- Fruit
- Alcohol

9 Why are young children and pregnant women referred to as vulnerable groups with regard to nutritional intake?

____

10 Why is it important to know exactly what ingredients are used to make a dish, or are contained within a pre-prepared food product, when serving the public?

____

____

5

Introduction to kitchen equipment

Unit 105 Introduction to kitchen equipment

LEARNING OBJECTIVES

On completion of this chapter you will be able to:

- **State the factors in selecting equipment and utensils for use.**
- **State how to use equipment and utensils correctly and safely.**
- **Identify associated hazards with using, cleaning and storing equipment and utensils.**
- **State how to carry out routine care and storage of equipment and utensils.**
- **Identify the different types of knives and cutting equipment and their uses.**
- **State the importance of correct and safe use of knives and cutting equipment.**
- **Describe how to clean, maintain and store knives and cutting equipment.**
- **Identify relevant age restrictions specific to the use of cutting equipment.**

Introduction

Equipment is designed with a purpose in mind. For example, scales were designed to weigh, refrigerators to keep food cold and ovens to cook food. Occasionally, we can be tempted to use equipment for the wrong purpose, perhaps because it seems convenient at the time or possibly due to a lack of experience and/or knowledge. It is when equipment is used incorrectly that the final result can be affected or accidents can happen.

There is a term 'a bad workman blames his tools', which to some extent is true. A chef with poor skills and/or a sloppy approach will not perform a task very well regardless as to the quality of his or her tools and equipment.

Factors required in selecting equipment and utensils

Equipment comes in all shapes and sizes and is designed to be used for certain tasks. For example, many frying pans have a non-stick surface so that foods, including delicate items such as eggs, can be cooked at fairly high temperatures without them sticking to the surface. This makes it much easier to handle and move foods without the risk of breaking or damaging them through having to use harsh movements. However, a frying pan would not be suitable for making soup due to its wide and shallow surface area; where a much deeper pan would be required to hold the amount of liquid required. There is also no requirement for the ingredients used in making the soup to be in direct contact with the surface area of the pan, as there is when shallow frying foods.

It is much easier to perform tasks if the equipment being used is of high quality and suitable for the task in hand. For this reason, it is essential that aspiring chefs learn to handle, maintain and care for their knives and equipment at an early stage of their learning and development.

How to use equipment and utensils correctly and safely

The following tables show how to carry out routine care and storage of equipment and utensils. It also identifies hazards with using, cleaning and storing equipment and utensils.

VIDEO CLIP Demonstration of a selection of large and small equipment.

TYPE OF EQUIPMENT	SAFE USES	ASSOCIATED HAZARDS	ROUTINE CARE AND STORAGE
Conventional oven	The temperature in the **oven chamber** is **thermostatically controlled** and the burners at the top of the oven can be set to provide a low or high heat. It has many uses including baking, roasting, stewing, braising and frying.	If the oven is powered by gas, it is very important that the gas is ignited once turned on. Ovens should be fitted with a flame failure device to prevent gas spillage and the risk of explosion.	Gas equipment should be checked and serviced on a regular basis to ensure that there are no gas leaks.

TYPE OF EQUIPMENT	SAFE USES	ASSOCIATED HAZARDS	ROUTINE CARE AND STORAGE
Fan assisted oven (convection)	A fan built in to the cooking chamber circulates hot air evenly through the oven, resulting in faster cooking times. Good for baking and roasting due to the accuracy and even nature of the temperature.	When cleaning, it is important that it is allowed to cool down sufficiently to avoid burns. Appropriate PPE, should be worn when using cleaning chemicals.	
Combination oven	Can be used for many purposes. It can be used as a convection oven, a steamer or a combination of both. It has computerized control which can control temperature and **humidity**. It also has the capacity to hold food at a specified temperature without additional cooking or drying. It can be used to **prove** and bake, braise and stew, roast, grill, steam, fry, hold hot foods and a combination of the above. Modern combination ovens can record their history and use for hazard analysis.	Foods often have to be placed into, or removed from, the oven at height. Great care and attention is required when performing such tasks. If the oven is being used as a steamer or in combination mode, it is also important that heat and steam are released slowly before attempting to place or remove items from the oven.	Modern combination ovens have a self-cleaning programme to ensure the oven stays in very hygienic, safe and efficient condition.
Microwave	Cooks food by disturbing the water molecules within foods. The microwaves energize these molecules and this reaction produces heat, which in turn cooks the food. A microwave, if not used correctly, can have the potential to dry foods out and produce undesired textures. A microwave is very good for reheating foods that have already been cooked.	Microwaves will deflect from metal surfaces and cause small explosions within the oven chamber. Metal should never be used in a microwave.	It is essential that any spillages or spluttering from cooking are cleaned up immediately to prevent cross-contamination or bacterial growth.
Induction hob	An energy saving and safety conscious invention. The hob will only heat up when a pan with a magnetic base is in direct contact. When contact is broken that heat retracts very quickly.	Reduces many of the hazards associated with conventional cooking methods. For example there is virtually no chance of burning from direct contact with an induction hob. Induction equipment tends to be very easy to clean.	Induction equipment tends to be quite expensive and the utensils have to be suitable (magnetic).
Solid top	The solid top is made of one large burner and a complete solid metal hob. A solid top provides an efficient use of surface area and pans can be moved around the cooking area to points where the heat is most suitable for the speed of cooking required (i.e. very hot in the centre and cooler at the edges).	Some solid tops, particularly those powered by gas, have removable rings in the centre of the plate. The rings, due to their thick metal structure are very heavy. Move and replace the rings carefully to avoid them falling. The surface also stays hot for a long time after it has been turned off.	Gas powered ovens should have flame failure devices to ensure gas does not leak. Thermostats need to be checked.

TYPE OF EQUIPMENT	SAFE USES	ASSOCIATED HAZARDS	ROUTINE CARE AND STORAGE
Grill	The heat source is underneath the food and food items are placed on the grill bars above the heat. This type of grill produces the enhancing grill lines on foods reflecting where the food has been in contact with the bars. Due to the desired outcome when grilling food in this way, gas is usually the preferred heat source as this produces a flame. Barbeques or charcoal fuelled grills will produce very similar results.	Care has to be taken when placing and removing food items on the grill. The use of sturdy tongs is recommended to protect the hands from burning. It is also necessary to be aware of flames rising if fats and/or oils drip onto the naked flame.	Has a tray for catching grease and cooking liquids. This also needs to be cleaned at the end of the cooking process.
Salamander	A **salamander** is also a type of grill. But the heat from a salamander comes from elements above the food rather than below the food as in the case of the flame grill. It is important that grills are operating at the correct temperature when the cooking process begins.	Salamanders are often placed at chest height or above. Therefore, it is essential that care is taken when placing and removing items to and from the grill. A thick cloth that is in good condition and is clean and dry, is also required when handling grilling trays when cooking using a salamander.	Salamanders also have a tray to catch grease. This needs to be emptied appropriately and cleaned using hot water and a cleaning chemical (detergent).
Pressure steamer	Steam is the vapour that is produced by boiling water. A steamer uses this vapour to cook food items. Pressure steamers have the capacity to increase the pressure within the steaming chamber and therefore increase the temperature.	The main hazard associated with the use of a steamer is scalding. When a steamer door is first opened, the steam will escape from the chamber and out into the open air. It is advised that the door is opened slightly at first while standing behind the door itself. Once the main body of steam has dispersed, the food items can be safely removed.	It is vital to keep a steamer clean. The water held within the steamer itself needs to be changed on a regular basis. All shelving needs to be cleaned after use to ensure a hygienic chamber.
Deep fryer	Potentially one of the most dangerous pieces of equipment in the kitchen. A deep fryer consists of a vessel which contains a depth of oil that will surround foods once they are placed into the vessel. The oil in a deep fryer reaches very hot temperatures (up to 200°C). Deep fryers contain a thermostatic control to avoid overheating to a point where the oil would catch fire. A deep fryer also has a 'cool zone' below the heat source. This is designed to catch any particles of food that fall away from the main item being cooked.	Placing items into a deep fryer can be quite a hazardous activity. Food items should never be thrown into a deep fryer or dropped from a height. This would cause splashing and the potential for a nasty accident. When changing the oil in a deep fryer, it is essential that it is allowed to cool first, and that suitable containers are in place to capture the oil.	The oil in a deep fryer needs to be kept as clean as possible to extend its life. Food debris should be removed to prevent spoilage and oil should not be overheated unnecessarily.

TYPE OF EQUIPMENT	SAFE USES	ASSOCIATED HAZARDS	ROUTINE CARE AND STORAGE
Refrigerator	A refrigerator's main function is to keep food items cold and in good condition for use. A refrigerator should function between 1°C and 5°C, a temperature that will not start to freeze foods but will help to prevent bacterial growth and spoilage and extend the life-span of the food.	Refrigerators are used to store a whole range of products. Therefore, it is essential that good storage practices are followed to ensure that cross-contamination from one product to another is avoided.	Temperatures should be closely monitored on a daily basis and all food items stored in a refrigerator should be covered, clearly labelled and dated.
Hotplate	Designed to keep plates and other service equipment hot during service periods. This equipment should be heated to a point that is manageable for staff to handle but also keep food in prime condition for service.	Although hotplates and heated lighting are designed primarily to maintain temperature rather than increase it, the elements and bulbs used are extremely hot and would cause a nasty injury if they ever came into direct contact with the skin.	Hotplates should be emptied and cleaned on a regular basis to provide a clean and hygienic environment.
Bain-marie	Bain-marie translates to mean 'water-bath'. The function of a bain-marie is to keep food items, particularly foods high in liquid content, such as soups, sauces and stews, hot during the service period.	It is important to monitor the amount of liquid that is present in a bain-marie. During the time that a bain-marie is functioning, water is being heated and will gradually vaporize (evaporate). This could cause the heating element to burn out, causing potential damage to the heating element and also a risk of fire.	A bain-marie should be monitored while in use to ensure that it has enough water. Once the service period is finished, the bain-marie should be switched off and emptied carefully. Once this is complete, the bain-marie should be cleaned thoroughly.
Proving cabinet	A proving cabinet is designed to provide a warm and **moist environment** in which dough products can prove (rise). The temperature in a proving cabinet is between 30°C and 40°C. The ideal temperature for yeast to ferment is around 37°C. This environment will allow the yeast to ferment and develop the gluten in the flour to produce dough capable of rising to provide an airy and springy product.	Modern proving cabinets are often plumbed in, removing the need to ensure that water is always present in the cabinet. Older proving cabinets may require a manual feed which will have to be monitored while the cabinet is in use.	Proving cabinets are not ovens and should not be exposed to the conditions that an oven receives. However, it is still important that the cabinet and its shelves are kept clean and hygienic for use.

CHEF'S TIP When holding food for service it is very important to keep the temperature of the food out of the danger zone. This is between 5°C and 63°C.

Make a poster showing the procedures for keeping foods either below 5°C or above 63°C. Include the type of equipment you would need.

Small equipment and its use in the kitchen

WEB LINK Look at the following website to find out more about hot and cold temperature control **http://www.food.gov.uk/multimedia** and search for 3. Houserules hot & cold temperature control.

PICTURE	TYPE OF EQUIPMENT	USE
	Scales	Used to accurately weigh ingredients for specific recipes.
	Measuring jug	Used to accurately measure volumes of liquids (water, wine, stock, milk, etc.).
	Liquidizers	Used to **blend** foods into liquids–soups and sauces, for example.
	Blenders	Blenders are similar to liquidizers but are usually larger and have additional functions – shredding vegetables, for example.
	Mixers	Mixers come in a variety of sizes. Mixing machines are used for making dough (e.g. bread) and other mixes (e.g. cakes).

PICTURE	TYPE OF EQUIPMENT	USE
	Pestle and mortar	A pestle and mortar is used to pound herbs and spices into pastes or purees. Oil or vinegar is sometimes used to help this process.
	Rolling pin	The main use of a rolling pin is to roll out pastry into the required shape. A rolling pin is sometimes used to roll out dough, when making Chelsea buns, for example.
	Spider	A spider is used to remove items (such as vegetables) from saucepans or deep-fried items from a deep-fryer. In both examples, the spider catches the food with the water or oil draining back into the cooking vessel.
	Slice	A slice is used to lift items safely from a tray. The slice has been designed to provide a very thin, usually square or rectangular platform, which slides between food items and the tray.
	Ladle	A ladle is used to serve or add liquids, such as stocks, soups and sauces.
	Whisk	Whisks are designed to add air and mix liquids and batters together. For example, a whisk is used when aerating egg whites to make meringues.
	Cutlet bat **VIDEO CLIP** Using a cutlet bat to prepare pork escalopes.	A cutlet bat is normally square or rectangular and made of sturdy metal. It is used to batten out meats to make them flatter and more even. An example of a product where a cutlet bat would be used is a pork escalope.
	Saucepans	Saucepans come in many different sizes and can be made of many different metals (stainless steel, copper, **alloys** – (a mixture of metals)). Saucepans play a massive part in the kitchen and have many uses.
	Sauté pan	**Sauté** is a method of frying and the term literally means to jump or toss. The process of 'sauté' is often applied to cuts of meat or poultry, 'sauté of chicken', for example, and also to make the famous dish, sauté potatoes.

PICTURE	TYPE OF EQUIPMENT	USE
	Griddle pan	A griddle pan is normally finished with a non-stick coating and has raised sections inside the pan itself to form lines of contact. When foods are placed into the pan, it is the raised sections that come into contact with the food, producing the griddled lines associated with this method of cookery.
	Wok	The wok is associated with Oriental cookery. It is round and deep and usually made of a steel based alloy. The metal surface of a wok is thin and therefore conducts heat very quickly.
	Bowls	Bowls come in many shapes and sizes and are used for many different purposes. One of the main uses of bowls is to mix foods, vinaigrette or mayonnaise for example. As the majority of bowls used in the professional kitchen are made of stainless steel, they can be used for hot and cold items both safely and hygienically.
	Cooling racks	Cooling racks are usually square or rectangular and are designed to provide a flat cooling point for baked items. The 'mesh' type design and raised feet on the cooling rack provides items placed upon it with a complete circulation of air.
	Moulds	Moulds come in countless shapes and sizes. Foods that are placed into moulds are intended to take on the shape of the mould. It is essential that moulds are cleaned properly to prevent cross-contamination or any bacterial growth. Moulds are used when making mousses (sweet and savoury), egg custard dishes, ice creams as well as moulding foods for presentation (rice for example).
	Sieves	Sieves are a very fine form of strainer. A sieve can be designed for dry goods, for sieving flour or cocoa powder, for example. Other sieves are designed for wet goods such as soups or sauces. The purpose of a sieve is to (1) aerate dry goods such as flour removing any unwanted particles or clusters during the process; or (2) to pass liquids (soups and sauces) where any items used as flavourings (e.g. **mirepoix**, bay leaves) are not intended to be served.
	Strainers/colanders	A strainer has similar properties to a sieve but tends to be larger in size and has larger holes. A strainer would be used to capture items such as boiled vegetables once they are cooked. A conical strainer with finer holes is used mostly to strain sauces and soups. This will produce a smoother and finer finish.

TASK At your place of work you are worried about an electric hob you use because you received a mild electric shock when you were using it. You have mentioned this to your employer and they have made this equipment 'out of bounds'. They also have asked you to find out what procedures they should follow regarding making sure all the electrical equipment is safe to use and to make a leaflet to promote this.

WEB LINK The following website gives you information about keeping electrical equipment safe **http://www.hse.gov.uk** and follow these links Guidance, Electrical safety at work, Simple precautions, Electrically powered equipment.

Different types of knives and cutting equipment and their uses

Knives have many different purposes and have been designed accordingly. Knives come in different shapes and sizes and a chef should know which knife to use for the job in hand. Beyond this, a chef needs to know how to use the knife selected safely and efficiently and also how to maintain the knife.

The following table identifies the various types of knives as well as other cutting equipment and their uses.

WEB LINK Chopping boards are a necessity when working with knives. Find out more about the different types of chopping boards and how you should look after them at the following website **http://www.cookeryonline.com/** and follow the link in 'What's on this site?' to kitchen health & safety.

TASK Make a list of the pros and cons of wooden chopping boards compared to plastic chopping boards.

PICTURE	TYPE OF EQUIPMENT	USE
	Paring knife	A paring knife is a small, multi-purpose knife used for small jobs such as 'topping and tailing' vegetables, removing skins from onions and preparing small fruits.
	Turning knife	A turning knife has a very small curved blade. This is designed to 'turn' vegetables into a barrel shape for presentation purposes. Mushrooms can also be 'turned' although the process is different. In this example, small reverse cuts/slices are made into the top of the mushroom producing a unique style of presentation.
	Filleting knife	A filleting knife has a medium length blade that is narrow and flexible. It is designed to be flexible so that it can bend while running along the bone structure of fish, particularly flat fish.
	Boning knife	A boning knife has a short to medium blade that is pointed at the end. A boning knife should be strong and rigid, not flexible like a filleting knife. The point is designed to get close to bones and cut away the meat.
	General chef's knife	A general chefs' knife is a multi-purpose knife. It can be used to prepare many different commodities such as vegetables and fruits as well as items such as meat and poultry. The knife can be used across a variety of cutting techniques including chopping, dicing, shredding and slicing.
	Palette knife	A palette knife is used for two main purposes. The first is to turn items over during the cooking process, for example, fillets of fish. Also used for lifting food from the pan to the plate. The second use is spreading. This could be butter onto bread, cream onto a cake or pâté on top of a canapé. A palette knife is usually quite long, although they vary quite a lot in length. It is also flexible in order to get underneath food items. The blade of a palette knife is rounded and therefore not designed for cutting purposes.
	Carving knife and fork	A carving knife usually has a long, thin blade. The edge of the knife should be very sharp to ensure neat, accurate and efficient cutting. A carving fork is usually a two-pronged fork that is substantially larger and stronger than a standard fork. It is designed to support meats, etc., during the carving process.
	Serrated edged knives	Serrated edged knives are designed to slice certain foods and therefore have a long thin blade to assist in the sawing type motion required when slicing. A serrated knife cannot be sharpened using conventional methods.

PICTURE	TYPE OF EQUIPMENT	USE
	Saws	Saws are used mostly in butchery. A saw is used to saw through bones when breaking carcasses and large cuts of meat down into smaller joints.
	Food processors	Many food processors come with an assortment of attachments that are used to **grate**, slice and chop food items extremely quickly. Food processors are also used as blenders to puree items and in the production of soups and sauces.
	Mincer	A mincer is used to pass meat, fish and other items such as offal through small holes, and in so doing produce a mince of the food being processed.
VIDEO CLIP Using a mandolin to prepare vegetable cuts.	Mandolins	A mandolin is used for manual slicing. It is made up of a flat platform with an adjustable blade. This is used by running an item of food, such as a potato, down the platform. The blade half way down the platform can be adjusted to different widths and will slice a piece of the food item as it passes the blade. This can be set to slice items such as potatoes at a regular thickness for a hot-pot, for example. A mandolin can also be set to slice items that are wafer thin such as crisps. Mandolins have different sorts of blades, some will produce a criss-cross effect. As a mandolin is a manual device, extreme care and attention is required to ensure that hands are not in danger when slicing. Mandolins often come with an optional guard which is designed to protect the hands from being cut by coming into contact with the blade.
	Graters	Graters are used to roughly **shred** foods. Graters often come with four different edges (one on each side) to produce course or finer gratings.
	Peelers	Peelers are used to remove the outer skins from hard fruits and vegetables.
	Corers	Corers are used to remove the core (the seeded and fibrous area) from fruits such as apples and pears. Corers have a long circular blade that **penetrates** through the core of the fruit. As this is pushed down, it encases the core and locks it inside the cutter. As the corer is retracted, the core from the fruit is removed.
	Can openers	In professional kitchens, can openers are usually table mounted and more robust. The blade is connected to a long handle which, when pushed down, breaks the seal in the can. The handle is then pulled down and turned to rotate the blade around the can until it can be removed. It is very important to take care when opening tins as the cut in the metal makes a very sharp and often jagged edge which could cause a nasty injury.

PICTURE	TYPE OF EQUIPMENT	USE
	Scissors	Scissors are an essential piece of equipment for a chef. Scissors used to cut the fins from fish need to be strong and robust to break through the bones without buckling. Scissors are also used for other tasks such as cutting string used for tying.
	Cleaver	A cleaver is a very heavy knife that is designed to cut through large bones.
	Gravity slice	A gravity slice is an electrical appliance that provides uniform cutting, **portion control** and a virtually waste-free method of cutting. For example, a gravity-feed slice will cut thin slices of ham to exactly the same thickness according to its setting.
	Steels and sharpeners	A sharpening steel is made of a long, thin, circular and slightly ridged metal. As the blade of a knife runs up and down the steel at a slight angle, the edge of the knife is sharpened. Sharpening stones are used when the edge of the knife is lost. In this event, a steel would not be sufficient to retrieve the edge of the knife as it is designed to increase the sharpness, rather than to create the edge.

VIDEO CLIP
Using a cleaver.

The correct and safe use of knives and cutting equipment

Knives are particularly dangerous pieces of equipment if used incorrectly. However, they are an essential item for a chef as well as being equipment that a chef must master and control in order to become efficient and skilled within the profession.

Well organized and efficient chefs work methodically and clean as they go. They will also clean, sharpen and handle knives throughout their working day. When placing knives on the table for use, it is good practice that the knife is placed in a parallel position to the chopping board, with the blade pointing inwards towards the board.

The condition of a knife has a massive impact on the finished product as well as the effort and energy that is required by the chef to prepare foods.

Hold the knife to the side of the body and with the blade of the knife pointing to the floor.

Safe practice for carrying a knife

Offer the knife to the receiver, who should have the handle pointing towards him or her, and the blade of the knife pointing towards the floor.

Safe practice for passing a knife

When a sharp knife is used to make a cut, regardless of the food item, the sharpness of the blade will penetrate through the food neatly and following the direction of the knife. The chef should be controlling the direction of the knife rather than having to use force to push the knife through the food to make the cut.

A blunt knife, however, produces a much more difficult scenario. In this case, because the blade is not sharp, it will not easily penetrate the food being cut and the chef has to increase the power being placed into the cut in order for the knife to get through the food. This will not only produce a poor quality cut but the chef is having to use much more energy and force to create a finished item that is likely to be inferior to the one cut using a sharp knife. The risk of injury by cutting yourself is therefore much higher when using a blunt knife.

Cleaning, maintaining and storing knives

Knives are one of the most important kitchen items because of their direct contact with foods. Therefore, a knife has to be clean and in a hygienic condition before it is used. Modern knives are usually made of stainless steel or a steel based alloy. Handles are usually manufactured from an easy-clean, waterproof material. Generally, the more expensive handles are 'riveted'. This is where the steel section of the knife continues from the blade, through the handle of the knife and two to three riveted sections come out from the handle at 90°. This forms part of the handle itself and makes it very secure.

The less expensive knives on the market tend to have moulded handles. In this case, the metal section of the knife continues from the blade to the handle but the handle is moulded around the handle section with a plastic or rubber based material. The handles on such knives are not as strong as those riveted to the handles and are generally not as well made, hence the difference in price.

There are many 'Oriental' style knives on the market. The metal base of the knife is actually formed into a handle itself, making the knife one continuous piece rather than a blade with a handle attached.

Care has to be taken when cleaning knives. Knives should be washed in hot, soapy water and then rinsed in clean hot water. **When cleaning the blade of a knife, it is essential that the blade of the knife is pointing away from your hand.** A sharp blade will easily cut through a cloth and into your hand or fingers if this rule is not followed. The same rule applies if you dry a knife – the blade must always point away from the hand drying the knife.

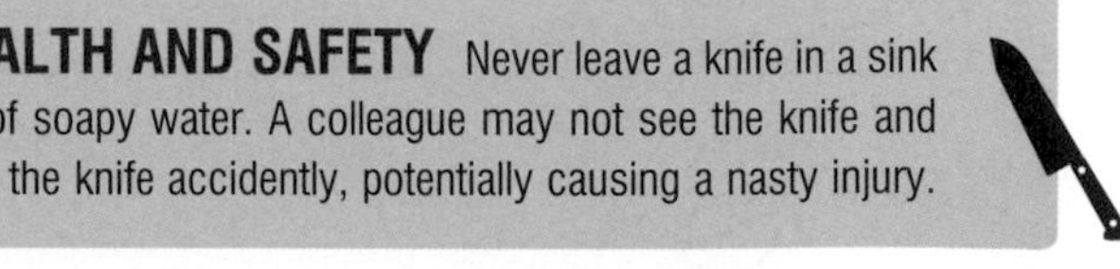

Maintaining knives in good condition is important for a number of reasons. First of all, there is the initial cost of buying knives. To maintain knives on a regular basis a steel is used. Occasionally, a carborundum stone can be used if the knife is starting to lose its sharp edge. A stone usually has a coarser edge than a steel and will take more of the surface of the blade away. Care has to be taken to ensure that a rough edge is not created by uneven application across the stone. For safety reasons, when using a stone, the blade of the knife should always be pointing away from the body.

Sharpening a knife using a steel

There are two main methods used to sharpen a knife using a steel. However, the angle at which the blade runs along the steel remains the same.

VIDEO CLIP Sharpening knives with steels.

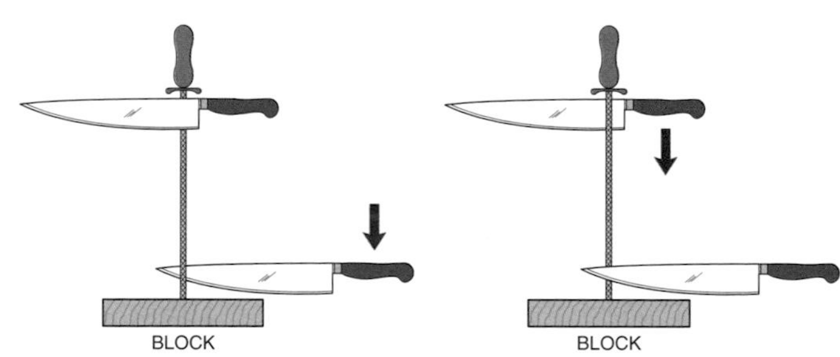

In the first method, the steel is placed downwards vertically onto a board. Holding the steel in one hand and the knife in the other, place the base of the knife at the base of the steel (just below the handle). Run the knife down the steel until the tip of the knife reaches the tip of the steel. This should be performed at an angle between 30° to 40°.

Once the tip of the knife has reached the tip of the steel, the knife should be moved so that the opposite side of the knife (tip) is placed at the same angle on the other side of the steel (tip). This time the knife should run up the steel until the base of the knife reaches the base of the steel. Once this stage is reached, run the knife back down the steel from base to tip and then switch sides again. Repeat this about ten times on each side.

In the second method, the steel is held pointing upwards at approximately 45°. With the other hand, the knife is run

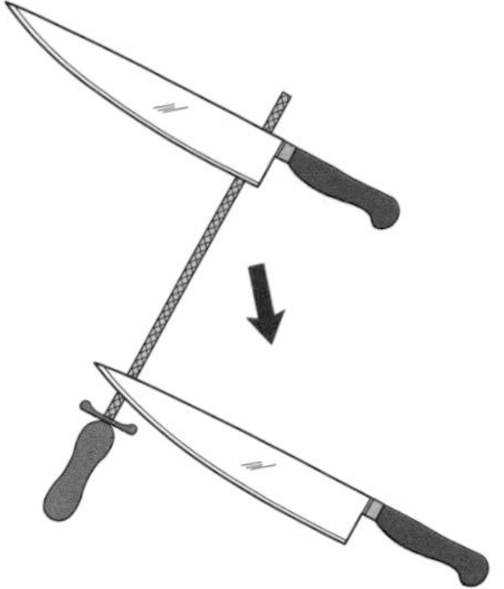
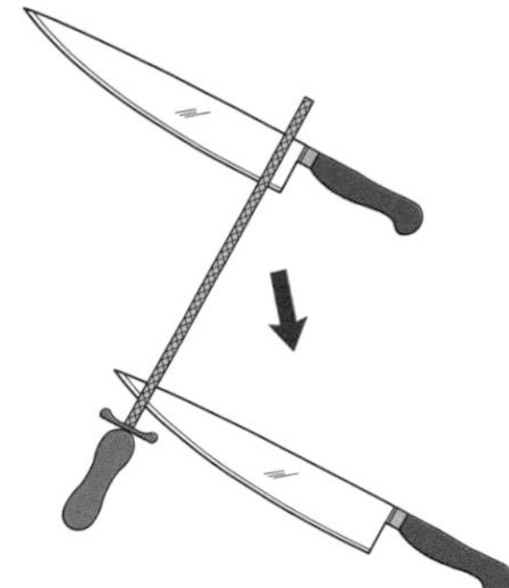

down the steel. In this method, the base of the knife starts at the tip of the steel working downwards until the tip of the knife reaches the base of the steel. As in the previous example, this is done at an angle between 30° and 40°.

The knife is then moved to the alternate side of the steel and runs back up the steel from the tip of the knife and base of the steel to the base of the knife at the tip of the steel. Once this is reached the knife runs back down the steel before switching back to the original side again. Repeat this about ten times on each side.

Age restrictions specific to the use of cutting equipment

Under health and safety legislation (law), young people have to be protected from potentially dangerous equipment. In a kitchen, this includes items such as electric gravity slicing machines. Such pieces of equipment should therefore not be used or cleaned by anyone less than 18 years old. For those over 18 years old, full training should be provided to ensure that the equipment can be used and cleaned safely.

WEB LINK Look at the following website again to find out more about the hazards in the kitchen and how to avoid them **http://www.cookeryonline.com** and follow link in 'What's on this site?' to kitchen health & safety.

TASK For the items listed below, describe how they could be dangerous if misused or mishandled, and the actions you can take to prevent accidents:

- cleaning chemicals
- deep fat fryers
- large heavy containers.

TEST YOURSELF

1 Provide three reasons why it is important to select the right piece of equipment for the job in hand.

i) ______

ii) ______

iii) ______

2 How does an induction hob save energy?

______

3 Which methods of cookery can be performed using a combination oven?

______

4 What is the difference between a salamander and a flame grill?

______

5 What is the purpose of the 'cool zone' in a deep-fryer?

______

6 Why would you want a 'spider' in the kitchen?

______

7 Name three food items that could be 'turned'.

i) ______

ii) ______

iii) ______

8 What features and qualities would you look for in a filleting knife?

______

9 Why would a 'mandolin' be useful in the kitchen?

______

10 Why is it safer to use a sharp knife rather than a blunt knife?

______

11 Name two ways in which a knife can be sharpened.

i) ______

ii) ______

12 Name one piece of equipment that you should not use or clean until you are over 18 years old and have received training.

______

6

Introduction to personal workplace skills

Unit 106 Introduction to personal workplace skills

LEARNING OBJECTIVES

On completion of this chapter, learners will be able to:

- **Identify the correct uniform for work and the reasons behind it.**
- **Describe the importance of personal hygiene and appearance, highlighting examples of poor practices.**
- **State the importance of punctuality, attendance and good time management.**
- **Identify the communication skills used in teams and the factors that make a good team in the workplace.**
- **Describe the importance of knowing your own limitations and asking for help and assistance.**
- **State the importance of effective communication with customers and how to deal with customer requests.**
- **Highlight some of the potential barriers to effective communication.**

Personal skills are very important in the hospitality and catering industry. You need to have a high standard of personal hygiene and wear clothing that will enable you to do your work safely (for your own sake and that of your customers). Kitchens are made up of teams, so communication, punctuality, time management and understanding your limits are all important, so the kitchen can run smoothly.

You are also providing a service for customers and may have contact with them. Dealing with customers properly is crucial for any catering and hospitality business or service. The skills described in this chapter will be those required by employers.

The correct uniform for work and the reasons behind it

VIDEO CLIP Showing correct uniform and personal appearance.

Chef's jacket

The chef's jacket is designed to provide a hygienic and functional piece of clothing in which to prepare and cook food. It also protects the chef from the physical dangers of the kitchen. Originally made of cotton and linen, the materials have evolved into modern, lightweight textiles. It is double-breasted to protect the chest and stomach from the heat from ovens and stoves, and also from burns and scalds. It acts as a barrier and gives a few vital extra seconds to protect the wearer should a spillage of hot liquid occur onto the upper body. The sleeves should be worn to the wrist for protection to the arms from burns.

IMAGES COURTESY OF RUSSUMS

Trousers

These are generally made of lightweight cotton or mixed material and Teflon coated fabric. They should not be worn tight-fitting to the leg as this creates a hazard if a spillage occurs. Loose-fitting trousers are also more comfortable for work in a kitchen.

IMAGES COURTESY OF RUSSUMS

Apron

Any difference in colour can be relevant to the operation. For example blue aprons usually indicate larder work or butchery. They must be worn at full length to protect the legs (always to below the knee). It is one of the most important items of protection. If a spillage of hot liquid occurs it is the first line of protection. It should be tied at the front to allow for quick release.

IMAGES COURTESY OF RUSSUMS

Necktie

The original use of the necktie was to mop the brow due to the lack of ventilation and the heat generated by solid fuel stoves. A system of coloured neckties can identify departments or seniority within the workplace, allowing for an assumption of ability and/or experience based on a quick visual inspection.

IMAGES COURTESY OF RUSSUMS

Chef's hat

The tall hat, known as a toque, has always epitomized the stature of the chef. Traditionally an apprentice cook would wear a skull cap and graduate to a toque when they reached the position of chef de partie. Nowadays even some head chefs prefer the skull cap. The main function of the hat is to stop loose hair falling into the food and help absorb perspiration on the forehead. When the hair is beyond collar length and it cannot be contained in a hat, a hair net should be worn.

Safety shoes

Shoes should be of a sturdy design with non-slip soles and steel toecaps. If clogs are preferred then they too should be protective and have a back strap to prevent slipping. The colour is usually dictated by the workplace. An important element is that footwear should be comfortable and give support to the chef who will be on their feet for many hours.

The wearing of trainers and non-specialist shoes should be prohibited.

IMAGES COURTESY OF RUSSUMS

Kitchen cloths

Kitchen cloths must be clean, dry and undamaged. They provide important protection between the hands and the sometimes very hot equipment that chefs handle on a regular basis.

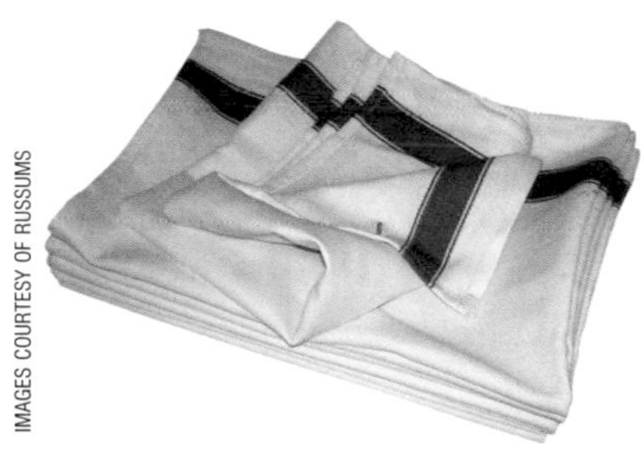

IMAGES COURTESY OF RUSSUMS

TASK Identify the correct uniform required for front-of-house staff. Discuss the quality points that would be expected for each item of the uniform.

Care and maintenance of uniforms

As a professional member of staff, regardless of the department you work in, uniform and appearance send out important messages to customers. Clean uniforms are also essential when dealing with food. In the hospitality industry, cleanliness, alongside a smart and professional appearance, provides the perception of high quality and this helps to reassure customers that they are being provided for by safety conscious, hygienic and professional staff.

To maintain the uniform to a high standard, it is important that it is looked after and cleaned on a regular basis. As well as being clean, to ensure the uniform looks crisp and fresh, it is important to iron clothes. After all, a wrinkled shirt or jacket looks scruffy.

The cleaning of uniforms is sometimes performed by a laundry service, which can be an in-house or external service. If this is not a service provided by your place of work, it is your responsibility to ensure that you clean and maintain your uniform to a professional standard.

As well as clothing, shoes are an important part of uniform and can easily let down someone's appearance if footwear is inappropriate or scruffy. Shoes should be safe for the type of work being performed and must be cleaned and polished on a regular basis.

Finally, uniform should be repaired or replaced as necessary. Clothing and shoes have a limited life and will become worn after time and will begin to look scruffy regardless of how clean they are. It is therefore essential that clothing and shoes are replaced before they get to this stage.

The importance of personal hygiene and appearance

The hospitality and catering industry is expected to prepare and serve food in very clean and hygienic conditions. The people working in the industry therefore have a personal and professional responsibility to present themselves properly and practice hygienic methods of work.

CHEF'S TIP Uniforms must be changed on a shift-by-shift basis. Clothing should be of an easily washable material. Generally all chef attire is white in colour to show when clothing has been soiled needs to be changed.

It is vital that a chef maintains a high standard of personal hygiene. Bodily cleanliness is achieved through daily showering or bathing. This removes stale sweat, dirt and bacteria which are the causes of body odour. An **antiperspirant** or **deodorant** may be applied to the underarm area to reduce perspiration and reduce the smell of sweat. Clean underwear should be worn each day. In terms of personal hygiene, the following points should be considered.

HEALTH & SAFETY Cuts and abrasions on hands should be covered with a clean, waterproof, blue coloured dressing to minimize the risk of secondary infection. Disposable gloves may be worn for additional protection.

Care of hair

Hair should be kept clean by washing on a regular basis. Chefs should cover their hair with a hat. Longer hair should be tied back and wrapped in a hairnet to avoid loose hair from falling into food that is being prepared. From a customer perspective, hair should be neat and tidy in a style that is appropriate for a customer-focused industry.

Care of mouth and teeth

There are many germs within and around the area of the mouth. Therefore, it is essential that the mouth does not come into contact with utensils or hands that will come into contact with food.

It is important that we keep our breath fresh and it is also advisable that we should visit the dentist regularly to maintain healthy teeth and gums.

VIDEO CLIP Washing hands correctly

Hands and nails

As chefs, the hands are used constantly in the preparation and cooking of food. It is therefore essential that they are kept clean. Hands, and everything that has been touched are covered with bacteria. Although most of these are harmless, some can cause ill-health. Hands must be washed regularly and frequently, particularly after visiting the toilet, before commencing the preparation of food and during the handling of food. Hands should be washed using hot water with the aid of a nail brush and an **antibacterial gel** or liquid.

Our nails have the potential to harbour dirt, grime and therefore bacteria. With this in mind, nails need to be kept short and clean. From a customer perspective, if a chef or the person serving food had dirty nails, it would raise a question about the safety of the food in terms of the bacteria present. This may be enough to put the customer off eating the food at all. It would certainly not promote the hygienic practices of the establishment concerned.

Nail varnish should not be worn!

HEALTH & SAFETY Wash your hands with a liquid gel from a sealed dispenser. Bar soap should be discouraged because it can accumulate germs when passed from hand-to-hand. **Disposable paper towels** or warm-air hand dryers should be used to dry the hands.

HEALTH & SAFETY To ensure good health and safety practice some employers insist on the use of plastic disposable gloves when preparing food items. Although you must remember that you should change gloves with every task to prevent cross-contamination.

Jewellery and cosmetics

Jewellery should not be worn. Even a plain wedding ring can harbour dirt and bacteria. There is also the potential for pieces of jewellery to become tangled in equipment or fall into food.

Cosmetics should not be worn either. In a hot kitchen make-up will reduce the effectiveness of the skin losing heat. It may possibly get on to clothing, hands and food. It also attracts dirt and bacteria.

Some examples of poor practice

Smoking

Smoking is not only proven to be bad for your health; it is also an unhygienic activity for a food handler. During the act of smoking, the hand regularly touches the lips as the cigarette is placed and removed from the mouth. During this action, the fingers pick up bacteria from the mouth, which could potentially be passed onto the food.

Chewing

The act of chewing while at work does not create a professional image. Chefs, by the nature of their work, also need to taste the dishes they are making on a regular basis to ensure that the quality of food being produced is of the required flavour, texture and **seasoning**, etc.

HEALTH & SAFETY Plastic disposable spoons should be used to taste food during preparation and cooking and then disposed of immediately, using a new spoon for each tasting.

Eating and drinking in the food preparation area

Although a chef should 'hygienically' taste foods being prepared to check quality, he or she should not eat and drink in food preparation areas during working times. This should be left for break times.

In working areas, if water is provided, this should be supplied in plastic glasses or bottles.

Wearing uniform outside the premises

Wearing uniform outside working premises not only looks unprofessional and unhygienic to customers, it potentially brings bacteria and dirt from the outside environment into the kitchen. This should be avoided at all times, unless it is required in the case of an evacuation or similar reason.

HEALTH & SAFETY When handling or preparing food, blue plasters should be used so that they are easily identifiable when lost. These dressings can feature an internal metal strip that allows them to be detected by electromagnet equipment and metal detectors in large food production units.

Punctuality, attendance and time management

Punctuality and attendance at work are vitally important. For example, chefs are continuously working against the clock, making sure sufficient ingredients are prepared, and that meals are served on time. Lateness reduces the amount of time to get ready, as there is no way that the service time can be put back to accommodate a chef's poor timekeeping. It is essential that targets are met in order to meet customer expectations.

Non-attendance at work simply makes this problem even worse as this will put pressure on the other members of the team to cover for the missing person. However, it must be noted that people miss work for genuine reasons, such as illness or for other valid personal reasons. In such cases, it is standard practice for the person to be covered by temporary cover. This could be someone within the organization or temporary contracted staff from an agency.

TASK Find out what the procedures are to report illness in your place of work or study.

CHEF'S TIP Most organizations have set procedures to report illness. It is important that this is followed and that you report any absence as early as possible, so cover arrangements can be made.

The key points of punctuality, attendance and good time management are as follows.

Dependability

As a chef you will normally work as part of a team. Your colleagues (team members) will be relying on you to do your job. Each person has a role to play in the overall performance of the team, regardless of position (rank) or experience.

As well as dependability, flexibility is a trait that is often required when working as a chef. Work patterns can vary due to the nature of demand and there may be occasions when you are asked to work a different shift to the one you normally cover. There may also be a particularly busy time when more staff are required than usual. A team member that offers flexibility is an asset to the team and this forms part of the reliability needed in a strong team.

Contractual expectation of employers

When you secure a position within an organization, your employers will expect you to perform to that position and meet the requirements of your contract of employment. If you are regularly late or absent from work without a valid reason, you will be breaking the conditions of your contract and will be at risk of losing your job.

CHEF'S TIP As you progress through your career, your working history follows you. Therefore, it is much better to leave a job on good terms and with a positive reference. This will increase your chances of securing future positions and develop routes of progression and opportunities for promotion during your career.

Expectation of colleagues

Your colleagues will expect you to perform your role in a professional manner. Your contribution at work will have an effect on the way that the team operates. **Interpersonal relationships** can be placed under pressure and sometimes break down if there are feelings that one member of the team is not pulling their weight. This would obviously have a negative impact on the way that the team would function.

Courtesy

Punctuality, regular attendance and good time management are traits that you should try to develop. It is courteous for us to become reliable and not let our colleagues down.

Working to deadlines and meeting targets

Working to realistic deadlines is an important factor for a chef, especially during a busy lunch or dinner service. Doing this effectively depends on the skills of estimating how long a task is going to take and being able to prioritize jobs. Once that is achieved, it may be helpful to set intermediate deadlines into relatively short chunks of time.

CHEF'S TIP Time management is an important skill for chefs working in the hospitality industry. In order to manage your time more effectively, you must have a realistic assessment of all the tasks required and then plan the workload accordingly.

The ability to set shared targets and make plans is vital to successful teamwork. If there is no real planning, progression cannot be properly monitored and the team may not be able to learn from the experience. It is during these stages that team members can support each other and provide help where necessary to achieve the end result.

Communication skills in teams

When working in teams, good communication is vital for all members of the team to be clear on what has been completed and what still needs to be done. If communication breaks down, for whatever reason, quite often many other things will go wrong as a consequence.

Communication takes many forms. The following points describe the main factors associated with communication.

TASK Identify three important examples of good communication relevant to the following teams:

- bar (e.g. acknowledging customers waiting to be served)
- reception
- food service
- housekeeping.

CHEF'S TIP As kitchens can be very busy places with lots of hustle, bustle and noise, it is important that verbal communications are clear. The clearer the message, the more likely it will be understood by the person receiving it.

Speaking

Speaking is the most obvious form of communication and one that chefs rely on very heavily. For example, during a busy service period, chefs are constantly communicating to ensure that orders are being prepared on schedule. There may also be times when parts of a dish are being prepared by more than one chef. In this situation, chefs need to inform one another of progress so that the final dish comes together at the same time to ensure a high-quality finished product.

Clarifying and confirming

The process of communication is at least a two-way process. Even if a person speaks clearly, using good pronunciation and at a sufficient volume, it does not guarantee that the message has been received and/or understood.

One way to show that a message has been received is to respond. This shows the other person that you have recognized that they are communicating with you.

Listening

Listening skills are crucial for effective communication and teamwork. They ensure that we obtain the right information from the right people and help us understand what information or support other people need to help them to work more effectively as a group.

CHEF'S TIP To be a good listener:

- clear your mind of other things
- spend a few minutes thinking about the topic before the meeting or discussion
- avoid distractions
- recognize how you are feeling (interested? bored? tired? cross?) and take this into consideration

- remember you are there to learn what the other person has to say, not the other way round
- focus on the speaker – look at them, nod, encourage, use non-verbal cues to acknowledge what is being said
- show interest, even if you disagree
- let the speaker finish what they are saying before you respond
- ask questions to increase your understanding
- confirm your understanding by expressing what was said in your own words, or summarizing. This is referred to as 'paraphrasing'

These points show that you are being 'active' in listening to the person with whom you are communicating. This is called 'active listening'.

Always remember that a good listener aims to get a thorough understanding of what the other person is saying before starting to form an opinion.

Other forms of communication

Other forms of communication include telephone conversations and in written formats (e.g. email, memorandum or letter). The telephone is a fast and effective way of communicating. For example, detailing specific requirements or placing orders with suppliers can be achieved quickly by talking to the supplier directly on the telephone.

CHEF'S TIP When using the telephone, your face cannot be seen so it is important to consider your tone of voice and to speak clearly.

With the arrival of information technology and email it is now easier than ever to communicate in writing and attach relevant documents. Suppliers can now usually accept orders electronically via email which makes it easier to see potential mistakes in the order or provide a greater sense of clarity.

CHEF'S TIP It is important to be aware of cultural variations in the meaning of some gestures, posture and facial expressions.

To become effective in communication such as speaking and listening, you should have an understanding of non-verbal communication (NVC), sometimes referred to as body language.

Non-verbal communication can take many forms:

- touch: greetings, agreements, apologies, goodbyes
- posture: sitting or standing straight, leaning forward or back
- proximity: distance between people, personal territory
- dress: clothes, hair, appearance
- eye contact: indicates interest and attention, or the opposite if eye contact is not made
- hand gestures: agreement, disagreement, impatience, welcome, excitement, disapproval
- facial expression: shows emotion and provides feedback.

When using verbal communication:

- briefly express your appreciation of the speaker, e.g. 'That was a really interesting point'
- briefly summarize the point made by the speaker, e.g. 'I was particularly reinterested in what you said about' …
- ask your question, if you need to, write it down and read it out and try to make it clear, concise, relevant, informed and non-aggressive

CHEF'S TIP Asking questions or making a point during discussions is an essential element to effective communication. Many people will want to ask questions but some will not do so because they lack the confidence to put their thoughts across at the right moment. It is a key sign of support if you can ask questions in a positive manner.

What makes a good team?

A team is made up of a group of individuals contributing to the work of the group as a whole. There is a phrase 'A team is only as good as its weakest link'. This is true to an extent but teams are usually made up of people with different skills and experience.

CHEF'S TIP A good team ethos will help members support one another, utilizing the strengths within the team to develop others.

A good team has to have direction so that it knows where it is going and what has to be achieved. Leadership is an important aspect here in providing a good example to others as well as the vision and support required to motivate other members of the team to perform to the desired standard.

Good teamwork increases **creativity** and makes the most of the available range of skills and knowledge. It also helps to improve understanding, communication and a sense of shared purpose which, overall, will improve efficiency. Good teamwork leads to the achievement of targets and goals.

TASK Think about the types of teams there are in hospitality and catering and make a list.

Knowing your own limitations and when to ask for help

Knowing your own limitations is not showing a weakness in your ability. In fact, it shows a strength!

As a chef, you are regularly working with foods, some of which can be very expensive. It could be costly to make mistakes in their preparation if they are then unusable.

If there is doubt over the way to prepare or cook certain food items, you should ask for assistance and let somebody demonstrate how to complete the task successfully. The same applies to the use of equipment. If you are unsure how a piece of equipment works, it is much better to ask than to run the risk of damaging the equipment or possibly injuring yourself.

It is always better to ask! It may seem hard at the time, and you may feel that you are disturbing your supervisor, but they would prefer to help you than for you to make mistakes which could be costly or dangerous.

WEB LINK Find out more about the skills employers are looking for at the following online community website **http://www.hospitality-crew.com/**

Search for 'What personal skills you need to work in hospitality' and the 'Jobs and skills' section.

Communication with customers

Customers are essential to a catering operation. Without customers, there is no business and therefore no need for the staff making up that business. It is essential that customers are treated well and enjoy their experience.

The catering world is very competitive and customers' expectations are getting higher all the time. Nearly all organizations have some sort of customer care or service policy and some have staff that are dedicated specifically to customer services.

This demonstrates the importance of customers and the revenue (money) that they spend when using the services of a catering organization. The staff representing an organization are the front line of contact for the customers they serve. For example, a hotel can have the most impressive reception area, bedrooms and swimming pool, but if staff do not perform to the customers' expectations, the customer may leave the organization disappointed.

A vast amount of money is spent by catering businesses trying to attract customers to use their services and much research is undertaken to study the ways in which customers behave. All of this time and investment is trying to attract new customers and keep existing customers. One negative experience can influence a customer enough so that they decide not to return to that organization and potentially tell their friends, family and acquaintances of their poor experience.

On the other hand, a positive experience is likely to encourage the customer to return in the future and they may inform friends, family and acquaintances of their great experience. Word of mouth recommendation from a neutral source is considered to be a very powerful form of marketing!

All staff, whether they are working in front-of-house or back-of-house operations, should be aware of the importance of customers. Many organizations will train their staff in customer service as part of their **induction** to the organization, regardless of their role within the organization. If everyone has a customer focus, the more likely it is that customers will receive good products and service.

The following points list some of the correct methods that should be used when dealing with customers.

Acknowledging the customer

It is very frustrating as a customer not to be acknowledged. Even if you are busy with another task or order, an acknowledgement of the customer will inform them that you are aware of their presence and that you will deal with them as quickly as you can.

Keeping the customer informed

Keep customers informed of how their requests or orders are being processed; of progress and the likely outcome. A lack of information can cause anxiety for the customer and perhaps give the impression that their request has been forgotten or even lost. The fact that someone is taking the time to communicate is also reassuring and sends the message that care and attention is being taken.

For example, during a busy service, there could be a slightly longer waiting time than usual between the end of one course and the service of the next. A simple message to apologize for the slight delay and to inform the customer that their order will be arriving soon or within a few minutes will reassure them of the staffs' attention.

CHEF'S TIP Value should not be associated directly with cost. It is possible to spend a lot of money and be disappointed with what has been received or experienced. It is also possible to spend a small amount of money and be very happy!

Providing the service or outcome

Essentially, it is the delivery of the service or product in a timely and efficient manner that is the ultimate expectation of the customer. The customer will also expect the product to be of good quality so that they consider the whole package of product and service as good value.

Potential barriers to effective communication

There are many barriers to effective communication. However, they can be overcome with effort and willingness from those involved.

The following points highlight some of the potential barriers to effective communication and recommendations as to how they can be overcome.

Verbal barriers

Verbal barriers can be present in many formats. If speech is unclear and almost impossible to hear, the chances of being able to understand what has been said are small.

In addition to this, within the catering industry, people of many different nationalities work together, and for some people, English is not always a first language. Imagine if you were working in a country using another language and the difficulties this could cause in communication.

Even people from the same country can speak in very different ways due to regional dialects. For example, someone from Scotland has a very different accent to someone from the south of England and this has the potential for misunderstanding.

It is important that we recognize that we need to maximize the potential for understanding in such situations. Speaking clearly and at a reasonable pace increases the likelihood of understanding. Look directly at the person and try to avoid slang or colloquialisms (informal language) that people from other areas or countries may not have come across before.

Hearing and listening barriers

Not everyone has perfect hearing, in which case an appropriate solution will have to be found to overcome the situation. The person may be able to lip-read, but he or she will need good sight of you speaking. The person may require you to speak up slightly and speak slower than usual. Whatever the situation, there is nearly always a solution provided that all parties concerned have the commitment and desire to overcome the problem.

Written barriers

Writing can cause difficulty as a method of communication. Ideally, it should be clear, simple and to the point. Written communication can break down for a number of reasons, including how words are spelt, the use of grammar and how legible the handwriting is. Other considerations include how the writing is presented and its structure.

Other barriers

There are many examples of how we can produce barriers in communication without speaking or writing. The way in which we present ourselves and act sends out messages to those around us, regardless of whether or not the message has been received as it was intended.

CHEF'S TIP In the hospitality and catering industry, personal appearance is very important. This is the case across all areas, whether front or back-of-house. If staff look clean, smart and professional, this communicates a professional image.

Our own personal level of confidence and experience can also provide a barrier to communication. A lack of confidence can make people withdrawn and shy. Limited experience may prevent a young or new member of staff from performing well, if they have not had sufficient training to prepare for the situations they are faced with. Although these examples are fairly common, the customer still expects to receive the service or product they are paying for. It is down to the organization and the teams within organizations to train and develop new or inexperienced people to perform to the required standard.

Body language sends out a multitude of signals, so it is extremely important that people are aware of the potential of their actions. Showing enthusiasm and interest to a customer will make them confident of your attention and increase the likelihood of a clear route for communication.

Other barriers to effective communication can arise from the physical or mental state of a person at a specific time. For example, if someone becomes intoxicated (drunk), their mood can be difficult to measure. People react differently under the influence of alcohol, sometimes by becoming giggly and continuously laughing, or becoming upset and even violent. Whatever the reaction, communication is affected as a consequence.

Guest Chef

Scarborough caught wild sea trout, served with whitby lobster and tarragon risotto, deep fried leeks

Chef *Rob Clark – Chef Lecturer*
Centre *Yorkshire Coast College, Scarborough*

Ingredients	*6 portions*
Wild sea trout	1.5 kg
For the Risotto	
Olive oil	200 mls
Onion – cut into fine brunoise	1
Arborio rice	150 g
Lobster stock	750 mls
Lobster tail cut into collops (slices)	1
Chilled butter – cut into cubes	100 g
Fresh tarragon – lightly chopped	1 tbsp
Freshly grated Parmesan cheese	50 g
Lemon juice	1/2 lemon
Double cream	4 tbsp
For the garnish	
Chive points	
Beurre Blanc	500 mls

METHOD OF WORK

1 Pre-heat the oven to 180°C and a deep fat fryer to 185°C.

2 Fillet the sea trout leaving the skin on. Remove the pin bones and cut the fillets into 6 x 150 g supremes.

3 **Sweat** the onion slowly in half the olive oil, add the rice and cook until nutty. Add the hot stock one ladle at a time until it is thoroughly absorbed. Cook for around 12 minutes until the rice is al dente. Cover and set aside.

4 Heat a non-stick frying pan on a medium heat, brush the fish with olive oil and season well. Sear skin side down for 3 minutes, when the skin is crisp, turn over and cook for a further 3 minutes.

5 Gently remove the fish from the pan and place on a non-stick tray and bake for a further 3 minutes. Once cooked allow the fish to rest.

6 When ready to bring the dish together, place the risotto in a saucepan with the ladle of lobster stock and bring to a **simmer**; fold in the cut lobster. Once the stock has reduced, add the butter, parmesan cheese, lemon juice, cream, then finally the tarragon and season to taste.

7 Arrange in a serving bowl with the lobster risotto in the centre, the wild sea trout on top, drizzle with olive oil, **garnish** with the chive points. Finish with ribbons of beurre blanc.

TEST YOURSELF

1 List three functions of a chef's uniform.

i) ______
ii) ______
iii) ______

2 How often should a chef change their uniform? Explain the reasons behind your answer.

______

______

3 As a chef, why is it important to keep nails short and clean?

______

______

4 Provide two reasons why a blue plaster should be used to cover small cuts and grazes.

______

______

5 Why should drinking from glass containers be avoided when working in the kitchen?

______

______

6 Provide three reasons why good timekeeping is important.

i) ______
ii) ______
iii) ______

7 List four types or methods of communication.

i) ______
ii) ______
iii) ______
iv) ______

8 List four traits or characteristics of a good listener.

i) ______
ii) ______
iii) ______
iv) ______

9 Describe why it is considered important for all staff to be aware of the importance of customers.

______

______

10 Provide three examples where communication can break down.

i) ______
ii) ______
iii) ______

7 Boiling, poaching and steaming

Unit 107 Prepare and cook food by boiling, poaching and steaming

Recipes

ONLINE RECIPES

LEARNER SUPPORT

Velouté
Creme patisserie
Leek and potato soup
Herbert Berger's poached fillet of lamb

LEARNING OBJECTIVES

At the end of this chapter you will be able to:

- **Describe the methods of boiling, poaching and steaming.**
- **Identify foods that can be boiled, poached and steamed.**
- **Identify the liquids that are used to boil, poach and steam.**
- **Select suitable techniques associated with boiling, poaching and steaming.**
- **Describe associated products that are made when boiling and poaching.**
- **List the quality points to look for in food that has been boiled, poached and steamed.**
- **List the general safety points to follow when boiling, poaching and steaming food.**

Boiling

What is boiling?

Boiling is the cooking of food by placing it into a liquid which is at, or brought to, boiling point. This can be achieved by using a variety of different liquids including water, stock, milk and a range of **infused** cooking liquids, for example, water enhanced with herbs, spices and vegetables.

In certain cases, such as with an egg, boiling changes the structure of the egg making it more pleasant to eat. The process also helps to ensure that the egg is safe to eat by destroying harmful bacteria such as salmonella.

The equipment used to boil foods

The equipment normally used to boil foods is quite standard in the kitchen. This includes saucepans of varying sizes and stockpots.

It is very important that the correct size of pan is selected to cook the food being boiled. Ladles used for **skimming**, fish slices, spiders and draining equipment are all useful for removing the cooked food from the boiling liquid.

If pans are too small:

- it will be difficult to place foods in and remove them from the liquid
- it could be dangerous as the liquid could overflow when the food is placed into it
- the food may not be covered with the liquid as there may not be enough space within the pan for the food items and enough liquid to cover them.

If the pan is too big, it will be an uneconomical and wasteful use of energy (gas, electricity), equipment, space and liquid.

CHEF'S TIP Simmering describes a gentle boiling motion. If the boiling is too rapid it could damage the food being boiled. Be careful to control and check the heat applied and movement of the liquid.

The methods used to boil foods

There are two methods used to boil food.

These are as follows:

1. The food is placed into cold liquid and brought to the boil. Once the liquid has reached boiling point, the heat source is **reduced**, so the liquid is simmering as described above. For example, when cooking potatoes, they are usually placed in cold water and brought to the boil. New potatoes are the exception to this rule. They are placed into boiling water.
2. The food is placed into boiling liquid. At this stage the cool or **ambient temperature** of the food entering the liquid will normally reduce the temperature of the liquid temporarily to below boiling point. The liquid is then heated back to boiling point and then reduced to a simmer.

Foods that are suitable for boiling

The most common type of food that is cooked by boiling is vegetables. Many vegetables can be boiled, although it is important that they are not boiled for too long. Overcooking vegetables leads to a loss of vitamins and nutrients and can also make the vegetables soggy and unpleasant to eat.

Other foods that are commonly boiled include eggs, pasta, pulses and grains. When cooking pasta, pulses and grains, the liquid is partially absorbed in the cooking process, improving the texture of the food and at the same time making them more digestible and easy to eat.

Tougher and generally cheaper cuts of meat are also suitable for boiling. This is similar to the way that meat is cooked when braising or stewing as the meat is also cooked slowly in moist surroundings. This helps to break down the **muscular structure** and connective tissue, making the meat tender to eat.

The advantages of placing food into cold liquid and bringing to the boil

- The process of bringing the liquid to the boil can help to extract flavours from the food and also help to make food tender.
- It is less likely to damage the shape and structure of the food as the liquid is not moving rapidly at the beginning of the heating process.
- Bringing a liquid to simmering point can help to clarify the cooking liquid if impurities are removed from the surface in the process.

The advantages of placing food into boiling liquid

- This prevents the reaction that causes the loss of vitamin C in vegetables.
- It helps to retain the colour when cooking green vegetables such as broccoli, fine green beans and cabbage. The addition of salt to boiling water helps to retain the colour in green vegetables.

TASK Excluding the examples given so far, name five other vegetables that are suitable for boiling.

VIDEO CLIP Boiling pasta.

Other techniques used when boiling

- *Soaking* – Most dried beans and pulses need to be soaked before cooking. Split lentils do not always need to be soaked before cooking but you need to follow the producer's instructions carefully to ensure that they can be cooked without soaking.
- *Blanching* – Blanching refers to the cooking of the food item followed by rapid cooling, normally in iced water, to stop the cooking process. This is referred to as 'refreshing'. When refreshed vegetables or pasta are ready to be served, they are placed back into boiling water, not with the intention of cooking the food any further, just to re-heat.

Step-by-step: Blanching pasta (spaghetti)

STEP 1 Add the pasta by spreading it into a saucepan containing deep, salted boiling water. This helps to keep the pasta separate during the cooking process.

STEP 2 Test to see if the pasta is cooked by removing some with a spoon. The pasta should be cooked through but retain a 'bite' referred to as 'al dente'.

STEP 3 Once cooked, the pasta should be drained and served.
Note – If a little of the pasta water is retained, this will help prevent the pasta from sticking. A little olive oil can also help to prevent sticking as well as adding a delicate flavour.

- *Skimming* – During the boiling process, the food being boiled may produce impurities in the form of froth or foam rising to the surface. Impurities are particles of dirt or grease that become a by-product during the cooking process. This is very common when making a stock, soup or a sauce. If impurities are not removed, they will go back into the liquid due to the natural movement of the boiling motion. This could result in the liquid going cloudy or becoming greasy and the flavour being spoiled.

  Removing impurities from a liquid is a simple process. As foam or froth rises to the surface of the simmering liquid, stir the liquid from the centre with the base of a suitably sized ladle. The foam will then move to the edge of the pan. Using the ladle, but this time from the lip of the cup of the ladle, move the ladle around the edge of the pan to remove the froth from the liquid and discard (throw away in a safe and hygienic manner).
- **Refreshing**, *storing, reheating and serving* – In the professional kitchen, it is essential to be well prepared for service periods when large numbers of customers are often served in short spaces of time. For example, when preparating and cooking vegetables as an example, if you tried to cook and serve vegetables as customers requested them (to order), it would be very hard work. You would find it very difficult to cook, hold at temperature and serve the vegetables in prime condition.

  To achieve these aims, the practice of blanching, refreshing and storing for service is used. The vegetables can then be re-heated and served very quickly and in an organized and structured manner.

CHEF'S TIP When cooking lentils with an acid ingredient, such as tomatoes, either allow extra cooking time or add the tomatoes at the end of the recipe. The natural acid in the tomatoes will prolong the cooking process.

Other products from boiling

Some of the most common products made by boiling are stocks, soups and sauces.

STOCK

Stock is a flavoured liquid, which is used as a base to make many soups and sauces. The flavour of a stock is influenced by the ingredients that are used to make it. There are three broad categories of stocks:

- *White stock* – Is made from bones of animals such as beef, veal and chicken with the addition of vegetables and herbs. This is covered with water, brought to the boil, simmered slowly and skimmed to remove impurities over a number of hours to develop flavour, on average between 6 and 8. This is then strained and passed through a chinois (conical strainer) at which point the stock is ready to use. Fish bones are used in the production of fish stock but due to their size and strength of flavour, the cooking time required is only 20 minutes. Any longer than this and the liquid will start to become cloudy and develop a sour taste.
- *Brown stock* – To make a brown stock, the same ingredients are used but the bones and vegetables are roasted, or fried, before starting to provide colour and a deeper flavour to the stock. Fish stock is always white and never made by this method.
- *Vegetable stock* – Vegetable stock can be made white or brown.

Step-by-step: Brown beef stock

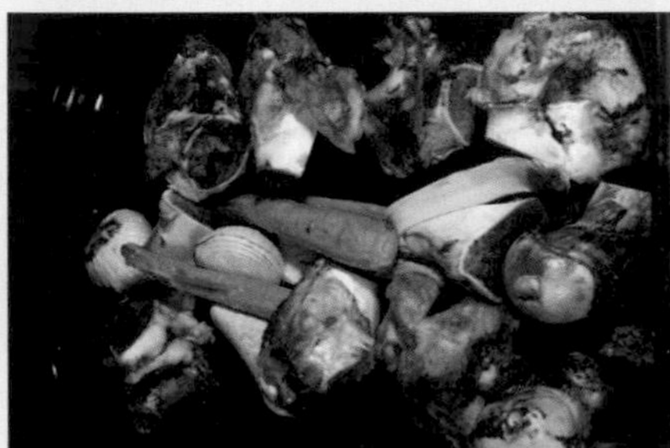

STEP 1 Remove excess fat from the bones and roast them in a roasting tray alongside the mirepoix of root vegetables to a deep golden brown colour.

STEP 2 Place the bones and vegetables into a stockpot, cover with water and bring up to a simmer. Add a bouquet garni to infuse.

STEP 3 Using the base of the ladle, gently stir the surface of the liquid which will push the impurities to the side of the stockpot. Use the cup of the ladle to skim and remove these impurities.

STEP 4 Simmer for 6 to 8 hours to develop sufficient flavour. Using a ladle and a chinois or strainer, ladle the stock into a clean pan.

STEP 5 As you get towards the end and it is safe to do so, lift the stockpot and pour the remaining stock through the chinois/strainer.

STEP 6 The finished stock, ready for use.

SOUPS

When making a soup, it is usual for the ingredients to be cooked in the liquid that will make up the soup itself. For example, if you were making a vegetable soup, the flavour would depend on the quantities of the vegetables used. For instance, in the case of a mushroom soup, the main ingredient would be mushrooms but it is likely that other ingredients such as onion, leek, celery and even potato could be used in smaller quantities to develop the flavours and texture of the soup. Herbs and spices would also add delicate flavours.

Soups are made into many styles and flavours, which is almost limitless. In some soups the vegetables and other ingredients are cut neatly and left suspended in the stock. This style of soup is known as a broth. In other styles the vegetables are cooked in the stock but then blended to make a purée. Puréed soups are often passed through a conical strainer (**chinois**) to make them smoother to eat.

CHEF'S TIP The soup could either be eaten with the vegetables left as they were originally cut, as in a broth, or placed into a liquidizer or food processor and made into a purée or cream based soup.

SAUCES

Sauces are offered with many dishes. They make a huge difference to a dish, making it moist and adding a lot of flavour. A good sauce also adds to the eating quality and enjoyment of the dish as well as helping to digest the food.

Sauces can be made from many bases including stock, wine, milk and, as in the case of a tomato sauce, the food item itself. In most cases, sauces will be simmered for the time it takes to develop the flavours and consistency looked for in the finished sauce.

Step-by-step: Making a cartouche

STEP 1 Take a sheet of greaseproof paper.

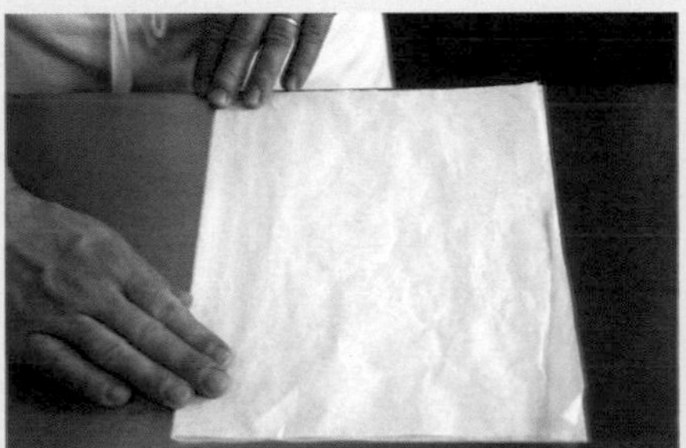

STEP 2 Fold it in half lengthways.

STEP 3 Fold in half again.

STEP 4 Keeping all the 'open' ends facing the same direction, fold in half again from the corner.

STEP 5 Repeat this process once or twice more depending on the size of the cartouche.

STEP 6 Measure the size of the item you are going to cover by placing the point of the folded cartouche in the centre of the item. Add a little extra to your measurement to go up the edge of the pan or bowl being covered.

STEP 7 Cut or tear along the line of your measurement.

STEP 8 Unfold to produce a cartouche that fits the size of the item you are covering. Some poaching techniques shown overleaf require the use of a cartouche. A cartouche is a circle of greaseproof paper used to prevent dishes from forming a skin or losing moisture.

Holding soups and sauces for service

Hot soups and many sauces can be kept hot by placing them in a bain-marie. This is a hot water bath, in which the sauce or soup (placed in a suitable container) is placed into the heated water. The heat from the water keeps the sauce or soup hot without cooking the soup or sauce any further.

To prevent a sauce or soup from getting a surface skin as a result of it coming into contact with the air, a cover, known as a cartouche (see above) is often used. This is made from greaseproof paper, folded in stages and cut into a circle slightly larger than the circumference of the pan. This allows full coverage of the surface area and a lip to go up the side of the pan itself.

Poaching

What is poaching?

Poaching is the cooking of foods by placing them into a prepared liquid, which has been heated to boiling point and then lowered, just below boiling point, to a very gentle simmer. Foods can be poached using a variety of different liquids including water, stock, wine, milk, stock syrup and a range of infused cooking liquids, for example, water enhanced with herbs, spices and vegetables.

The liquid also helps to develop flavour and texture. In some cases, the poaching liquid is reduced to become the sauce that is served with the poached item of food. A practical example of this is 'Poached Smoked haddock Florentine' (see recipe on page 90).

VIDEO CLIP Deep poaching salmon.

Step-by-step: Poaching smoked haddock in the preparation of 'Poached Smoked Haddock Florentine'

STEP 1 A fillet of smoked haddock with the poaching ingredients, milk, white peppercorns, parsley stalks and bay leaves.

STEP 2 Place the haddock, skin-side down, into the infused milk (milk with the parsley, stalks, etc).

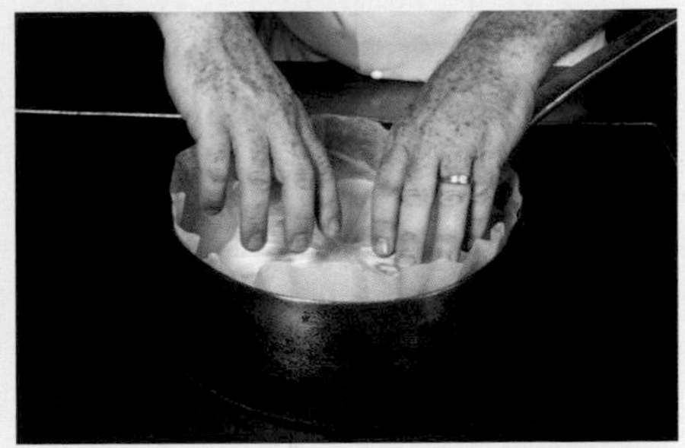

STEP 3 Place a buttered cartouche on top of the poaching liquid and bring the poaching liquid to a gentle simmer.

STEP 4 Poach the fish gently for 5 minutes and then remove carefully using a fish slice.

CHEF'S TIP Use a wide and fairly shallow saucepan when poaching. This will provide easy access to place and take out the food item being poached.

STEP 5 Place on a tray and gently brake down the fillet into the natural flakes.

STEP 6 Fill a shallow ring with some lightly sautéed spinach and top with flakes of the poached haddock.

STEP 7 Cover with Mornay sauce. The recipe and a picture of the finished dish can be seen on page 89.

The equipment used to poach foods

The equipment normally used to poach foods is a shallow or deep-sided poaching pan. It is important that the pan is quite wide to allow foods to be poached together at one level (rather than on top of one another) and also to allow easy access to place and remove the items of food being poached. A spider, perforated (slotted) spoon and slice or fish slice are all useful for removing the poached food from the pan.

The methods used to poach foods

There are two methods used to poach food. These are as follows:

1 The food is placed into a shallow poaching liquid. In this situation, the food is placed into the minimum amount of liquid. In some cases, the poaching process is started on the top of the oven and then finished by placing the whole pan into a medium oven between 170°C and 180°C. This temperature will keep the poaching liquid just below boiling point. Foods cooked by shallow poaching often use the poaching liquid as the base for the sauce that is served with the food item being poached.

2 The food is placed into a deep poaching liquid. For example, an egg is poached in simmering water which is two or three times as deep as the shelled egg. A poached egg can be blanched, refreshed and reheated for service in a similar way to the way that vegetables are re-heated for service. The sequence below demonstrates an egg being poached.

VIDEO CLIP Poaching eggs.

Step-by-step: Poaching an egg

STEP 1 Break an egg into a small dish or bowl. Make sure that the egg is fresh and has no blood spots. The albumen (egg white) will be much thicker and stick close to the yolk if the egg is fresh. This becomes much thinner and runnier as the egg gets older.

STEP 2 Using a shallow poaching pan, fill two-thirds full with water and bring to the boil. Stir the water to produce a circular movement before carefully adding the egg.

STEP 3 This picture shows the egg white surrounding the yolk as it poaches. Usually, a poached egg is ready when the egg white is firm and the yolk is left soft.

STEP 4 Once the egg is sufficiently cooked, remove the egg carefully using a perforated (slotted) spoon.

CHEF'S TIP The addition of vinegar to the poaching liquid will help to coagulate the egg white and keep this surrounding the yolk as it poaches.

CHEF'S TIP If the egg is to be served at a later time, it can be refreshed and stored by placing it into ice-cold water.

Foods that are suitable for poaching

TASK Other foods that are commonly poached include fruits, fish and chicken.

In the categories below, find two dishes that are poached for each type of food.

FOOD	DISH EXAMPLE	
Eggs	1. ______	2. ______
Fish	1. ______	2. ______
Chicken	1. ______	2. ______
Fruit	1. ______	2. ______

VIDEO CLIP Poaching fruit.

VIDEO CLIP Poaching a whole chicken.

Other techniques used when poaching foods

A number of techniques help to achieve a good quality and consistent finished dish when poaching foods. These are as follows:

- *Cutting into uniform size* – Cutting to uniform size helps to ensure that food items cook evenly in the same amount of time. Accurate cutting helps with portion control, making sure that enough portions are produced. Presentation is also improved by accurate and uniform cutting skills.
- *Tying* – Tying helps to make sure that foods stay in the required shape while they are poached. Tying food items also makes it easier to handle the food during the whole cooking process.
- *Folding* – As in tying, folding food items such as fish fillets helps the items stay in the required shape. Folding can help to make the thickness of the food items more even, allowing the food to cook in an even time. Presentation can also be improved if the food has been folded neatly.

Step-by-step: Poaching a pear in red wine (see recipe on page 90)

STEP 1 The ingredients for poaching a pear in red wine – (red wine, sugar, cinnamon stick, star anise and the pears).

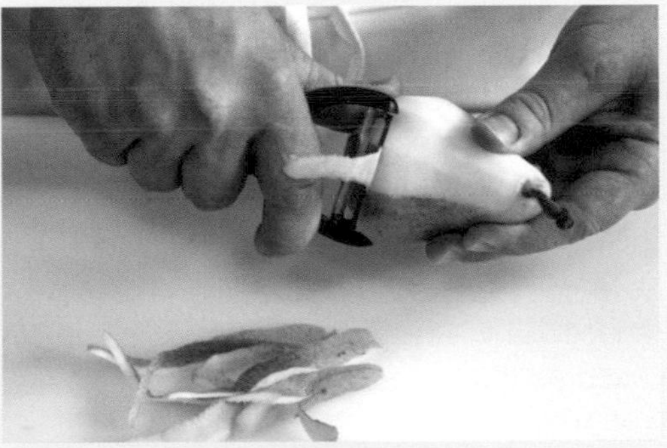

STEP 2 Carefully peel the pears.

STEP 3 Place the pears into the poaching liquid, ensuring that the liquid covers the pear and bring to a gentle simmer (a slightly deeper saucepan can be used in this instance).

STEP 4 Poach the pears until cooked (this will depend on how ripe they are) and remove using a perforated (slotted) spoon.

Step-by-step: Poaching chicken

STEP 1 Prepare a white mirepoix (chopped onions, leek and celery) and gather aromatics (parsley stalks, peppercorns, bay leaves and sliced garlic).

STEP 2 Place the mirepoix and aromatics into a poaching pan, bring to a gentle simmer and then carefully place in the skinned chicken breast.

STEP 3 Cover with a cartouche and poach until cooked through.

STEP 4 Once cooked, remove the chicken breast with a slotted slice and use as required.

- *Draining* – When poaching, as the food is placed in a liquid, it is important that the food is dried properly before it is served. If the food is not dried properly and is being served with a sauce, the poaching liquid would appear separately from the sauce or possibly make the sauce thinner.
- *Reducing for sauce* – With some poached dishes, the liquid is strained and reduced in volume by boiling it rapidly. It can then be used as the base of the sauce to accompany (be served with) the poached item of food.
- *Holding for service* – Once the food item is cooked, there may be a period of time before the item is served. For example, this could be the time that it takes to prepare the sauce. It is very important that the food is kept hot and in good condition during this time. As many poached foods are quite delicate, this has to be done carefully so that the food remains in prime condition.

CHEF'S TIP A hotplate, or very low oven, can provide a good place to keep the food at the appropriate temperature while you are preparing the finishing touches to the accompaniments.

CHEF'S TIP Prime condition means:

- hot
- sufficiently cooked without overcooking e.g. vegetables with a bite – referred to as 'al dente')
- good colour retained
- well seasoned
- well presented.

Steaming

What is steaming?

When steaming, the food is cooked by placing it in the steam produced as a by-product (side effect) of boiling water, rather than the water itself. The food is being cooked in an atmosphere of moist or wet heat.

CHEF'S TIP Steaming is considered as a good method of preserving colour and nutrients in foods.

Methods and equipment used to steam foods

A Chinese bamboo steamer

There are two main methods of steaming. The method used will determine the type of equipment that is needed. This is described below.

1 *Atmospheric or low-pressure steaming* – The food is cooked in the steam produced by boiling water. It is either in direct contact with the steam (the food is placed into the steam itself) or the process is indirect, and the food item is protected from the steam by sealing it in a mould or container. The equipment required to steam food by this method is very basic. For example, a rack in a pan of water will make a good steamer (as long as the rack is higher than the water level or else the food will cook in the water rather than the steam). A Chinese bamboo steamer is also a low-cost way of producing a very good atmospheric steamer.

2 *High pressure steaming* – Some steamers (pressure cookers) trap the steam, which increases the pressure. This means the steam is at a higher temperature. This enables the food to be cooked faster than using a normal steamer, which is at atmospheric (normal) pressure.

Foods that are suitable for steaming

- Most vegetables can be steamed, particularly if using a high-pressure steamer.
- Fish that can be poached are also suitable for cooking by steaming.
- Sponge and suet puddings are steamed to produce a light and moist texture.

Step-by-step: Preparing cauliflower florets for steaming

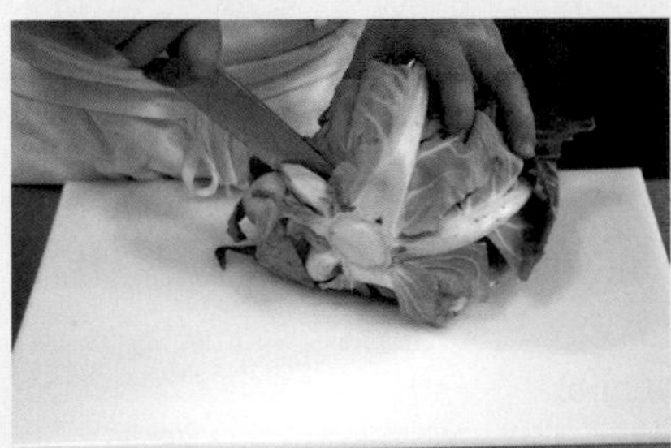

STEP 1 Place the cauliflower securely on a chopping board and, using a large knife, cut the root from the base of the cauliflower.

STEP 2 Using a paring knife, trim the remaining leaves from the base of the cauliflower leaving the white florets of the cauliflower intact.

STEP 3 Cutting squarely across each floret, cut into evenly sized florets.

STEP 4 Place neatly onto a steaming tray and steam.

STEP 5 Finished steamed cauliflower florets.

TASK For each category below, research two dishes that are steamed.

FOOD	DISH EXAMPLE	
Vegetables	1. ________	2. ________
Fish	1. ________	2. ________
Chicken	1. ________	2. ________
Sweet and savoury puddings	1. ________	2. ________

VIDEO CLIP Steaming fish.

Step-by-step: Steamed délice of plaice (en papillote)

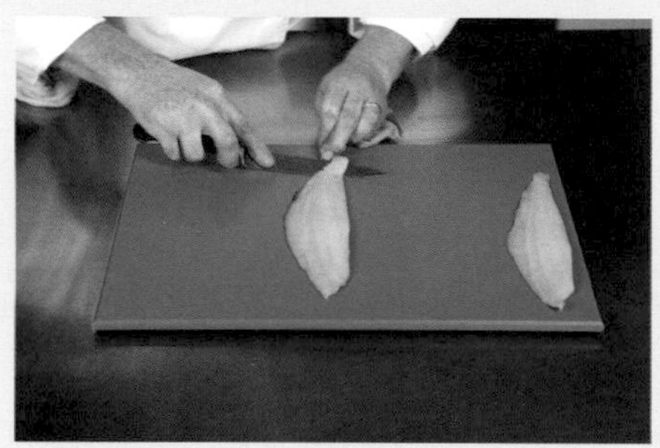

STEP 1 Using a sharp filleting knife, cut into the tail end of the fillet at an angle to free the flesh, holding onto the skin for leverage.

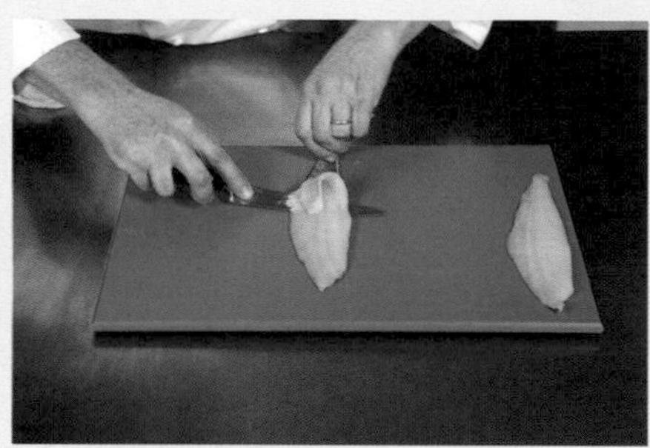

STEP 2 Continue to remove the fillet by holding the blade at a slight angle towards the skin, whilst sliding the knife along the skin.

STEP 3 Fold the fillet into a délice as shown, ensuring that the fillet is skin-side upwards.

STEP 4 Trim the outside of the root ginger.

STEP 5 Cut the trimmed ginger into fine slices.

STEP 6 Cut the slices in to fine strips (**julienne**).

STEP 7 Cut the spring onion into matchstick-sized lengths. Cut each piece in half lengthways and slice into julienne.

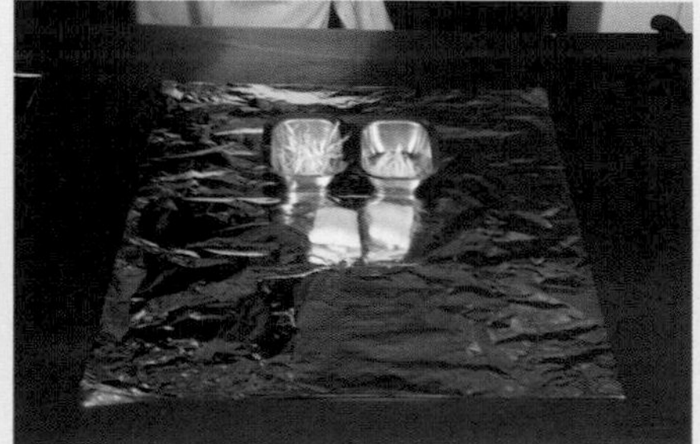

STEP 8 The prepared fish and julienne of ginger and spring onion.

STEP 9 Wrap in foil or greaseproof paper.

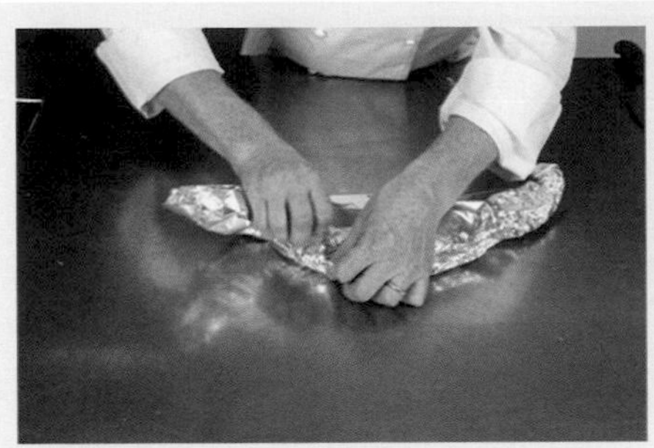

STEP 10 Crimp the edges to ensure the package is sealed.

STEP 11 Steam for 4 minutes.

STEP 12 The finished dish – Steamed paupiette of plaice with ginger and spring onion (en papillote).

Other techniques used when steaming foods

A number of techniques help to achieve a good quality and consistent finished dish when steaming foods:

- *Preparing the container or mould* – It is important that the container used to steam the food is in good condition and the right size for the job.
- *Greasing* – Lightly coating the inside of the mould with oil or fat will provide a non-stick surface to allow the food to come free from the mould when ready to be served.
- *Moulding* – This refers to the food being placed into the mould itself. It is important that the food is added evenly to take on the shape of the mould. A gentle tap of the filled mould onto a table can help the food to spread out around the mould.
- *Waterproofing* – Foods that are steamed in containers or moulds are usually sealed to prevent the steam (water vapour) from getting into direct contact with the food item itself. This enables the food item to be cooked by the steam without taking in the moisture and becoming soggy. To produce a waterproof seal, the mould is usually covered with greaseproof paper and kitchen foil. When covering, a fold in the centre of the paper and foil will allow room for the food (such as a steamed pudding) to expand.
- *Traying up* – Sometimes many items are needed to be steamed at the same time. For example, if serving an individual steamed pudding as a dessert for 30 covers, 30 moulds would need to be filled and covered. Rather than placing each mould individually into the steamer, it would be much easier and more efficient to place the moulds onto a tray and steam the puddings together in one batch.
- *Loading* – This refers to the moulds, or trays of moulds, being placed into the steamer. When working with steam, it is very important that you keep a safe distance from the steam itself. Steam can produce a nasty scald if in direct contact with skin. Particular attention is required when opening the doors of high-pressure steamers.

Step-by-step: Steamed sponge pudding

STEP 1 The ingredients and basins for producing steamed sponge puddings – Plain (soft) flour, butter, eggs, caster sugar, baking powder. Note that self raising flour can be used but this flour already has the raising agent added, so the baking powder would not be necessary.

STEP 2 Cream the butter and sugar together in a suitably sized bowl.

STEP 3 Beat the eggs in a separate bowl and add the creamed mixture gradually whilst continuing to beat. Adding the eggs gradually should prevent the mixture from curdling.

STEP 4 Mix the baking powder with the flour and sieve into the butter, sugar and egg mix. Fold this in gently using a large metal spoon.

STEP 5 Line the pudding basins by brushing with melted butter and finely coating with flour. This will prevent the cooked puddings from sticking to the basins when removing to serve.

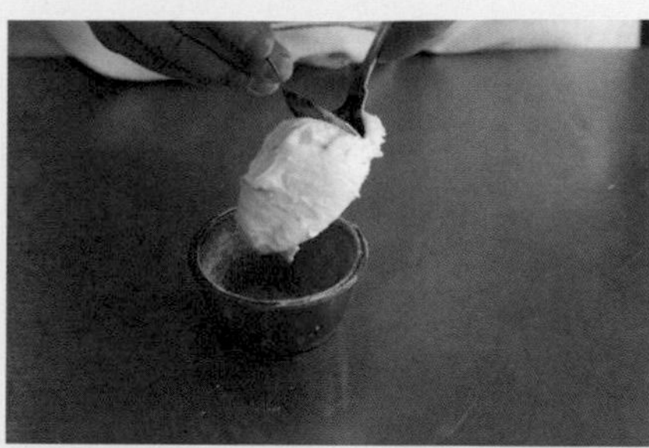

STEP 6 Using two spoons, as shown, place the sponge mix into the pudding basins leaving some room at the top of the basins for rising.

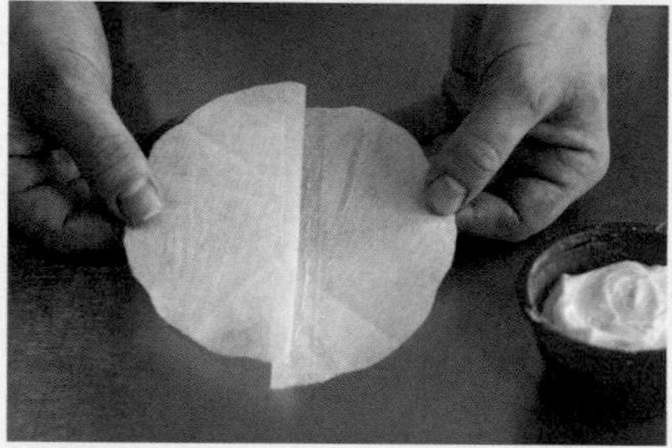

STEP 7 Prepare a suitably sized cartouche, brush one side with melted butter and make a fold in the centre of the cartouche as shown. The cartouche will protect the sponge mixture from moisture in the steamer and the fold will allow the mixture to rise.

STEP 8 Place the cartouche, butter-side down, over the basin and secure by tying with a piece of string or elastic band.

STEP 9 Place in the prepared steamer and steam until cooked (approximately 40 minutes for a pudding of this size).

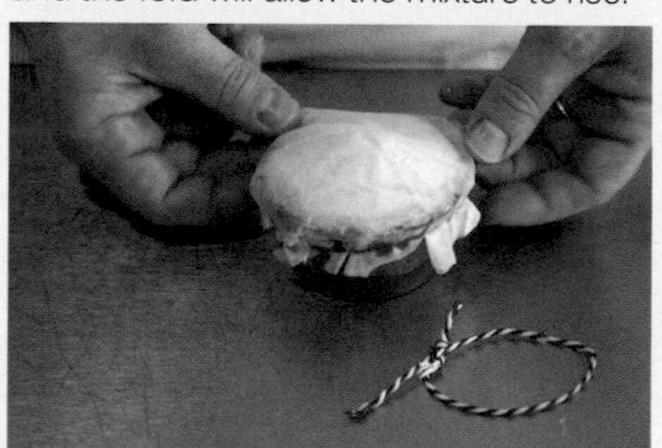

STEP 10 Once cooked, remove from the steamer, untie the string and carefully peel off the cartouche.

STEP 11 To serve, demould the puddings by releasing from the basins as shown.

STEP 12 Coat with an appropriate sauce (e.g. lemon, orange, etc.), garnish and serve.

HEALTH & SAFETY When opening a high pressure steamer, the steam from the chamber will pump out from the door. Therefore, it is good practice to stand away from, or behind, the door to let the steam out before removing the moulds or trays from the steamer.

CHEF'S TIP Some items, such as sweet steamed puddings, will rise during the steaming process. Do not fill the mould to the top, fill to about two-thirds of the way up the mould to allow space for the sponge to rise.

VIDEO CLIP Steaming sweet puddings.

TASK Take three vegetables of the same type, such as sticks of celery, small leeks or fennel.

Boil, poach and steam the chosen vegetable. Once cooked, evaluate the colour, texture and cooking time.

After tasting, which is your preferred method for the chosen vegetable? Give reasons behind your choice.

QUALITY POINTS TO LOOK FOR DURING THE SELECTION OF FOOD ITEMS

When selecting ingredients, it is essential that they are checked for various quality points, including:

- Freshness – To ensure the correct flavours come through the dish.
- Appearance – Checking that the ingredients are in good condition and of the right colour and size.
- Smell – Checking that the ingredients smell how they are expected to smell. Our sense of smell is very powerful and quickly detects strong and/or rancid odours.
- Temperature – The temperature of food items needs to be checked to ensure they are at the appropriate temperature for the type of food, e.g. chilled, frozen or ambient.

QUALITY POINTS DURING PREPARATION

- Cut to **specification** – When producing a broth, for example, it is important that the vegetables are cut neatly in the required shape (e.g. diced) and of an even size.
- Trimming – When preparing vegetables, it is important that they are washed, peeled and re-washed, neatly trimmed and that waste is minimized.
- Recipes are closely followed and any small equipment is prepared in advance (e.g. pudding basins when steaming).

QUALITY POINTS DURING COOKING

There are many points to consider during the cooking of foods by boiling, poaching and steaming. This includes checking:

- the texture of the food
- the taste and flavour of the food
- its appearance and colour
- the degree of cooking
- the temperature throughout the cooking process.

QUALITY POINTS IN THE FINISHED DISH

After the hard work put into the selection of ingredients and their preparation and cooking, it is important to complete the process by serving them to the highest standard possible. The following points should be considered at this point:

- colour(s)
- flavour
- temperature
- taste
- appearance
- consistency
- seasoning
- portion control
- cleanliness of serving equipment
- saucing, if a sauce forms part of the dish
- garnishes
- final presentation.

Working safely

It is important to follow safe working practices when boiling, poaching and steaming food items. The following points should be considered.

When boiling and poaching

- Use the right sized pan for the job in hand.
- Handle hot pans with care!
- Make sure that handles from pans do not stick out from the stove!
- Be careful when placing and removing items from the liquid!

When working with steamers

- Make sure that there is enough water in the steamer before turning it on.
- Ensure that steam is released in a controlled manner!

Guest Chef

Fillet of sole Véronique

Chef *Mathew Shropshall*
Centre *University College Birmingham*

Ingredients	*4 portions*
Lemon sole	1 whole
Salt and pepper	
Fish stock	200 ml
Lemon juice	1/2 lemon
Butter	50 g
Flour	25 g
Double cream	30 ml
Egg yolk – free range	1 egg
Cream, lightly whipped	2 tbsp
White seedless grapes,	50 g skinned
Staffordshire baby	100 g spinach, washed & picked
tomatoe concasse,	10 g finely sliced
home grown fresh	2 sprigs parsley, washed

METHOD OF WORK

1. Skin and fillet sole, trim and wash.
2. Butter and season an earthenware dish.
3. Add the fillets of sole.
4. Season, add the fish stock, wine and lemon juice.
5. Cover with a buttered greaseproof paper.
6. Poach in a moderate oven (150°C) or regular 2 for 10 minutes.
7. Drain the fish well, dress neatly on a flat dish or earthenware dish.
8. Bring the cooking liquor to the boil and strain. Heat flour and butter together to form a **roux** then, with the fish stock, mix in to form a **velouté**.
9. Correct the seasoning and consistency and pass through a **muslin** cloth or a fine strainer. Make a **liaison** by mixing together the egg yolk and cream. Add this to the sauce but do not allow the sauce to re-boil as this will scramble the egg and curdle the sauce.
10. Blanch the baby spinach for 30 seconds in boiling salted water and drain. Reheat in a pan with butter and seasoning and tomato concassé.
11. Pour some sauce over the sole fillet, Glaze under the salamander.
12. To present, sit spinach and tomato on a 25 cm fish bowl/plate, rest sole on top, surround with sauce and glaze under the salamander, Garnish with grapes and red amaranth (or other suitable micro-salad) and finish with a sprig of curly parsley.

TEST YOURSELF

1 Briefly describe the processes of:

boiling ______

poaching ______

steaming ______

2 When boiling raw green vegetables, why are they placed into salted boiling water?

______

______

3 Why is it important to cut vegetables into a uniform size when cooking them by boiling?

______

______

4 Name three liquids that can be used as the base for a sauce.

i) ______
ii) ______
iii) ______

5 When making a sauce or a soup, why is it important to skim the impurities (foam and froth) from the top of the liquid?

______

______

6 What is steam?

______

______

7 What are the two main methods used to steam foods?

i) ______
ii) ______

8 Name a poached fish dish that uses the cooking liquid to make the accompanying sauce.

______

______

9 Name a sauce that is made from milk.

______

______

10 If poaching in the oven, at what temperature would you set the oven?

______

______

11 When poaching or boiling, why is it important that pan handles are not left to stick out from the oven?

______

______

12 If steaming food in a mould, how would you prevent steam from getting into direct contact with the food?

______

______

13 If a fish can be poached, it can be steamed.
☐ True ☐ False

Recipes

Lemon tart filling lemon curd

Ingredients	*Will fill 1 × 8 inch tart or 8–10 individual tartlets*
Granulated sugar	450 g
Grated zest of 2 lemons	
Freshly squeezed lemon juice	240 ml
Large eggs	8
Large egg yolks	2
Unsalted butter-cut into pieces	350 g

energy	cal	fat	sat fat	carb	sugar	protein	fibre
2152 kJ	516 kcal	34.6 g	19.9 g	47.6 g	47.6 g	6.5 g	0.1 g

METHOD OF WORK

1 Place the sugar into a bowl. Grate the zest of 2 lemons into it and rub together.

2 Strain the lemon juice into a non-reactive pan. Add the eggs, egg yolks, butter and zested sugar. Whisk to combine.

3 Place over a medium heat and whisk continuously for 3–5 minutes, until the mixture begins to thicken.

4 At the first sign of boiling, remove from the heat and strain into a bowl and cool.

Spaghetti carbonara

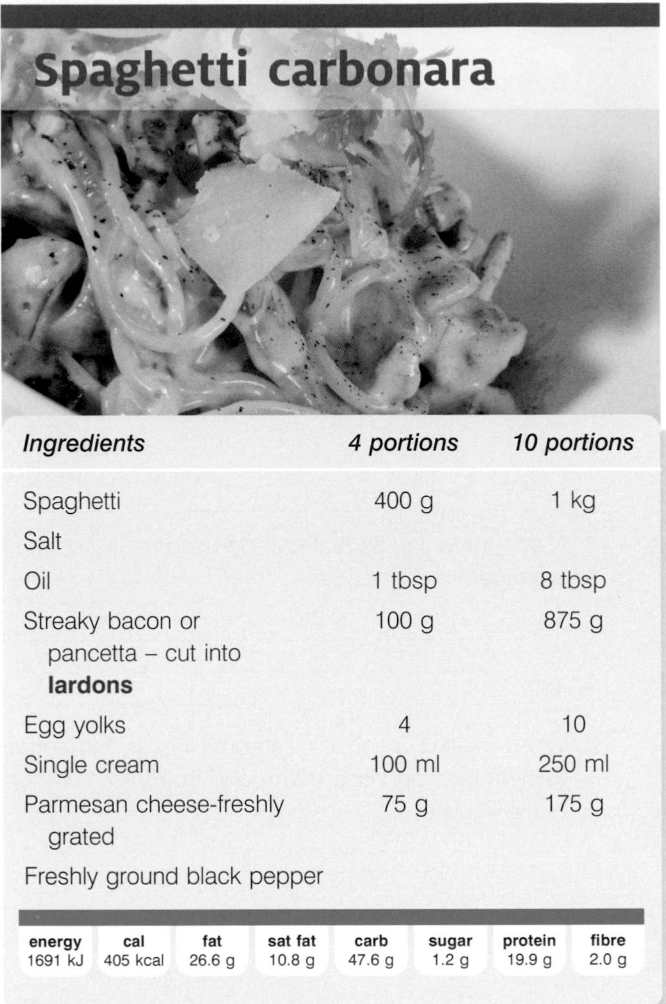

Ingredients	*4 portions*	*10 portions*
Spaghetti	400 g	1 kg
Salt		
Oil	1 tbsp	8 tbsp
Streaky bacon or pancetta – cut into **lardons**	100 g	875 g
Egg yolks	4	10
Single cream	100 ml	250 ml
Parmesan cheese-freshly grated	75 g	175 g
Freshly ground black pepper		

energy	cal	fat	sat fat	carb	sugar	protein	fibre
1691 kJ	405 kcal	26.6 g	10.8 g	47.6 g	1.2 g	19.9 g	2.0 g

METHOD OF WORK

1 Spread the spaghetti and drop into a pan with plenty of rapidly boiling salted water.

2 Heat the oil in a fairly large frying pan, add the bacon and fry lightly over a medium heat until the fat has melted.

3 Remove the pan from the heat and set aside, keeping it warm.

4 In a separate bowl, whisk the egg yolks with the cream and half the parmesan cheese. Season generously with the pepper.

5 When the spaghetti is still firm to the bite (al dente), drain it and transfer it to the pan with the bacon.

6 Place over a medium heat and pour the egg mixture over it.

7 Stir quickly and turn off the heat. (Do not let this mixture boil as it will curdle the eggs!)

8 Serve immediately offering the remaining Parmesan cheese.

Béchamel and Mornay sauce

Ingredients	*4 portions*	*10 portions*
For the Béchamel sauce		
Butter	50 g	125 g
Plain flour	50 g	125 g
Milk	500 ml	1250 ml
Pinch of freshly grated nutmeg (optional)		
Salt and freshly ground white pepper		
For the Mornay sauce		
Egg yolk	1	3 small or 2 large
Double cream	100 ml	250 ml
Recipe Béchamel sauce	1	1
Freshly grated Gruyère cheese	25 g	65 g
Freshly grated Parmesan cheese	25 g	65 g
Salt and freshly ground white pepper		

Béchamel sauce

energy	cal	fat	sat fat	carb	sugar	protein	fibre
814 kJ	195 kcal	12.7 g	7.9 g	15.9 g	6.2 g	5.7 g	0.5 g

Mornay sauce

energy	cal	fat	sat fat	carb	sugar	protein	fibre
1600 kJ	385 kcal	31.3 g	19.2 g	16.4 g	6.7 g	10.7 g	0.5 g

METHOD OF WORK

For the Béchamel sauce

1 Melt the butter in a saucepan over a low to medium heat.

2 Add the flour and mix to a paste (white roux).

3 Pour the milk in gradually (a small amount at a time), **mixing** constantly until it comes to the boil. The milk should bind well with the mix to form a smooth paste. This will become thinner as more milk is added.

4 Reduce the heat, cover with a cartouche and simmer gently, stirring occasionally, for at least 45 minutes. Béchamel sauce should not taste floury.

5 Remove the saucepan from the heat and season with salt, pepper and/or nutmeg.

6 If the sauce is too thick, add a little more milk. If too thin, return to the heat and add a knob of butter mixed with an equal quantity of plain flour. For a richer Béchamel sauce, replace half the milk with the same amount of cream.

For the Mornay sauce

1 Beat the egg yolk with the cream in a small bowl.

2 When the Béchamel sauce is ready, remove the saucepan from the heat and stir in the Gruyère and Parmesan.

3 Stir in the egg yolk mix.

4 Season to taste with salt and pepper.

5 Use for poached eggs, fish dishes and gratins.

Note: Mornay sauce can be made using Cheddar in place of Gruyere and Parmesan.

Pears poached in red wine

Ingredients	4 portions	10 portions
Water	100 ml	250 ml
Red wine	300 ml	750 ml
Granulated sugar	125 g	300 g
Redcurrant jelly	1 tbsp	3 tbsp
Lemon – zest	1	2
Cinnamon stick	1	3
Firm pears (Williams/ Comice)	4	10

energy	cal	fat	sat fat	carb	sugar	protein	fibre
1044 kJ	247 kcal	0.2 g	0.0 g	50.9 g	50.3 g	0.9 g	4.0 g

METHOD OF WORK

1 Place the water, wine, sugar and jelly in a saucepan and heat gently until the sugar has dissolved.

2 Add the lemon zest and cinnamon.

3 Peel the pears very neatly without removing the stalks.

4 Place upright in the pan and cover with a lid. The pears should be completely covered by the wine and water mixture, so choose a suitable pan.

5 Bring the liquid up to the boil and simmer until the pears are cooked. The pears should be a cherry-red colour and tender when pricked with a small sharp knife.

6 Remove the pears from the pan and allow to cool.

7 Reduce the wine liquid by boiling to a syrupy consistency and strain it over the pears.

8 Allow to cool, then chill in the refrigerator and use accordingly.

Poached smoked haddock florentine

Ingredients	4 portions	10 portions
Smoked haddock	400 g	1 kg
Milk	500 ml	1250 ml
Bay leaves	2	5
Parsley stalks		
Bouquet garni	1	3
Studded onion – studded with 2 cloves	½	1½
Spinach	500 g	1250 g
Poached eggs	4	10
Mornay sauce	250 ml	625 ml

energy	cal	fat	sat fat	carb	sugar	protein	fibre
830 kJ	197 kcal	8.3 g	5.1 g	8.1 g	7.7 g	23.3 g	0.4 g

METHOD OF WORK

To poach the haddock

1 Place the haddock into the milk (with herbs) and simmer gently for 5 minutes.

2 When cooked, take out of the milk and remove the backbone.

3 The flesh should now break into firm flaky pieces.

4 Retain the milk to make the Mornay sauce.

To complete the dish

1 Poach, refresh and re-heat eggs as shown earlier in the chapter.

2 Remove the stems from the spinach.

3 Wash well in cold water until clean. Drain.

4 For larger leaves, blanch by placing in boiling salted water for 30 seconds and remove using a spider.

5 Refresh in iced water and squeeze dry into a ball.

6 To serve, place the spinach into a pan containing 50 g heated butter.

7 Mix with a fork and re-heat quickly without colouring.

8 Season lightly with salt and freshly ground white pepper.

9 Serve by neatly arranging the spinach on a plate.

10 Arrange the flakes of haddock on top of the spinach.

11 Place the re-heated eggs on top and coat each egg carefully with Mornay sauce.

Steamed sponge puddings

Ingredients	*10–12 portions*
Basic sponge	
Individual moulds buttered and floured	12
Unsalted butter	200 g
Caster sugar	300 g
Eggs	4
Egg yolks	2
Self-raising flour	400 g
Milk (if needed)	2–3 tbsp

energy	cal	fat	sat fat	carb	sugar	protein	fibre
1724 kJ	410 kcal	19.0 g	10.9 g	57.1 g	29.4 g	6.3 g	1.2 g

METHOD OF WORK

1. Beat the butter and sugar until creamed.
2. Add the eggs and egg yolks gradually and continue to beat.
3. Fold in the sifted flour, adding the milk if necessary.
4. Spoon the mixture into the prepared moulds (three-quarters full) and cover with greaseproof paper (fold in the centre to allow for the rising pudding).
5. Steam for 40 minutes.

Steamed treacle sponge

Add a spoonful of golden syrup to the mix with a spoonful at the base of the moulds.

Brown beef stock

Ingredients	*5 litres*	*10 litres*
Raw beef bones – chopped	1 kg	2.5 kg
Water	6 litres	12 litres
Onion, carrot, celery, leek	400 g	1.5 kg
Bouquet garni	1	2
Peppercorns	8	16

energy	cal	fat	sat fat	carb	sugar	protein	fibre
250 kJ	60 kcal	4.8 g	2.0 g	0.3 g	0.2 g	3.5 g	0.1 g

METHOD OF WORK

1. Brown the bones well on all sides by placing in a roasting tin and placing in a hot oven. Alternatively, brown by frying the bones carefully in a little fat in a large frying pan.
2. Drain the bones from all fat and place in a stockpot.
3. Brown the sediment that may be in the bottom of the tray before deglazing (swill out) with half litre of boiling water. Simmer for a few minutes to maximize the flavour and add to the bones.
4. Cover the bones with the cold water and bring to the boil whilst skimming any impurities from the surface.
5. Wash, peel and roughly cut the vegetables (mirepoix) and fry in a little fat until brown. Alternatively, the vegetables can be roasted in the same way as the bones. Strain from fat/oil and add to the bones.
6. Add the bouquet garni and peppercorns and simmer for 6–8 hours, skimming off any impurities throughout the cooking process.
7. Strain through a conical strainer (chinoix) into a suitable container.

Note: This stock can be made using other types of bones, such as lamb or veal.

White chicken stock

Ingredients	5 litres	10 litres
Chicken **carcass**/wings	5 kg	10 kg
Onion, carrot, celery, leek	400 g	1.5-kg
Bouquet garni	1	2
Cold water	6 litres	12 litres

energy	cal	fat	sat fat	carb	sugar	protein	fibre
6 kJ	1 kcal	0.0 g	0.0 g	0.3 g	0.2 g	0.1 g	0.1 g

METHOD OF WORK

1 Remove excess fat from the chicken carcasses and wash in cold water.

2 Place all the bones into a suitably sized stockpot.

3 Add all the other ingredients and cover with the cold water.

4 Bring to the boil skimming all the impurities as they rise to the surface.

5 Reduce the heat to simmer and continue to skim throughout the cooking process.

6 Simmer for 6 to 8 hours then pass through a conical strainer into a suitable container.

Note: To enhance the flavour of a stock, reduce the strained stock rapidly until the stock has reduced by 50 per cent. Pass again through a fine sieve.

Vegetable broth

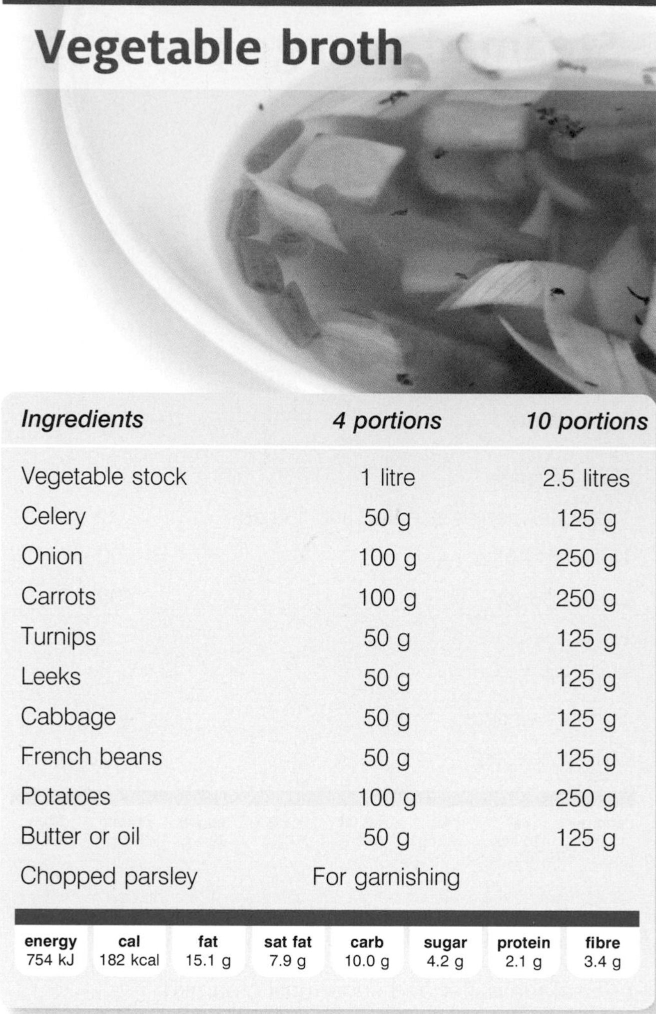

Ingredients	4 portions	10 portions
Vegetable stock	1 litre	2.5 litres
Celery	50 g	125 g
Onion	100 g	250 g
Carrots	100 g	250 g
Turnips	50 g	125 g
Leeks	50 g	125 g
Cabbage	50 g	125 g
French beans	50 g	125 g
Potatoes	100 g	250 g
Butter or oil	50 g	125 g
Chopped parsley	For garnishing	

energy	cal	fat	sat fat	carb	sugar	protein	fibre
754 kJ	182 kcal	15.1 g	7.9 g	10.0 g	4.2 g	2.1 g	3.4 g

METHOD OF WORK

1 Cut all of the vegetables and potatoes into a neat paysanne.

2 In a suitable saucepan, add the butter or oil and heat gently.

3 Add the onion, leeks and celery and sweat for 2 to 3 minutes.

4 Add the remaining vegetables.

5 Add the stock and bring to the boil. Simmer until all the vegetables are cooked.

6 Adjust the seasoning with salt and freshly ground white pepper.

7 Sprinkle over some finely chopped parsley before serving.

Chasseur sauce

Ingredients	4 portions	10 portions
Butter or oil	25 g	50 g
Shallots-chopped	10 g	25 g
Garlic clove – chopped	0.5	1
Button mushrooms – sliced	50 g	125 g
Dry white wine	60 ml	150 ml
Tomatoes – skinned, deseeded and diced (concassé)	100 g	250 g
Jus-lié or reduced stock	250 ml	625 ml
Parsley and tarragon – chopped	For flavour and garnishing	

energy	cal	fat	sat fat	carb	sugar	protein	fibre
585 kJ	141 kcal	11.4 g	5.0 g	4.0 g	2.4 g	3.3 g	1.4 g

METHOD OF WORK

1. Melt the butter or oil in a saucepan.
2. Add the shallots and sweat for 2 to 3 minutes without colour until soft.
3. Add the garlic and the mushrooms, cover and cook gently for two to three minutes, **straining** off any excess fat.
4. Add the white wine and reduce by 50 per cent.
5. Add the jus-lié or stock and simmer for 5 to 10 minutes.
6. Add the diced tomato and the tarragon and parsley.
7. Adjust the seasoning with salt and freshly ground white pepper.

Note: Chasseur sauce is often served with sautéed chicken, steaks or pork chops, etc.

Jus-lié is a thickened brown sauce which is often used as a base for other sauces.

Tomato sauce

Ingredients	4 portions	10 portions
Butter or oil	10 g	25 g
Onions, carrots, celery, leek (for mirepoix)	100 g	250 g
Bacon scraps (optional)	25 g	75 g
Flour	10 g	25 g
Tomato pureé	50 g	125 g
Bouquet garni	1	1
Vegetable or chicken stock	375 ml	1 litre
Garlic clove	1	2

energy	cal	fat	sat fat	carb	sugar	protein	fibre
326 kJ	78 kcal	5.3 g	2.3 g	5.2 g	2.8 g	2.9 g	1.1 g

METHOD OF WORK

1. Melt the butter or oil in a saucepan.
2. Add the vegetables (mirepoix) and bacon scraps (if using) and brown slightly.
3. Add the garlic and cook gently to soften.
4. Add the flour and mix to produce a roux.
5. Cook the roux for 1 minute allowing it to colour slightly.
6. Mix in the tomato pureé.
7. Gradually add the stock, stirring to the boil after each batch.
8. Simmer for 1 hour.
9. Correct the seasoning and cool.
10. Pass through a fine conical strainer (chinoix).

Note: Tomato sauce is very versatile and is often served with pasta and egg dishes as well as meat and fish dishes. Tomato sauce can also be made without using flour. To make a tomato sauce using fresh or canned tomatoes, omit the flour and use 75 g of tomatoes per portion instead. The amount of stock required will also be reduced due to the water content of the tomatoes.

Délice of flat white fish Bercy

Ingredients	4 portions	10 portions
Fillets of flat white fish (sole, plaice)	400-600 g	1-1.5 kg
Butter – for the ovenproof dish and greaseproof paper	To cover	
Shallots – finely chopped and sweated	20 g	50 g
Fish stock	60 ml	150 ml
Dry white wine	60 ml	150 ml
Lemon juice	¼	½
Fish velouté	250 ml	625 ml
Button mushrooms – quartered/sliced	40 g	100 g
Tomatoes – skinned and neatly diced	2	4
Butter	50 g	125 g
Cream – lightly whipped	2 tbsp	5 tbsp

energy	cal	fat	sat fat	carb	sugar	protein	fibre
1729 kJ	416 kcal	28.8 g	16.5 g	7.2 g	3.5 g	28.5 g	1.8 g

METHOD OF WORK

1. Skin and fillet the fish, trim and wash. Fold the fillets neatly ensuring the skin side is outside facing (délice).
2. Butter and season an earthenware dish.
3. Sprinkle with the sweated chopped shallots and mushrooms and add the folded fillets (délice).
4. Season, add the fish stock, wine and lemon juice.
5. Cover with buttered greaseproof paper.
6. Poach in a moderate oven at 160°C for 7 to 10 minutes.
7. Drain the fish well; dress neatly on a flat dish or clean service dish or plate.
8. Bring the cooking liquor to the boil and mix in the velouté.
9. Correct the seasoning and consistency, and pass through a fine strainer into a clean pan.
10. Bring to a simmer and add the neatly diced tomatoes (concassé). Be careful not to overcook at this stage as the tomatoes will begin to disintegrate (break down) if heated for too long.
11. Mix in the butter and finally the cream.
12. Coat each délice with the sauce.

Rice pudding

Ingredients	4 portions	10 portions
Pudding rice – washed	50 g	125 g
Caster sugar	50 g	125 g
Milk	½ litre	1 ¼ litre
Butter	10 g	25 g
Vanilla pod/good quality vanilla essence	1 pod/2-3 drops	2 pods/6-8 drops

energy	cal	fat	sat fat	carb	sugar	protein	fibre
601 kJ	142 kcal	4.2 g	2.7 g	22.7 g	19.0 g	4.7 g	0.0 g

METHOD OF WORK

1. Bring the milk to the boil in a thick based pan.
2. Add the rice and stir continuously to the boil.
3. Turn down and simmer very gently, stirring frequently until the rice is cooked.
4. Mix in the sugar, vanilla and butter.
5. Pour into individual dishes.

Note: A wide range of additional ingredients can be added at this stage, diced rhubarb or apple poached in vanilla syrup, for example. Traditionally, fresh nutmeg is grated over the top of the rice just before serving.

Recipes

8 Prepare and cook food by stewing and braising

Unit 108 Prepare and cook food by stewing and braising

LEARNING OBJECTIVES

On completion of this chapter learners will be able to:

- **Describe the methods of stewing and braising.**
- **Identify foods that can be stewed and braised.**
- **Identify the most suitable equipment for stewing and braising.**
- **Describe the techniques associated with stewing and braising.**
- **State the points that need considering when stewing and braising food.**
- **List the quality points to look for in food that has been stewed and braised.**
- **List the general safety points to follow when stewing and braising food.**

Stewing

What is stewing?

Stewing is described as pieces of food that are cooked slowly in a liquid. The liquid is then served as a sauce to accompany the food that has been stewed.

There are many varieties of stews and methods used to produce them. With meat-based stews, this includes stews where the meat is cooked within a pre-thickened sauce that will be served as part of the dish, such as **ragout** of beef or boeuf bourguignon. In other methods, the liquid used is thickened at the end of the cooking process. An example of this is a blanquette of lamb. There are also stews that are thickened naturally by the ingredients within the stew itself. An Irish stew provides a good example.

Other food items can also be made into stews. This includes fish, vegetables and fruit. Due to the structure of these items, the cooking time is much less than for meat-based stews.

CHEF'S TIP Examples of stews made from these food items include:

Vegetables – ratatouille

Fruit – stewed fruit or fruit compote

Fish – bouillabaisse (Level 2/3 dish)

VIDEO CLIP Making ratatouille.

Step-by-step: Ratatouille

STEP 1 Place some olive oil into a suitably sized pan (e.g. sauteuse) and heat.

STEP 2 Add the onion and sweat for a few minutes before adding the garlic and peppers.

STEP 3 Add the courgette and aubergine and continue to cook, stirring on a regular basis. Some chopped herbs (e.g. marjoram, basil, parsley) can be added to enhance the flavour.

STEP 4 If intended to serve as a vegetable stew, a few ladles of tomato coulis/pasatta (strained tomatoes) can be added at this point to provide a binding sauce.

STEP 5 Continue to cook, stirring gently.

STEP 6 Just before serving, add some diced fresh tomato (concassé) and stir in gently.

Step-by-step: Stewing fruit

STEP 1 Cut the plums from the core all the way around the stone, twist to split in half and remove the stone.

STEP 2 Place the fruits to be stewed into suitably sized saucepans and add sugar.

STEP 3 Add water – this will produce a syrup with the sugar when dissolved and heated.

STEP 4 Heat the saucepans and gently stew the fruit.

STEP 5 Apples being stewed with cinnamon and cloves added for additional flavour.

STEP 6 Stewed plums, apples and blackberries.

Stewing meat

As stewing is a slow method of cooking, cheaper cuts of meat can be used with excellent results. When making meat-based stews for example, the cubes of (diced) meat are coated with the sauce that will eventually be served alongside the meat itself. This produces a moist environment and a gentle heat in which the connective tissues within the structure of the meat are slowly broken down, making the meat tender to eat. As this happens over a long cooking time the natural flavours and juices from the meat fall into the sauce, increasing its flavour. This is also true of any other food items that are added to the stew, some of which may have been added purely to release flavour, not to be served as part of the finished dish. Examples of this include a mirepoix, a rough cut of root vegetables (onion, celery, leek, carrot) used to flavour the dish rather than to be served as part of the dish. Additional flavours can be developed with herbs and spices. This can be achieved by adding a **bouquet garni** during the stewing process. A bouquet garni is a package of herbs, see page 98 to see how to make one.

Step-by step: Making a bouquet garni

STEP 1 To make a bouquet garni, you collect the herbs, usually parsley stalks, bay leaf and thyme with the addition of a few peppercorns. Place on a square of muslin.

STEP 2 They are then wrapped in either strips of leek or within a parcel of muslin. Take each corner and bring to the centre to form a package.

STEP 3 Tie the parcel with string.

STEP 4 The bouquet garni is placed carefully within the liquid during the cooking process. As the liquid is left to simmer, the delicate flavours are released.

VIDEO CLIP Making a bouquet garni. 

The methods and equipment used when stewing foods

Searing

This describes the initial cooking to sear the outside surface of the meat and to develop initial flavour, usually using a frying pan. This can be achieved to various degrees of colour.

SEARING WITH COLOUR (BROWNING)

In this situation the meat is placed into hot oil or fat so that it is seared while developing a good colour. This will also help to develop natural flavours. This is a requirement when making a brown stew.

SEARING WITHOUT COLOUR

When making a fricassée of chicken for example, the chicken is placed into moderately (gently) heated oil or fat. This will start to cook the surface of the chicken, helping to develop flavour, but in this case without colouring. As a fricassée is a white stew, additional colour is not sought from the initial searing process.

Blanching and refreshing

When making a blanquette, for example, the initial process involves the meat (lamb/veal) being placed into cold water which is brought to the boil. On reaching boiling point, the meat is refreshed by placing it under running cold water until all impurities have been washed away. The meat is now ready for the main cooking process.

The addition of liquid

Liquids can be added to stews at different points, for example a blanquette is made differently to a fricassée, ragout or navarin in that the sauce is thickened once the meat has been cooked. At this stage, the meat is strained from the liquid and, using a roux, the liquid is made into a velouté sauce. This is then cooked out by simmering for approximately 30 minutes. The sauce is then corrected for seasoning and consistency before being passed through a fine chinois. This is then re-heated and the meat is placed back into the sauce. The sauce is finished with cream or a liaison of cream and egg yolks.

Liquids–(for stewing and braising)

Stewing can take place using a variety of liquids. Liquids other than stock that are commonly used to stew foods include:

- *Stock syrup* – A water and sugar base that is often flavoured with other ingredients to infuse with the item being stewed. Examples include lemon, cinnamon and star-anise. A stock syrup would be used to stew fruits such as apricots and plums.
- *Wine* – The alcohol within wine is destroyed during the cooking process leaving behind its rich flavours. Wine makes an excellent base for a sauce and, when stewing, this is enhanced even more during a lengthy cooking process. A famous stew using red wine as its base is boeuf bourguignon. This stew uses red wine from the Burgundy region of France.
- *Beer and cider* – As with wine, the alcohol content is destroyed during the cooking process. Beer and cider also make very tasty sauces when used as a base in stews. Many regional dishes are produced using local beers and ciders. For example, in Devon and Cornwall (South West England), cider is often used in pork-based stews.
- *Sauce* – There are many ready-made sauces in which meats can be stewed. As with all ready-made or convenience products, this saves time but does not always produce a product of the same quality as when freshly made.

CHEF'S TIP The amount of liquid used should be sufficient to cover the food item(s) being cooked to keep them moist throughout the cooking process. The consistency of the liquid also needs to be considered and monitored. As cooking liquids are often turned into the accompanying sauce, there should be an appropriate amount of sauce of the right consistency to serve with each portion.

Associated techniques when stewing foods

- *Skimming sauces* – During the cooking process, impurities, grease and fat will rise to the surface of the sauce. It is good practice to remove such impurities to improve the overall quality of the sauce. If sauces are not skimmed, the impurities will be cooked into the sauce due to the natural movement of the liquid in the cooking process. This will reduce the quality and flavour of the finished sauce and potentially leave the sauce with a greasy finish. A ladle is usually used to skim sauces.
- *Straining* – For a more refined presentation and to increase the balance of flavours and consistency, stews are often strained to separate the meat and vegetables from the sauce. The sauce is then adjusted to correct seasoning, consistency and flavours. Once this is complete, the meat is then returned to the heated sauce and is ready to serve. It is optional whether the mirepoix (root vegetables used primarily to flavour the stew) would be served or left out. Other garnishes, such as button mushrooms or neatly cut spring vegetables may be used to enhance the dish and add contrast. A chinois (conical strainer) or a sieve are usually used to strain sauces.
- *Reducing* – Reducing a sauce will **intensify the flavour** and naturally thicken the sauce in the process. This is one method of adjusting a sauce once it has been strained. To achieve this, the sauce is placed over a high heat source (flame, hob) and boiled rapidly.

CHEF'S TIP It is very important that sauces to be reduced are not seasoned with salt and pepper until the reduction is complete. If seasoned in advance of reducing, the amount of seasoning will remain the same but in less liquid, making it too severe and potentially ruining the sauce.

- *Enriching white stews* – To enrich and thicken the sauce of a white stew, a combination of egg yolk and cream can be added at the very last moment. This is referred to as a 'liaison'. It is good practice that a small amount of the hot sauce is added to the liaison and mixed before adding this back into the sauce.

CHEF'S TIP Once a liaison has been added to a sauce, the sauce cannot be allowed to boil as this would scramble the egg yolks and spoil the sauce. Therefore, it is recommended that the liaison is added at the latest possible moment before service.

Health and safety requirements

When making a stew, it is necessary to stir the food throughout the cooking process from the searing and browning of meat to the production of the accompanying sauce. Therefore, selecting a saucepan of the appropriate size is essential to allow space for stirring without spillage or splashing.

Extreme care is required when moving a large saucepan, particularly when using the oven. Once removed from the oven, place the saucepan onto a suitable surface that is safe to check the sauce. If placing on the hob, make sure that it is not being placed on top of a fierce flame or heat. This would bring the stew to a rapid boil and potentially burn the base of the pan, catching the ingredients in this area and spoiling the flavour of the stew.

Some kitchens use signage to communicate a hot pan. A small sprinkle of flour on the lid or handle is sometimes the method used to show that the saucepan is very hot.

Always communicate with others in the kitchen when leaving hot saucepans on surfaces. It is very hard to identify the temperature of a saucepan by its appearance and a hot saucepan could cause a very nasty injury.

HEALTH & SAFETY Take care when opening the lid of the saucepan when checking progress or finishing the stew as steam will escape and could cause scalding.

HEALTH & SAFETY When stewing on the hob/range, ensure that the saucepan handle is not over a flame or direct heat source. If it was, this would become extremely hot and cause a nasty scald if touched by an unprotected hand.

HEALTH & SAFETY It is also good practice to have saucepan handles directed inwards from the stove to avoid people colliding with them.

Quality points to look for in stewed items

- Items are of even size (e.g. meat).
- The appropriate colour is reached (e.g. for brown stews, the meat has colour; for white stews, the meat has been seared without colour).
- Food items are tender.
- There is a good ratio of sauce to items of food (meat, fish, fruit, etc.).
- The sauce has a good consistency (not too thick or thin).
- The sauce is not greasy.
- The stew has a good depth of flavour and is well seasoned.
- The stew is well presented at the correct temperature and in the correct, even portion sizes.

Basic principles when making a stew

The flowchart below shows the basic method for making a brown meat stew:

Using a medium to large saucepan, sear the meat by frying with colour

↓

Add mirepoix and continue to fry to gain colour

↓

Add flour and stir in

↓

Add tomato purée and stir in

↓

Gradually add the appropriately flavoured stock, stirring consistently

↓

Add a bouquet garni and cover with a lid

↓

Cook slowly until the meat is tender
85°C to 90°C – simmering on the hob
160°C to 170°C – in a gentle moderate oven

Dishes cooked by stewing

- Ragout (brown beef stew) – Sauce thickened at the beginning of the cooking process.
- Navarin (brown lamb stew) – Sauce thickened at the beginning of the cooking process.
- Fricassée (white stew – chicken/veal) – Sauce thickened at the beginning of the cooking process.
- Blanquette (white stew – lamb/veal) – Sauce thickened at the end of the cookery process.

Other examples include

1 Goulash (of Hungarian origin – flavoured with paprika) – beef

2 Curries – any meat or poultry, can also be made using fish, vegetables or vegetable protein – e.g. quorn)

3 Irish stew – lamb

TASK Stews form traditional dishes from around the world. Research a stew from the following areas.

Africa ____________________
Carribbean ____________________
USA ____________________
India ____________________

And from Europe:

Italy ____________________
France ____________________
Hungary ____________________
Ireland ____________________

Can you find any other stews from European countries? If so, from which country and what is the name of the dish?

Step-by-step: Navarin of lamb

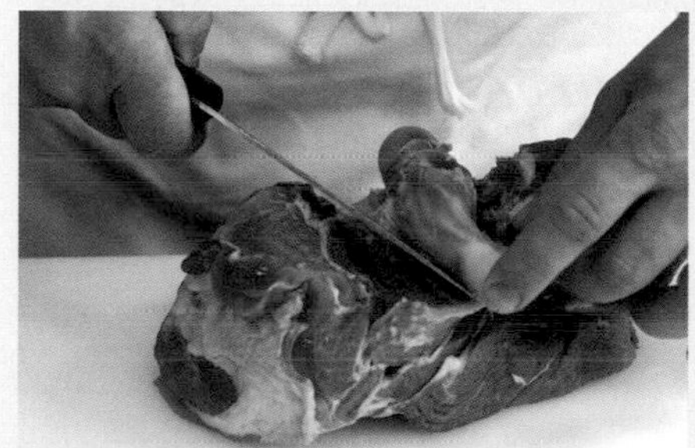

STEP 1 Carefully remove any bones (bone out) from the lamb. In this example, half a leg of lamb has been used.

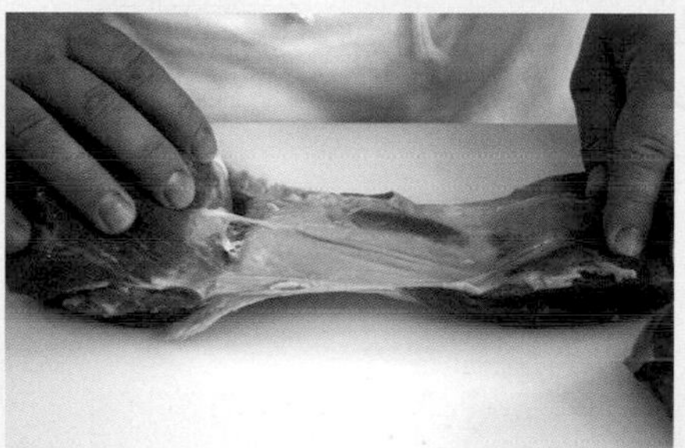

STEP 2 Remove any skin and excess sinew and cut or pull into the natural cushions (sections) of meat.

STEP 3 This shows the natural cushions of meat next to the bone and skin.

STEP 4 Cut the meat into fairly large dice.

STEP 5 Lightly oil a frying pan, heat though and fry the diced meat quickly to brown (sear) the outside surface of the meat.

STEP 6 Once browned, remove the meat with a perforated spoon and place into a bowl. Tip away any excess oil and deglaze the pan by heating the sediment (deposits) and adding some red wine. This will absorb the flavour from the pan into the liquid and maximize the flavour of the stew. Pour onto the meat placed into the bowl.

STEP 7 Fry the mirepoix (carrots, onion, leek and celery) until browned.

STEP 8 Pour the browned mirepoix into the stewing pan, heat gently and stir in the tomato purée and flour.

STEP 9 Pour in the wine from the meat and stir into the mixture until smooth. Continue to repeat this process but adding stock, stirring consistently until the liquid reaches the boil. At this point, the liquid should resemble the consistency of a sauce.

STEP 10 Add the browned meat to the sauce and mirepoix and stir.

STEP 11 Add a bouquet garni, and place a lid on top of the pan. Stew gently either on the hob or place in a pre-heated oven at 170°C until cooked (tender).

STEP 12 Once tender, remove the meat from the sauce and place into a clean pan. Strain the sauce through a chinois back onto the meat. This will remove the mirepoix and any other particles left in the sauce during the stewing process.

STEP 13 Cook (e.g. sauté) any other garnishes, e.g. button onions, mushrooms, and add to the stew.

STEP 14 Season with salt and freshly ground black pepper, adjust the consistency of the sauce, if necessary, and serve.

STEP 15 Plated version of Navarin of lamb with turned, glazed, spring vegetables.

VIDEO CLIP Demonstration of how to turn and glaze vegetables.

TASK Complete the following table stating the quality points that you would look for in the following stewed items.

ITEM/QUALITY POINTS	SIZE	COLOUR	TEXTURE	FLAVOUR/ TASTE	APPEARANCE/ PRESENTATION
Fricassée of chicken					
Navarin of lamb					
Bouillabaisse					
Fruit compote					

Braising

What is braising?

Braising is a very similar process to stewing. However, when braising, meat is usually left in joints or portion-sized cuts rather than cut into pieces or dice, as it is when stewing. Braising always takes place in the oven and for the majority of the cooking time, the cooking vessel will have a lid on to seal in the liquids and flavours.

Braising meats also helps to kill harmful bacteria during the process, making the food safe to eat.

The methods and equipment used to braise foods

Most meat-based braises follow the same basic steps. The meat or poultry is browned in hot fat. This helps to sear the surface of the meat and develop flavour as well as providing an **appetizing** appearance. **Aromatic** vegetables (mirepoix) are usually browned as well. The cooking liquid is then added, which often includes an acidic element, such as tomatoes or wine. The pot is then covered and cooked in a gentle, moderate heat in the oven until tender. Often the cooking liquid is finished to create a sauce.

HEALTH & SAFETY Braising meats, like other cooking methods, helps to kill harmful bacteria during the process, making the food safe to eat.

When braising commodities other than meat and poultry, the process is slightly different. This includes items such as vegetables (onions, leeks, celery), offal (sweetbreads, liver, oxtail) and rice.

For example, when braising vegetables such as onions and celery, the vegetable is usually **blanched** and then **refreshed**.

CHEF'S TIP A bed of roots consists of vegetables such as carrots, leeks, celery and onions, normally sliced at an angle or into chunks to provide a large, flat cut, suitable to create a 'bed' for the item to be placed upon.

Temperature needed for braising

When braising foods it is important that the temperature of the oven is carefully controlled. A braised item should cook slowly in liquid that is barely simmering. The ideal temperature for braising is usually 160°C.

Time required for braising

Time is also important to ensure that the item is cooked to the degree required without drying or burning. The structure of the item has to be taken into consideration when braising. For example, a large item, such as a leg of lamb, will require a longer cooking time than smaller items, such as braised steaks. In addition to this, if the item is to be braised on the bone, this will also have to be taken into consideration. Checking the degree of cooking is essential during the braising process to ensure that the food remains in good condition and the cooking liquid is sufficient i.e. not dehydrating, boiling too rapidly, etc.

Equipment for braising and dealing with whole braised items (multi-portion)

Upon removing the saucepan or braising vessel from the oven, the braised item will have to be taken out in order to carve it for service. This should also be planned before undertaking the task. Clean and appropriate tools should be used to remove the meat, such as a carving fork and spoon. This does not mean that the item is necessarily pierced with the fork. Ideally, it is best that the item retains its natural juices and flavours. Some of these would be lost if pierced, resulting in the potential loss of moisture and flavour.

Boards, knives and other small equipment should be clean and suitable for working with cooked meat products. Raw and cooked meats require different boards to avoid cross-contamination from the raw to cooked food.

Associated techniques when braising foods

The techniques identified in stewing would also apply when braising. In addition to this, the following techniques are more applicable to braising.

- *Trussing and tying* – Trussing refers to the tying of poultry (chickens, ducks, etc.) to make them compact and to retain shape during the cooking process. This ensures that the bird will cook more evenly and presentation will be enhanced. Joints of meat are often tied to retain their shape during the cooking process. Joints are also tied when they have been boned out (had the bone removed). Examples of this include a boned and rolled shoulder or leg of lamb or silverside of beef.

- *Basting* – Basting refers to the regular spooning of sauce over the outside surface of the food item during the cooking process. This helps to keep the item moist and will enhance the colour of the item as it cooks.
- *Relaxing before carving* – Before carving meat or poultry, it is advisable to let it relax. This means that the meat or poultry can adapt to the change in temperature from the oven and its structure will begin to settle. Meat and poultry are very difficult to carve straight from the oven, not only due to the extremely hot temperature but because of the contraction of the muscle structure. Relaxing on a board in a hygienic and safe environment for up to 20 minutes will make the carving process much easier and therefore portion control and presentation much better.

Associated products

Sauce

As with stewing, it is common practice that the braising liquid is served as a sauce to accompany the braised food item. This can be thickened at the beginning or the end of the cooking process depending on the recipe in question. For example, when braising steaks, it would be more likely that the sauce would be thickened at the beginning of the process whereas, when braising a joint of beef, a stock would be used as the braising liquid and this would be thickened towards the later stages of the cooking process.

Quality points

- Not all cuts of meat are suitable for braising.
- As with stewing, it is the tougher and generally cheaper cuts that are particularly suitable for braising.

TASK Research the various joints and cuts of beef and lamb that are most suitable for braising and stewing. From each one, provide a braised or stewed dish that can be made from the joint or cut in question. The following websites will help you:

http://www.virtualweberbullet.com/meatcharts.html

www.simplybeefandlamb.co.uk and follow the links to buying beef and lamb then beef cuts or lamb cuts.

Step-by-step: Braised rice

STEP 1 The ingredients for braised rice – long-grain rice, onion, bay leaf, saffron (strands and ground), star-anise and fresh thyme. Hot (boiling) stock is also required. A white chicken or vegetable stock can be used.

STEP 2 Melt the butter (or oil) in a saucepan and then add the chopped onions. Fry gently until soft.

STEP 3 If making a spiced variety, add the spices and herbs. If making plain braised rice, leave these ingredients out.

STEP 4 Stir in the additional flavourings to ensure an even coverage.

STEP 5 Add the rice and stir in well to take on the flavourings from the onions and spices. This will also ensure the rice takes on the colour from the spices.

STEP 6 Pour on the boiling stock to a ratio of two parts liquid (stock) to one part rice.

STEP 7 Cover with a cartouche and place in a pre-heated hot oven (220°C) for 17–18 minutes.

STEP 8 After this period of cooking, the rice will have absorbed the stock and no liquid should be left in the saucepan.

STEP 9 Well braised rice should leave the grains individual and fluffy and will have taken on the additional flavourings from the spices (if used) and the stock.

VIDEO CLIP Rice pilaf. 

VIDEO CLIP Braised celery. 

Step-by-step: Braised celery

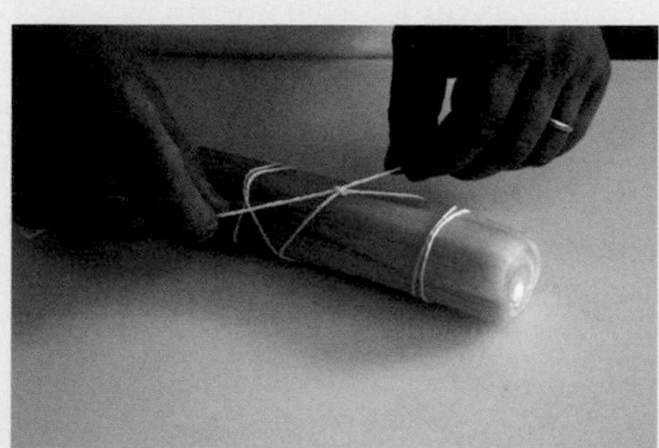

STEP 1 Cut the root and tips from the celery. Wash and peel the outside of the celery before tying into portions.

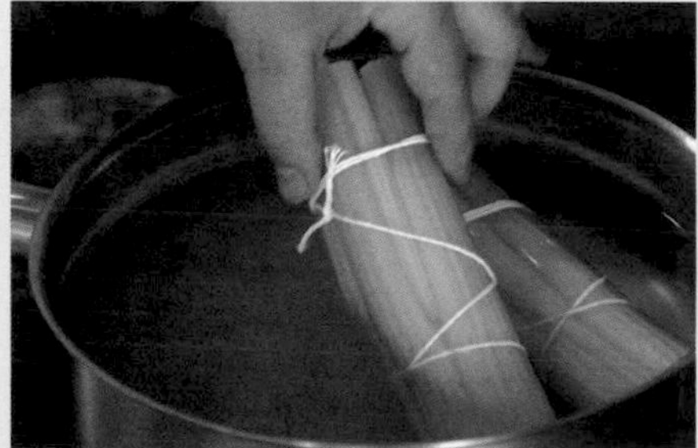

STEP 2 Blanch the celery in plenty of boiling salted water for approximately 10 minutes.

STEP 3 Refresh by placing into ice-cold water.

STEP 4 Sweat a mirepoix in a wide pan (large enough to fit the celery).

STEP 5 Add vegetable stock and a bouquet garni.

STEP 6 Place the blanched celery into the stock and bring up to a simmer.

STEP 7 Cover with a cartouche ensuring that the celery is **submerged** in the water.

STEP 8 Cover with a lid and place in a medium oven (160°C) until tender.

STEP 9 When cooked, remove with a slice. Remove the string, place into the serving dish or plate and strain the sauce into a clean saucepan.

STEP 10 Dissolve some arrowroot or corn flour (starch) in a little cold water and stir to ensure that the starch is fully dissolved.

STEP 11 Pour the arrowroot mixture gradually into the sauce, bringing the sauce to the boil each time until the correct consistency is achieved.

STEP 12 Season the sauce with salt and freshly ground white pepper, pour over the celery and serve.

Guest Chef

Parsnip-stuffed roast saddle of Powys lamb with roast beetroot, roasted vine tomatoes and Penarth red wine sauce

Chef *William Burgoyne*

Centre *Coleg Powys – Newtown*

The lamb is locally sourced in Powys. Penarth Wines is a local vine yard within Newtown producing award-winning red, white and sparkling wines. They provided the red wine in the sauce.

Ingredients	*1 portion*
For the lamb	
olive oil	1tbsp
parsnips, cut into	100 g 3 cm x 10 cm (1¼ in x 4 in batons)
honey	2 tbsp
fresh thyme	2 sprigs
fresh rosemary	2 sprigs
salt and freshly ground black pepper	
saddle of Powys lamb	250 g
For the roast beetroot	
beetroot, cut into wedges	1 large
olive oil	1 tbsp
salt and freshly ground black pepper	
vine tomatoes	4
For the sauce	
Penarth red wine	200 ml/7 fl oz
beef stock	300 ml/11 fl oz
salt and freshly ground black pepper	
butter	50 g/2 oz

METHOD OF WORK

1 Pre-heat the oven to 200°C/400 F/Gas mark 6. Bone out and prepare the saddle of lamb.

2 Heat the oil in an ovenproof frying pan and add the parsnips. Fry for 2-3 minutes, then add the honey, thyme and rosemary. Stir to coat and season, to taste, with salt and freshly ground black pepper.

3 Transfer to the oven and roast for 20–25 minutes, or until just tender and golden brown. Remove from the oven and allow to cool.

4 Open up the lamb and season with salt and freshly ground black pepper. Place the parsnips down the centre of the lamb. Fold the lamb over the parsnips, then turn over so that the join is on the bottom and tie securely with string to enclose the filling.

5 Heat a large frying pan until hot. Place the lamb into the pan and cook on each side for 2–3 minutes, until lightly browned all over. Place in the oven for 30–40 minutes, until the lamb is cooked throughly but still pink, or until cooked to your liking. Remove from the oven and leave to rest for 5 minutes.

6 Meanwhile, for the roast beetroot, place the beetroot into a roasting pan, drizzle with olive oil and season with salt and freshly ground black pepper. Place in the oven along with the lamb and roast for 30 minutes, or until just tender.

7 For the sauce, heat the red wine in a small pan. Bring to the boil, then reduce the heat and simmer until reduced by half.

8 Add the beef stock and simmer until reduced by two-thirds. Season, to taste, with salt and freshly ground black pepper and whisk in the butter.

9 To serve, slice the lamb and place onto the serving plate with the fondant potatoes, beetroot and vine tomatoes. Pour over the sauce.

TEST YOURSELF

1 Why it is important that meat is cut into even-sized pieces when making a stew?

____

2 Why is it important to use good quality stock when making a stew or braise?

____

3 Identify four cooking liquids that can be used as a base for stews and braises.

i) ______________________________
ii) ______________________________
iii) ______________________________
iv) ______________________________

4 State two differences between a stew and a braise.

i) ______________________________
ii) ______________________________

5 What is the main purpose of a 'mirepoix' when making a stew or braise?

____

6 What is the ideal oven temperature for cooking meat-based stews or braises?

____

7 State the two ingredients that make up a liaison.

i) ______________________________
ii) ______________________________

8 Why is it essential not to allow a sauce to boil once a liaison has been added?

____

9 Which cooking liquid would you associate with the production of a carbonnade?

____

10 Name four commodities, other than meat or poultry, that can be braised.

i) ______________________________
ii) ______________________________
iii) ______________________________
iv) ______________________________

11 What type of heat is associated with braising?

a. Convection ☐

b. Conduction ☐

c. Radiant ☐

d. Induction ☐

12 Why is braising considered to be a nutricious cookery process in terms of healthy eating?

____

13 Name four vegetables that can be braised successfully with menu examples.

i) ______________________________
ii) ______________________________
iii) ______________________________
iv) ______________________________

14 What steps could you take to ensure that meat does not dry out during the braising process?

____

15 Name three pieces of small equipment that would be commonly used when braising foods.

i) ______________________________
ii) ______________________________
iii) ______________________________

Recipes

Boeuf bourguignon

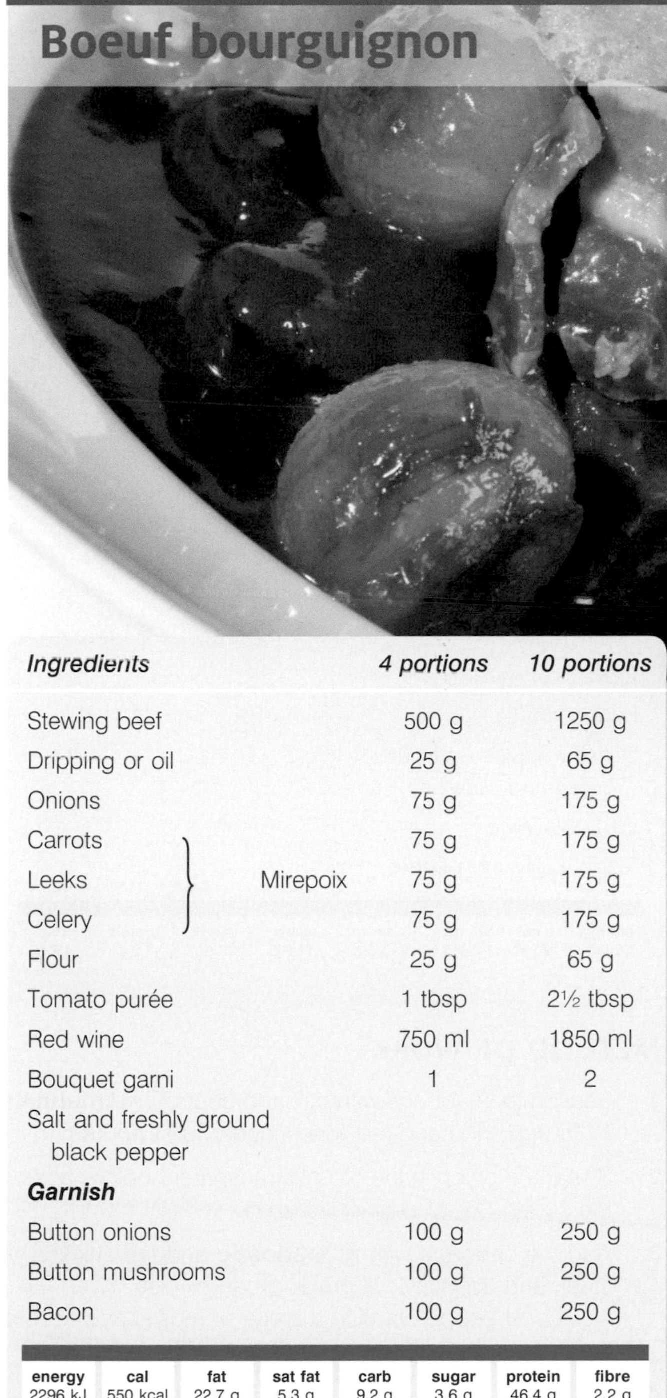

Ingredients		*4 portions*	*10 portions*
Stewing beef		500 g	1250 g
Dripping or oil		25 g	65 g
Onions		75 g	175 g
Carrots	Mirepoix	75 g	175 g
Leeks	Mirepoix	75 g	175 g
Celery	Mirepoix	75 g	175 g
Flour		25 g	65 g
Tomato purée		1 tbsp	2½ tbsp
Red wine		750 ml	1850 ml
Bouquet garni		1	2
Salt and freshly ground black pepper			
Garnish			
Button onions		100 g	250 g
Button mushrooms		100 g	250 g
Bacon		100 g	250 g

energy	cal	fat	sat fat	carb	sugar	protein	fibre
2296 kJ	550 kcal	22.7 g	5.3 g	9.2 g	3.6 g	46.4 g	2.2 g

METHOD OF WORK

1 Cut any excess sinew and fat from the beef and cut into 1 inch cubes.

2 Season the meat and seal quickly in hot fat until browned and remove from the pan.

3 Fry the mirepoix to a golden brown colour before mixing in the flour.

4 Add the tomato purée and stir using a wooden spoon.

5 Gradually mix in the wine and bring to the boil.

6 Using a ladle, skim away any impurities.

7 Add the bouquet garni and replace the sealed cubes of meat.

8 Cover with a lid and simmer gently in the oven set at 160°C for 1½ to 2 hours (or until tender).

9 When cooked, place the meat into a clean pan, straining the sauce through a sieve into a separate pan.

10 Correct the consistency and seasoning of the sauce and pass on to the meat.

To prepare the garnish

1 Peel and trim the button onions before boiling for 10 minutes. Place in a frying pan with heated oil or butter and sauté until glazed.

2 Cut the button mushrooms in half and fry in a little oil or butter.

3 Cut the bacon into lardons (thin strips) and blanch by placing them into cold water and bringing them up to the boil. Refresh immediately, separating the lardons, before frying in a pan.

Note: Traditionally, heart-shaped croutons are served with Boeuf bourguignon. To achieve this, a stale loaf is carved into a heart shape and is then sliced. These slices are then fried in butter until crisp and lightly golden brown.

To serve

Place a portion of the beef dish on a plate or bowl and garnish with the glazed button onions, mushrooms, bacon lardons and croutons (if appropriate).

Braised celery

Ingredients		4 portions	10 portions
Heads of celery		2	5
Onions		75 g	175 g
Carrots		75 g	175 g
Leeks	Mirepoix	75 g	175 g
Celery		75 g	175 g
Bouquet garni		1	2
White stock (vegetable/chicken)		250 ml	600 ml
Salt and freshly ground white pepper			

energy	cal	fat	sat fat	carb	sugar	protein	fibre
208 kJ	49 kcal	2.3 g	0.7 g	5.1 g	4.5 g	2.2 g	4.6 g

METHOD OF WORK

1. Trim the celery heads and the root.
2. Peel the outside stalks and cut the heads to approximately 15 cm lengths.
3. Wash well under running cold water.
4. Place in a pan of boiling water and simmer for approximately 10 minutes. Refresh and re-wash.
5. Place the mirepoix in a wide flat pan (e.g. sauteuse) and place the celery heads folded lengthways on top.
6. Barely cover with the stock and add the bouquet garni.
7. Cover with a buttered cartouche and a tight lid.
8. Bring to the boil and braise gently in the oven at 160°C until tender (approximately 1 hour).
9. Remove the celery from the pan, drain well and place in the serving dish.
10. Reduce the cooking liquor (an equal amount of jus can be added at this stage to enhance the flavour of the sauce. However, this would make the dish unsuitable for vegetarians).
11. Correct the consistency and seasoning.
12. Coat the celery with the sauce and serve.

Braised red cabbage

Ingredients	4 portions	10 portions
Red cabbage – thinly sliced	600 g	1.5 kg
Red wine	80 ml	200 ml
Red wine vinegar	20 ml	50 ml
Onion–sliced	20 g	50 g
Vegetable oil	25 ml	60 ml
Brown sugar	10 g	25 g
Chicken stock	150 ml	400 ml
Clove	½	1
Peppercorns	25	60
Dessert apples – peeled, cored and sliced	1	2
Dry white wine	40 ml	100 ml
Salt and ground pepper		

energy	cal	fat	sat fat	carb	sugar	protein	fibre
500 kJ	120 kcal	5.7 g	3.3 g	11.3 g	10.5 g	1.5 g	4.9 g

METHOD OF WORK

1. Season the cabbage with salt and pepper and **marinate** in the red wine and red wine vinegar for 4 hours.
2. Sweat the onion in the oil until transparent before adding the sugar. Sweat until well glazed.
3. Add the cabbage with its **marinade** and the chicken stock and transfer to a braising pan or dish. Wrap the clove and peppercorns in a piece of muslin and add to the cabbage.
4. Cover and braise at 170°C/325°F/Gas mark 3 for 40 minutes, stirring occasionally.
5. Add the apple slices and white wine to the cabbage.
6. Braise for a further 30 to 40 minutes or until the cabbage is tender and all the liquid has evaporated.
7. Remove from the oven, take out the muslin bag and season to taste.
8. Serve.

VIDEO CLIP Braised red cabbage.

Carbonnade of beef

Ingredients	4 portions	10 portions
Lean beef topside	400 g	1 kg
Salt, pepper	To taste	To taste
Flour (white or wholemeal)	25 g	70 g
Vegetable oil	25 ml	70 ml
Onions, sliced	200 g	500 g
Beer	250 ml	625 ml
Caster sugar	10 g	25 g
Tomato purée	25 g	60 g
Brown stock		

energy	cal	fat	sat fat	carb	sugar	protein	fibre
1838 kJ	439 kcal	23.6 g	7.1 g	8.5 g	3.2 g	48.1 g	1.7 g

METHOD OF WORK

1. Cut the meat into thin slices.
2. Season with salt and pepper and pass through the flour. Tap each slice to remove excess flour
3. Sear each slice on both sides in hot fat and place in an oven-proof saucepan or casserole dish.
4. Caramelise the onions by frying to a light brown colour and add to the meat.
5. Add the beer, sugar and tomato purée and sufficient brown stock to cover the meat.
6. Cover with a tight-fitting lid and simmer gently in a moderate oven at 150–200°C until the meat is tender (approx 2 hours).
7. Skim the sauce, correct the consistency and seasoning and serve.

VIDEO CLIP Braised steaks.

Braised lamb shanks

Ingredients	4 portions	10 portions
Lamb shanks	4	10
Vegetable oil	30 ml	70 ml
Onions – sliced	50 g	125 g
Garlic – cloves, crushed, finely chopped	2	5
Plum tomatoes (canned)	200 g	500 g
Lamb stock	250 ml	625 ml
Red wine	200 ml	500 ml
Fresh oregano, chopped	1 tbsp	2½ tbsp
Fresh rosemary, chopped	1 tbsp	2½ tbsp
Clear honey	1 tbsp	2½ tbsp
Salt, pepper		

METHOD OF WORK

1. Season the lamb shanks, heat the oil in a suitable braising pan and sear by frying the shanks on all sides until golden brown. Remove from pan and set aside.
2. Add the sliced onion and garlic, sweat until soft.
3. Stir in the chopped plum tomatoes, stock and red wine.
4. Place the lamb shank back in the sauce. Bring to the boil, reduce heat, cover and braise in the oven for 1 hour to 1 hour 30 minutes until tender.
5. Remove the lamb from the sauce, add the herbs and honey and bring back to a simmer.
6. Reduce the sauce by one third before correcting the seasoning and consistency of the sauce.
7. Replace the lamb and allow to steep in the sauce.
8. Serve with creamed potatoes or other suitable accompaniments.

Fricassée of chicken

Ingredients	*4 portions*
Chicken	1.5 kg
Butter	50 g
Vegetable oil	10 ml
Flour	35 g
Chicken stock	½ litre
Bouquet garni	1
Egg yolks	2
Cream or yoghurt	4 tbsp
Salt and freshly ground white pepper	

energy	cal	fat	sat fat	carb	sugar	protein	fibre
3745 kJ	896 kcal	49.6 g	19.0 g	7.8 g	0.9 g	105.1 g	0.8 g

CHEF'S TIP Due to the fact that one chicken cut for sauté will provide four portions (four cuts from the leg and four from the breast), multiples for this recipe will always have to be in four.

METHOD OF WORK

1. Cut the chicken for sauté and season with salt and pepper.
2. Place the butter in a sauté pan with a little vegetable oil and heat gently.
3. Add pieces of chicken in the order of thighs and drumsticks, followed by the two central breast pieces and the two half 'supremes'.
4. Cook gently on both sides without colouring and remove from the sauté pan, placing on a clean tray.
5. Mix the flour into the pan oils to form a paste (roux) and **cook out** carefully without colouring.
6. Gradually mix in the stock, stirring constantly to form a smooth and silky sauce.
7. Once sufficient stock has been added, bring to a simmer and skim off any impurities with a ladle.
8. Replace the chicken, add the bouquet garni and simmer gently until cooked.
9. Once cooked, remove the chicken and place into a clean pan.
10. Mix the egg yolks and cream in a small bowl. (This is referred to as a liaison.)
11. Pour a little boiling sauce on to the liaison and mix well.
12. Pour the liaison mixture back into the sauce and mix thoroughly. The sauce must not reboil at this stage or the egg yolks will curdle, spoiling the sauce.
13. Correct the sauce for seasoning and pass through a strainer over the chicken.
14. Re-heat very carefully without boiling.
15. Each portion is made up of one piece of dark (leg) meat and one piece of light (breast meat). Serve with appropriate accompaniments and garnishes.

VIDEO CLIP Fricassée of chicken.

Gary Rhodes' beef and potatoes braised in Guinness

Ingredients	*4 portions*
Olive oil for cooking	
Large onions, sliced	3
Pieces of chuck steak or braising beef	4 × 175 g (6 oz)–225 g (8 oz)
Flour for dusting	
Dalt and pepper	
Guiness	440 ml
Muscovado sugar	1 tblsp
Tin of beef consommé or stock	400 ml
Large potatoes, peeled and halved	4

METHOD OF WORK

1 Pre-heat the oven to 170°C 325°F/Gas mark 3. Heat some olive oil in a large frying pan. Add the onions and cook over a moderate heat for a few minutes, until tender and golden brown. Transfer the onions to an oven-proof braising pot or casserole dish.

2 Toss the beef in the flour and season with salt and pepper. Heat a little more oil in the frying pan and fry the steaks until well coloured on all sides then transfer to the dish.

3 Pour the Guinness into the hot frying pan, stir to lift the residue from the base, sprinkle in the sugar. Add the consommé and simmer for 1 minute before pouring over the beef. Cover tightly with a lid and braise in the oven for 1½ hours. Add a little water if necessary to keep the meat covered with the liquor during cooking.

4 Add the potatoes and continue to braise for a further 1 to 1½ hours until the potatoes have absorbed and thickened the sauce and the beef is soft and tender.

Note: Serve the beef and potatoes with any green vegetable, such as steamed spinach or buttery cabbage. The sauce can be finished with chopped parsley.

Ratatouille

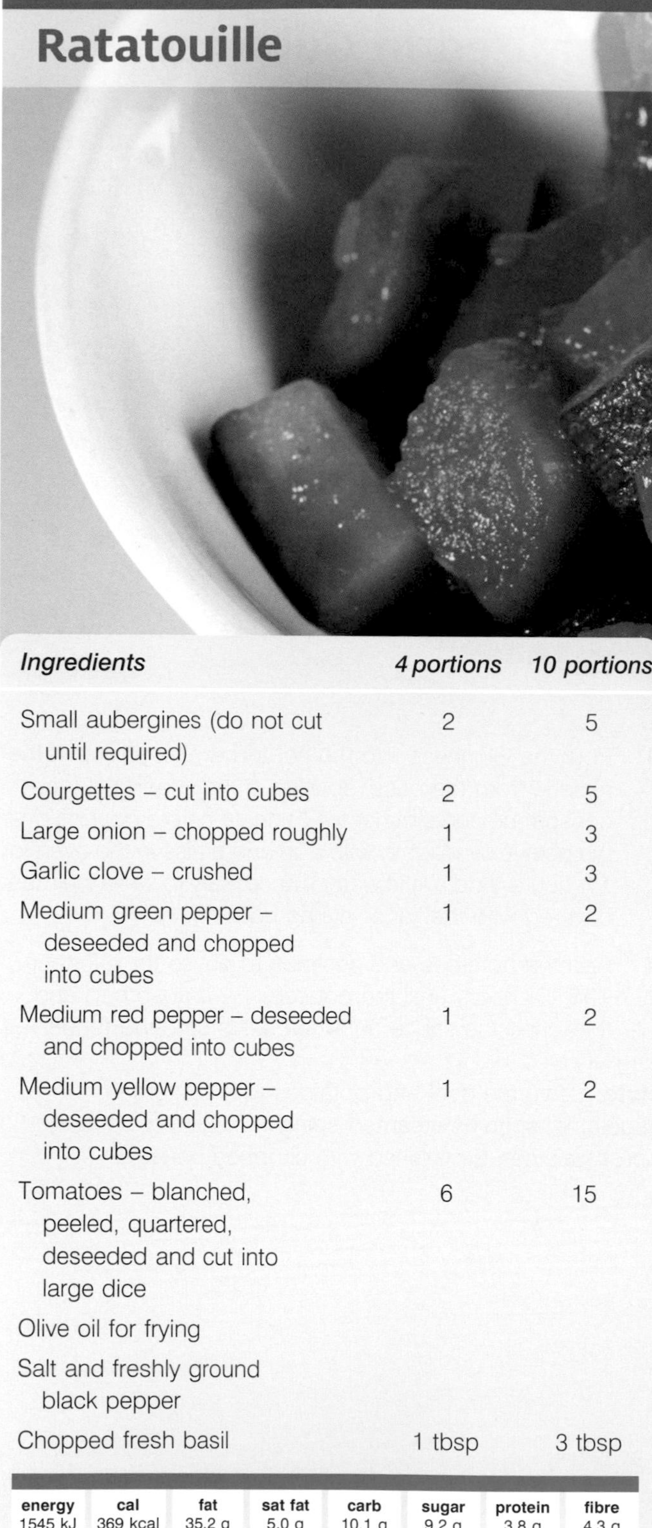

Ingredients	4 portions	10 portions
Small aubergines (do not cut until required)	2	5
Courgettes – cut into cubes	2	5
Large onion – chopped roughly	1	3
Garlic clove – crushed	1	3
Medium green pepper – deseeded and chopped into cubes	1	2
Medium red pepper – deseeded and chopped into cubes	1	2
Medium yellow pepper – deseeded and chopped into cubes	1	2
Tomatoes – blanched, peeled, quartered, deseeded and cut into large dice	6	15
Olive oil for frying		
Salt and freshly ground black pepper		
Chopped fresh basil	1 tbsp	3 tbsp

energy	cal	fat	sat fat	carb	sugar	protein	fibre
1545 kJ	369 kcal	35.2 g	5.0 g	10.1 g	9.2 g	3.8 g	4.3 g

VIDEO CLIP Ratatouille.

METHOD OF WORK

1. Gently heat a little olive oil in a large heavy wide saucepan (e.g. sauteuse).
2. Add the onions and garlic and fry until translucent (see- through).
3. While the onions and garlic are frying, cut the aubergines into cubes.
4. Add the peppers, aubergines and courgettes, cover and cook over a low heat for 25 minutes.
5. Add the tomatoes and continue cooking for a further 5 minutes. Serve sprinkled with freshly chopped basil.

Note: A little fresh tomato sauce can be used to bind the vegetables together to produce a more 'stew'-like dish. This would be added after the addition of the peppers etc.

Braised button onions

Ingredients	*4–6 portions*
Button onions	200 g
Vegetable oil	20 ml
White stock (vegetable or chicken). A little more stock may be required depending on the size or the braising vessel.	
1 bouquet garni	200 ml

METHOD OF WORK

1 Peel, wash and cook the onions in lightly salted boiling water for 5 minutes. Alternatively the onions could be steamed.

2 Drain the onions and place in a pre-heated pan or casserole lined with a coating of vegetable oil. Suitable for use in the oven.

3 Lightly brown the onions by allowing them to fry for 2 minutes to develop colour.

4 Half cover with stock and add a bouquet-garni.

5 Bring to the boil place a lid to cover and braise gently in the oven at 180–200°C until tender.

6 Reduce the cooking liquor to a syrupy consistency. Correct the seasoning and mask the onions with the liquor.

7 Serve neatly in a vegetable dish or as a garnish.

Vegetable curry

Ingredients	*4 portions*
Ghee (clarified butter) or vegetable oil	75 ml
Garlic purée	1.5 tbsp
Ginger purée	1 tbsp
Puréed	3 Onions
Tinned tomatoes and their juice	400 g
Tomato purée	2 tbsp
Salt	1 tsp
Sugar	1 tsp
Spices	
Masala mild curry powder	1 tbsp
Paprika	0.5 tbsp
Turmeric	0.5 tbsp
Mixed vegetables	
Mixed blanched vegetables (e.g. florets of cauliflower and/or broccoli, large dice of courgette, potato, sweet potatoes, button onions, button mushrooms, sliced haricots verts, mange tout)	750 g

energy	cal	fat	sat fat	carb	sugar	protein	fibre
894 kJ	215 kcal	17.4 g	1.7 g	12.9 g	4.6 g	3.5 g	5.2 g

METHOD OF WORK

1 Mix the spices with water to make a paste the consistency of tomato ketchup. Let it stand.

2 Using a large saucepan, heat three tablespoons of the oil. Stir-fry the garlic purée for 30 seconds, then add the ginger purée and cook for 30 seconds more. Add two or three more tablespoons of oil and when hot add the spice paste and stir-fry for 30 seconds more. Add the remaining oil and the onion purée and stir-fry gently for around 10 minutes.

3 Mulch down the tinned tomatoes in a blender then add with the tomato purée to the pan. Mix in well and add enough water to achieve a medium thick, soup type, consistency. Add a little sugar and salt to taste.

4 Simmer gently for at least 30 minutes and at most 1 hour. Aim for a reduction to a thickish but easily pourable texture. But if it starts to get too dry add a little water from time to time.

5 Add the blanched vegetables and stir gently until thoroughly reh-eated.

6 Serve garnished with roughly chopped coriander.

CHEF'S TIP The base sauce can be frozen and stored in batches and re-heated to be used as and when necessary.

Braised white cabbage

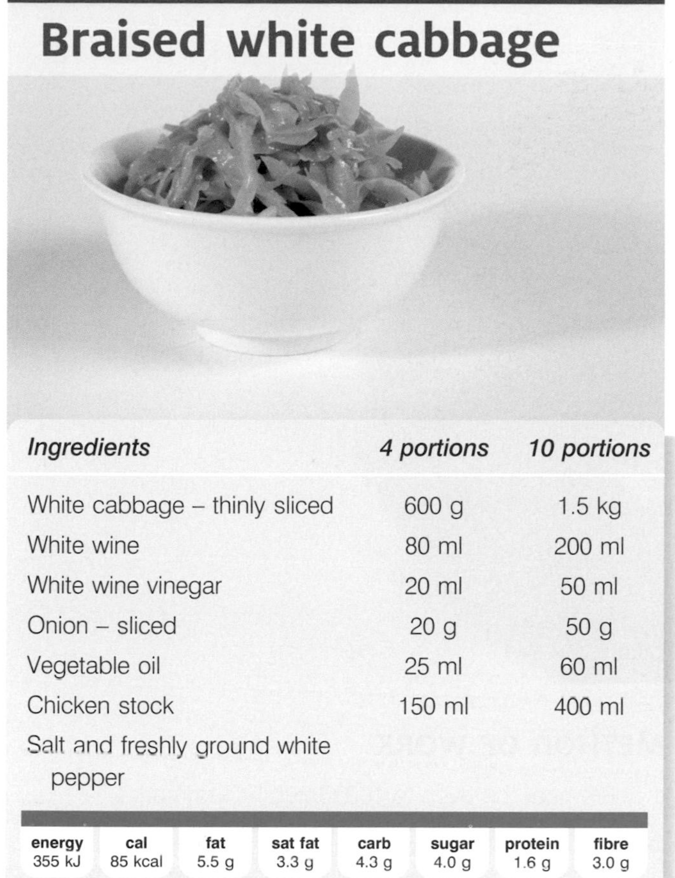

Ingredients	4 portions	10 portions
White cabbage – thinly sliced	600 g	1.5 kg
White wine	80 ml	200 ml
White wine vinegar	20 ml	50 ml
Onion – sliced	20 g	50 g
Vegetable oil	25 ml	60 ml
Chicken stock	150 ml	400 ml
Salt and freshly ground white pepper		

energy	cal	fat	sat fat	carb	sugar	protein	fibre
355 kJ	85 kcal	5.5 g	3.3 g	4.3 g	4.0 g	1.6 g	3.0 g

METHOD OF WORK

1 Cut the cabbage into quarters, removing the root from each quarter to leave the leaves of the cabbage.

2 Slice the cabbage finely (chiffonade).

3 Using a suitably sized pan lined with the vegetable oil, sweat the sliced onion over a gentle to moderate heat until the onion becomes transparent.

4 Add the cabbage and stir.

5 Add the chicken stock, along with the white wine and white wine vinegar and stir.

6 Bring to the boil gently before covering with a lid and braising in the oven at 170°C/325°F/ Gas mark 3 for 45 minutes to 1 hour, stirring occasionally until nearly all the liquid has evaporated.

7 Remove from the oven and season to taste before serving.

Irish stew

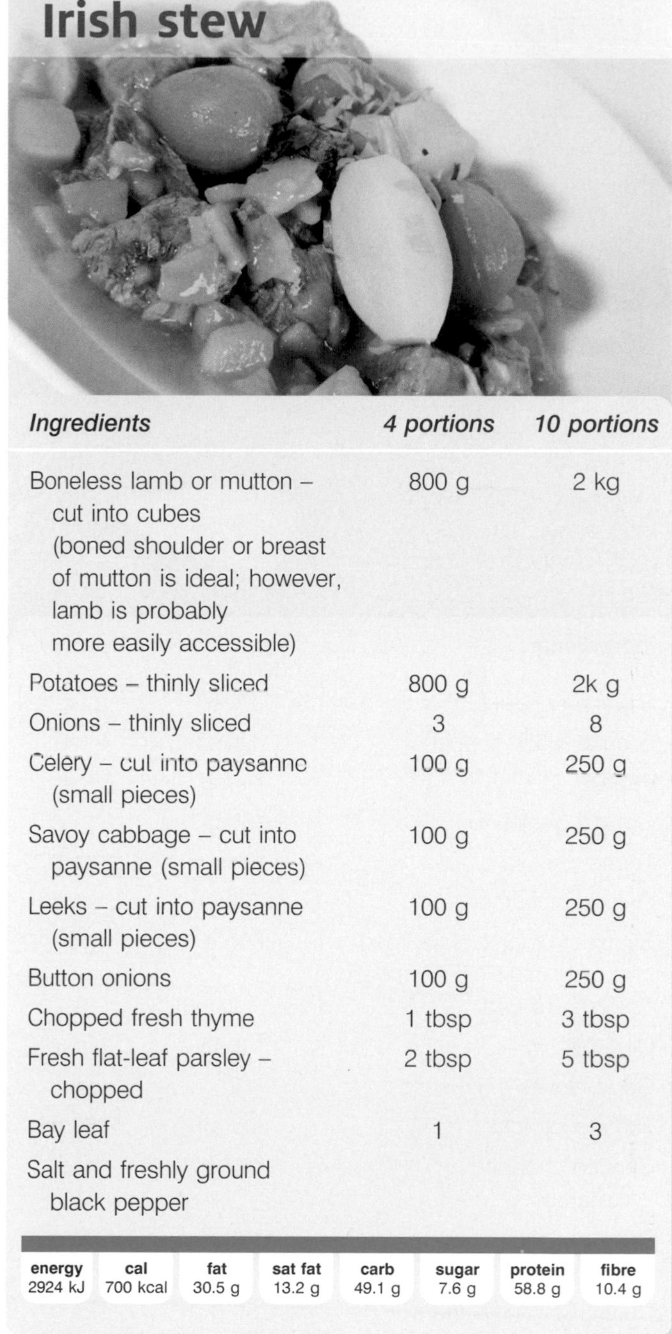

Ingredients	4 portions	10 portions
Boneless lamb or mutton – cut into cubes (boned shoulder or breast of mutton is ideal; however, lamb is probably more easily accessible)	800 g	2 kg
Potatoes – thinly sliced	800 g	2k g
Onions – thinly sliced	3	8
Celery – cut into paysanne (small pieces)	100 g	250 g
Savoy cabbage – cut into paysanne (small pieces)	100 g	250 g
Leeks – cut into paysanne (small pieces)	100 g	250 g
Button onions	100 g	250 g
Chopped fresh thyme	1 tbsp	3 tbsp
Fresh flat-leaf parsley – chopped	2 tbsp	5 tbsp
Bay leaf	1	3
Salt and freshly ground black pepper		

energy	cal	fat	sat fat	carb	sugar	protein	fibre
2924 kJ	700 kcal	30.5 g	13.2 g	49.1 g	7.6 g	58.8 g	10.4 g

METHOD OF WORK

1 Arrange alternate layers of meat, sliced potatoes and onions in a flameproof casserole dish.

2 Season each layer with salt, pepper, thyme and parsley.

3 Add the bay leaf and pour in just enough water to cover.

4 Bring to the boil over a high heat, cover, lower the heat and simmer for ½ hour.

5 Add the remaining vegetables and continue to cook for 1 to 1 ¼ hours or until tender.

6 Skim off any impurities, correct the seasoning of the sauce and serve.

Lamb Tagine

Ingredients	*4 portions*	*10 portions*
Cayenne pepper	1 tsp	2 tsp
Ground black pepper	1 tsp	2 tsp
Paprika	1 tbsp	2 tbsp
Ground ginger	1 tbsp	2 tbsp
Turmeric	1 tbsp	2 tbsp
Ground cinnamon	1.5 tbsp	2.5 tbsp
Shoulder of lamb – trimmed and cut into 5 cm (2 in) chunks	600 g	1500 g
Onions – sliced	2	5
Olive oil	1 tbsp	2 tbsp
Garlic cloves – crushed	2	4
Tomato juice	500 ml	1250 ml
Canned chopped tomatoes	400 g	1 kg
Dried apricots cut in half	100 g	250 g
Dates – cut in quarters	50 g	125 g
Sultanas or raisins	50 g	125 g
Flaked almonds	40 g	100 g
Saffron stamens soaked in cold water	0.5 tsp	1 tsp
Lamb stock	500 ml	1250 ml
Clear honey	1 tbsp	2.5 tbsp
Coriander – roughly chopped	1 tbsp	2.5 tbsp
Flat leaf parsley – roughly chopped	1 tbsp	2.5 tbsp

energy	cal	fat	sat fat	carb	sugar	protein	fibre
3414 kJ	816 kcal	46.2 g	17.4 g	45.1 g	35.4 g	55.4 g	14.3 g

METHOD OF WORK

1. Pre-heat the oven to 150°C/300°F/Gas mark 2.
2. Place the cayenne, black pepper, paprika, ginger, turmeric and cinnamon into a small bowl and mix to combine. Place the lamb in a large bowl and toss together with half of the spice mix. Cover and leave overnight in the fridge.
3. Heat half of the olive oil in a tagine/braising pan. Add the sliced onion and the remaining spice mix and cook over a gentle heat for 10 minutes so that the onions are soft but not browned. Add the crushed garlic and cook for another 3 minutes.
4. In a separate frying pan, heat the remaining oil and sear (brown) the cubes of lamb on all sides.
5. Add the browned meat to the tagine (casserole dish/ braising pan), de-glazing the frying pan with a ¼ pint of tomato juice. Add these juices to the pan.
6. Add the remaining tomato juice, chopped tomatoes, apricots, dates, raisins or sultanas, flaked almonds, saffron, lamb stock and honey to the tagine. Bring to the boil, cover with a fitted lid, place in the oven and cook for 2 to 2 ½ hours or until the meat is tender.
7. Serve the lamb in the tagine or large serving dish and sprinkle over the chopped herbs.

Risotto with smoked haddock and peas

Ingredients	*4 portions*	*10 portions*
Fish, chicken or vegetable stock	1.2 litres	3 litres
Butter	80 g	200 g
Onion, peeled and finely chopped	½	1
Arborio rice	240 g	600 g
Flaked smoked haddock	200 g	500 g
Peas (petits pois) cooked	100 g	250 g
Parmesan (½ grated and ½ shaved)	75 g	180 g
Salt, pepper	To taste	To taste

METHOD OF WORK

1 Bring the stock to a simmer and place at the side of where you intend to cook the risotto.

2 Take a wide, heavy based pan and put in half the butter over a medium heat to melt.

3 Add the onion and sweat until it softens and becomes translucent (without colour).

4 Add the rice and stir until it is thoroughly coated in the butter (about 2 minutes).

5 Pour a ladle of hot stock into the rice and stir gently until the stock has been absorbed by the rice (approximately 2 to 3 minutes).

6 Repeat this procedure several times until the rice has swollen and is nearly tender. The rice should retain a bite but should be just cooked through. Usually, the whole process will take approximately 20 minutes from the first ladle of stock.

7 When the final ladle of stock has been added, add the peas and stir into the rice. After 30 seconds, add the smoked, flaked haddock and stir very gently to heat the haddock through being careful not to break the fish too much.

8 Remove from the heat and stir in the remaining butter the grated Parmesan.

9 Season and cover, leaving the rice to rest for 1 to 2 minutes to swell a little more.

10 Serve immediately in soup or pasta bowls with Parmesan shavings offered separately.

Note: Any of these stocks will work well but will produce a different flavour to the finished dish. A fish stock will increase the intensity of the fish flavour whereas a chicken or vegetable stock will provide an interesting combination of flavours.

Recipes

ONLINE RECIPE

LEARNER SUPPORT
Gary Rhodes' bread and butter pudding

9 Baking, roasting and grilling

Unit 109 Baking, roasting and grilling

LEARNING OBJECTIVES

On completion of this chapter learners will be able to:

- **Describe the processes of baking, roasting and grilling.**
- **Identify foods that can be baked, roasted and grilled.**
- **Identify the most suitable type(s) of equipment for baking, roasting and grilling.**
- **Describe the techniques associated with baking, roasting and grilling.**
- **State the points that need considering when baking, roasting and grilling food.**
- **List the quality points to look for in food that has been baked, roasted and grilled.**
- **List the general safety points to follow when baking, roasting and grilling food.**

Baking

What is baking?

Baking refers to foods that are cooked by placing them in a pre-heated oven. Food items to be baked are usually placed on a lightly oiled baking tray to prevent them from sticking during the cookery process. There are mats available which can sit on top of a baking tray and do not require the addition of oil. This is efficient in that it saves time, the cost of oil and promotes healthy eating.

Baked items have a variety of textures based on the type of food being produced. For example, a bread roll or loaf usually has a crust on the outside with a soft, light and airy texture to the cooked dough in the centre. On the other hand, a biscuit or pastry would have a firmer and snappier (shorter) texture. Baked fruits and vegetables, such as an apple or potato, the skin would crisp while the centre would become moist and soft in texture.

The colour of baked items makes them pleasing to the eye and increases the desire to eat them. For example, many breads and pastry products are light, golden brown in colour and crisp in texture. On the other hand, the egg custard in a baked crème caramel, should be creamy in colour with a very soft, smooth and velvety texture.

Step-by-step: Baking a potato – 'Arlie'

STEP 1 Clean the baking potato and **score** around the centre with a small sharp knife.

STEP 2 Place the potato onto a baking tray and bake in the oven until the potato is cooked. To test if the potato is cooked, insert the blade of a small, sharp knife. It should have little resistance beyond piercing the skin.

STEP 3 Cut the cooked potato in half lengthways.

STEP 4 Using a spoon, scoop out the flesh from the potato.

STEP 5 Using a scraper, press the cooked potato flesh through a drum sieve.

STEP 6 Season the sieved potato with salt and freshly ground white pepper and enrich the potato mix with a little melted butter.

STEP 7 The ingredients for the potato filling – chopped onions, quartered button mushrooms, diced chicken breast, lardons of pancetta (dry cured crispy bacon), thyme, cheddar cheese and double cream.

STEP 8 Sweat the onions, add the chicken breast followed by the mushrooms, pancetta and thyme. Pour in the double cream and bring to the boil. The cream will thicken as it cooks. Once this is ready, add the grated cheddar.

STEP 9 Place the empty potato skins onto a baking tray and fill the shells with the chicken based filling.

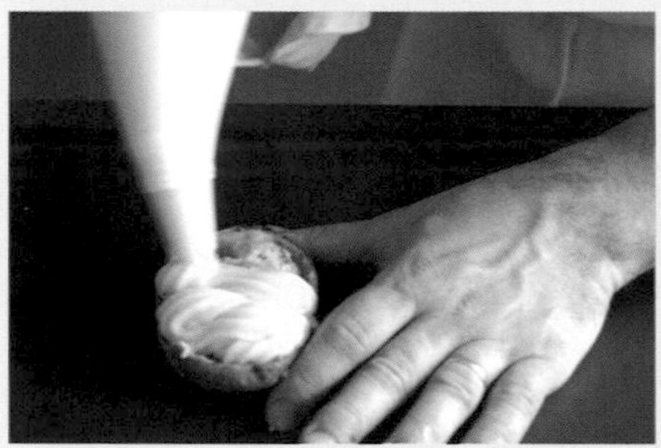

STEP 10 Pipe the pureed potato neatly on top of the filling.

STEP 11 An example of the filled potato and one with the potato piped on top.

STEP 12 Gratinate under a medium salamander and serve.

The methods and equipment used to bake foods

Many baked items require preparation before they are baked. This is particularly the case when making fresh bread, pastry or baked egg custard dishes. The baking process is merely the cookery of the prepared item.

The preparation of equipment when baking products is very important. For example, having the oven pre-heated to the correct temperature is essential so that the product starts to cook as soon as it is placed into the oven. Failure to do this will have a damaging effect on the finished product.

The heat, when baking, is often described as a dry heat and sometimes referred to as convection. In this case the oven can be assisted by a fan within the oven itself to circulate the heat evenly throughout the oven chamber (fan oven). This helps to ensure that foods are cooked evenly.

Some baked products benefit from the addition of steam within the oven chamber. This is referred to as a 'humid' oven. In modern baking ovens, this facility is a built-in feature. An example of a product that can benefit from the addition of steam is bread. In this instance, an injection of steam in the final stages of cooking produces a crusty surface to the bread.

BAKING IN A BAIN-MARIE

A third method of baking uses a water bath, referred to as a 'bain-marie'. This is particularly good for egg based products, such as egg custards, and hot mousses, when a crust is not wanted. These types of products are usually moulded before they are cooked. The water is placed in a suitable tray and is there to protect the egg custard or mousse from burning, scrambling or drying.

Baking is a versatile method of cookery as there are so many products that can be produced using this method. This applies to both savoury and sweet products.

Step-by-step: Bread rolls

STEP 1 The ingredients to make a batch of bread rolls – strong flour, salt, warm water (35–37°C), sugar, fresh yeast, butter (or oil), milk powder.

STEP 2 Dissolve the yeast in half the water. With the other half of the water, add the salt, milk powder and oil.

STEP 3 Make a well in the flour and add the yeast water. This will begin to ferment (bubble). Carefully add the other water.

STEPS 4 and 5 Mix until it forms a dough.

STEP 5

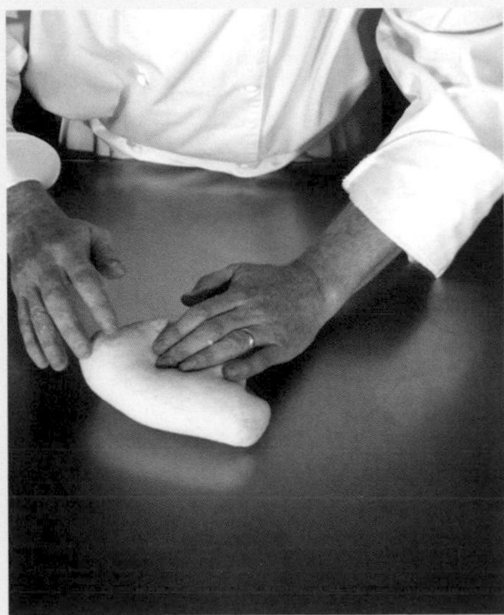

STEPS 6 and 7 Place the dough onto a clean surface and **knead** to stretch the gluten. The dough should be slightly moist and elastic.

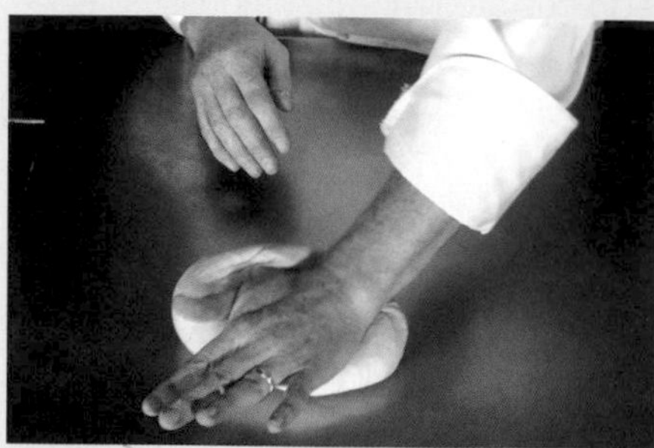

STEP 7

STEP 8 Form the kneaded dough into a ball and place into a clean bowl. Cover with a warm damp cloth and leave to prove, ideally in a proover. The dough should double in size.

STEP 9 Prove the dough in a warm and moist environment (ideally a prooving cabinet) until the dough has doubled in size. This is referred to as the bulk fermentation time (BFT).

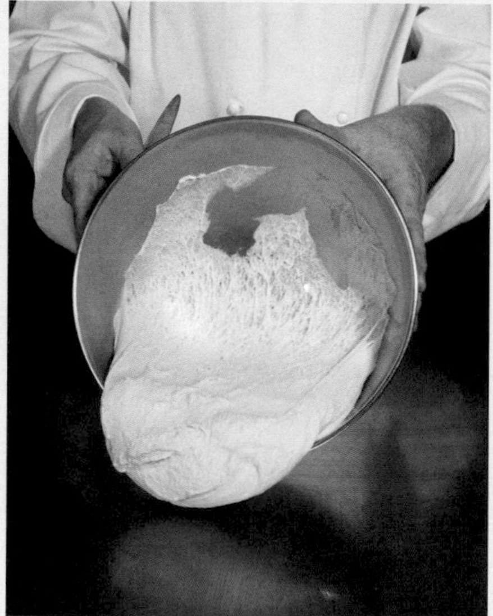

STEPS 10 and 11 Once proven, take the dough from the bowl and gently knead to remove the carbon dioxide produced during the initial fermentation.

STEP 11

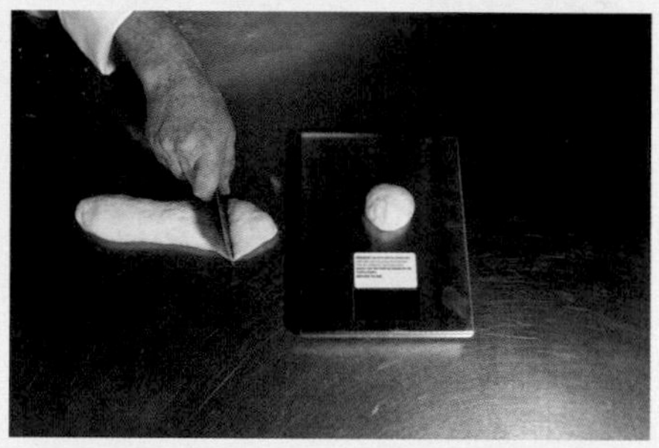

STEP 12 Roll into a log thin piece of dough and cut into evenly sized pieces using a pastry cutter/scraper.
These can be weighed to ensure evenly sized and weighted rolls.

STEP 13 Press each piece of dough firmly into a lightly floured work surface and shape into a roll by rolling in the palm of your hand. Mould, prove until doubled in size, **egg wash** and decorate some rolls with seeds. The rolls can be shaped into knots, plaits, etc. at this stage if desired.

STEP 14 Bake at 230°C (with steam). The rolls should be light golden brown and sound hollow when tapped at the bottom of the roll. Place the cooked rolls onto a cooling rack to cool down before serving.

CHEF'S TIP Popular seeds that are often sprinkled on bread rolls include:

- Sesame seeds
- Poppy seeds
- Caraway seeds
- Fennel seeds

TASK Look through the recipes within this chapter and name a dish or item that is baked in the following categories:

CATEGORY	DISH/ITEM
Savoury dough product	
Sweet dough product	
Fruit	
Potato dish	
Sweet pastry	
Short pastry	
Savoury egg custard	
Sweet egg custard	

Associated techniques when baking foods

- *Aeration* – To create the light texture of many baked items such as sponges, scones and dough products, the products are aerated. This can be through manual aeration (e.g. whisking eggs and sugar), through chemical aeration (e.g. by using baking powder) or through the fermentation process when using yeast.
- *Mixing* – Baked products require mixing to ensure that they have the right properties from which to produce the desired texture, e.g. short, sponge or dough.
- *Resting* – For certain baked items, such as scones, biscuits and pastry items, a period of relaxing prior to baking will help the items to hold a better shape.
- *Greasing* – Grease, usually oil or butter, is lightly brushed around the surface of the tray or tin to prevent food items from sticking. This is sometimes coated with a light dusting of flour.
- *Rolling and shaping* – In the case of dough products, such as bread rolls, they will need to be carefully rolled and shaped prior to baking.
- *Marking* – Certain baked items are marked to aid presentation of the finished item. An example of this is shortbread. Marks can also provide an indication as to where the item should be cut, if being cut or split into portions.
- *Cutting* – Bakery products such as scones and Chelsea buns need to be cut to shape and size before they are baked.
- *Glazing* – To create additional colour and a glaze to the baked product, a glaze is often brushed over the product. This could be egg wash, for example.
- *Loading* – This refers to the loading of the oven, making efficient use of the space available on the oven tray and of the shelves within the oven itself.
- *Brushing* – Brushing baked items with egg wash, milk or sugar syrup will enhance the presentation and, in the case of the sugar syrup, sweeten the flavour of the item. Egg wash will enhance the colour of the item whereas the sugar will produce a shiny finish. Baked items are brushed at different stages of the cooking process according to the finish required. For example, to enhance the colour of a loaf of bread, it could be brushed with egg wash and/or milk in advance of cooking, whereas to provide a shine to a fruit bun, the glaze would be brushed on at the end of the process.
- *Cooling* – To prevent baked items from becoming soggy, they are placed onto cooling racks once they have been taken out of the oven. This will stabilize the item, helping, for example, bread rolls to relax into their shape and pastry items to become crisp (short).

Step-by-step: Crème caramel

STEP 1 To make the caramel, place granulated sugar into a heavy saucepan (ideally a copper sugar pan) and dissolve in a little water. Bring this to the boil and cook until a light caramel is achieved.

STEP 2 Once a caramel is achieved, stop the cooking process by placing the pan base into cold water. A little cold water can also be added to the caramel itself. Pour a little caramel into the base of the dariole moulds and leave to set.

STEP 3 The ingredients for making the egg custard – eggs, milk, sugar and vanilla.

STEP 4 Cut the vanilla pod in half lengthways and, using the tip of a small knife, scrape the tiny seeds from the pod.

STEP 5 Place the milk into a saucepan and add the vanilla seeds and bring to the boil.

STEP 6 Beat the eggs and sugar together in a bowl.

STEP 7 Once the milk has boiled, pour over the egg and sugar mixture whilst whisking to ensure even distribution and so that the eggs do not cook (scramble) as you add the hot milk.

STEP 8 Strain the mixture through a fairly fine chinois to remove any bits of coagulated egg etc. and then ladle on top of the set caramel in the dariole moulds.

STEP 9 Place the moulds into a water bath (bain-marie) and bake in a low oven until set (150°C for approximately 30 minutes).

STEP 10 Once the custard has set, remove the tray from the oven and carefully take each mould out of the bain-marie. Cool before serving.

- *Finishing*–This refers to the final steps to make the product as appealing as possible. Some baked items will benefit from dusting with icing sugar, whereas others, such as a fruit tartlet, will be enhanced by brushing with a glaze, such as apricot.

HEALTH & SAFETY Always have a thick, dry cloth to handle a hot saucepan. Always stand back from the caramel when adding water as the caramel is likely to spit a little.

Considerations when baking foods

Baking is quite a technical process. It is scientific in the way that the ingredients are proportioned and also in the way they are prepared. Both of these points will have an effect as to how the item will react when placed into heat. Any adjustment to the recipe, method of preparation, the temperature and cooking time will result in differences to the finished product – e.g. texture (light, heavy, soft, crisp, airy, tight), colour (light, dark), etc. This is why the following points are so important:

1 Pre-heat ovens to the temperature specified in the recipe.
2 Use a reliable set of scales and weigh ingredients accurately.
3 Prepare all other pieces of equipment required, such as bowls, mixing machines, spoons, trays and tins, cooling racks, etc.
4 Follow the recipe accurately, handling items according to instructions, e.g. kneading bread or lightly mixing pastry.
5 Have any finishing or decorative items ready to complete the process.

CHEF'S TIP Avoid opening oven doors too often as this will reduce the temperature inside the oven and could affect the item being baked. It is also important that oven doors are not slammed closed as the air movement can have a damaging affect on more delicate items, such as cakes and sponges.

Quality points to look for in baked items

Depending on the product being made, the desired finishes can be very different in colour, texture and flavour.

TASK Using the recipes in this chapter to help you, list three quality points for each of the following baked products:

- Pastry items, biscuits and cakes
- Bread products
- Vegetables and fruit
- Meat dishes
- Fish dishes

VIDEO CLIP Making pastry.

Step-by-step: Apple tart

STEP 1 The ingredients to make the apple puree (marmalade) – peeled and sliced apple, water, sugar, butter and ground cinnamon.

STEP 2 Add all the ingredients to a suitably sized saucepan.

STEP 3 Cook over a low to moderate heat, stirring constantly until the apple has softened. Using a wooden spoon, beat to a puree and cool.

STEP 4 The ingredients to make the pastry – soft flour, butter, sugar and water. Note: For a richer pastry, egg can be used to replace the water.

STEP 5 Sieve the flour and cut the butter into small dice. Lightly crumb these two ingredients together.

STEP 6 Add the sugar and water (or egg) together and add to the crumbed mixture.

STEP 7 Gently bring the mix together (do not knead!) and form into a ball. Wrap in cling film and leave in the refrigerator to relax.

STEP 8 On a cool, lightly floured surface, form the pastry into a circular shape and gently roll out, turning by 90° after each roll.

STEP 9 Check to ensure that the pastry is rolled enough to cover the base and sides of the **flan** ring.

STEP 10 Roll around a rolling pin and then out and across the flan ring. Note: The flan ring and baking tray should be lightly greased to prevent sticking.

STEP 11 Push the pastry into the inside corners of the flan ring to take on the shape of the ring.

STEP 12 Using a rolling pin, roll over the top of the flan ring. This will take off the excess pastry at the top of the ring.

STEP 13 For a decorative finished effect, the edge of the pastry can be crimped between the fingers as shown.

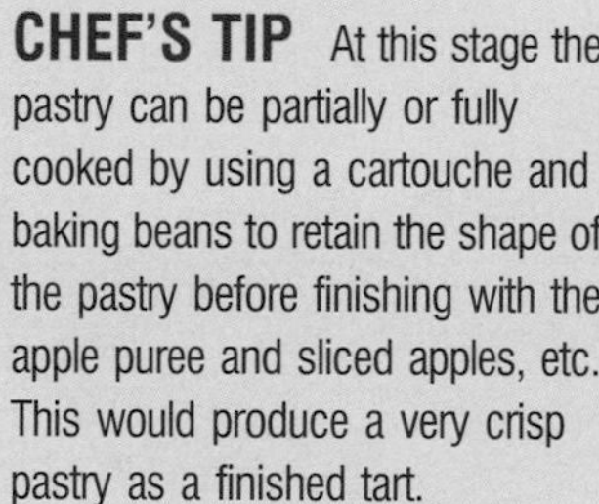

CHEF'S TIP At this stage the pastry can be partially or fully cooked by using a cartouche and baking beans to retain the shape of the pastry before finishing with the apple puree and sliced apples, etc. This would produce a very crisp pastry as a finished tart.

STEP 14 Fill with the apple puree.

STEP 15 Peel and core apples for the topping and slice neatly. Carefully arrange the sliced apple on top of the apple puree.

STEP 16 Brush with some sugar glaze and sprinkle with a little more sugar.

STEP 17 Bake in a pre-heated oven at 200°C until cooked. The sliced apples should lightly brown at the edge of each slice.

Roasting

What is roasting?

Roasting is one of the methods associated with the traditions of British cookery. Roast beef with Yorkshire pudding and horseradish sauce is known throughout the culinary world as a Great British classic.

Roasting is the cooking of food in a dry heat with the addition of oil or fat. Roasting can take place either in an oven or on a spit, e.g. spit roasted pig. Roasting enhances the natural flavours in foods, particularly meats. The smell of roast beef or a roast chicken is very distinguishable. For people who enjoy eating meat and poultry, this can certainly whet the appetite.

Roasting meats also helps to kill harmful bacteria during the process, making the food safe to eat. The usual process for roasting is to sear the outside of the food. Once seared, the oven temperature is usually reduced to finish the cooking process without drying the surface of the meat.

Roasting as a process, also enhances the presentation of foods. A roast chicken, for example, has an appealing light golden brown appearance. Roasted vegetables also present well. When roasting bell peppers, for example, the skin blisters and colours while the flesh naturally sweetens. Roasting is therefore an excellent process to enhance the presentation of foods whilst naturally developing their flavours.

CHEF'S TIP When turning roast meats in the oven, do not puncture the flesh by inserting a carving fork. This will puncture the flesh, resulting in the loss of natural juices.

The methods and equipment used to roast foods

There are two main methods associated with roasting:

1 Oven roasting

2 Spit roasting

Oven roasting

The first method is roasting using a conventional oven or convection oven, in which the heat is distributed throughout the oven chamber to produce an even heat. In this example, food items are usually placed into a roasting tray with the addition of oil or fat. Depending on the items being cooked, the tray and oil might be heated before adding the food items. Roast potatoes provide a good example where the oil or fat would usually be heated first. This ensures that the potatoes immediately start to lightly colour on the outside surface, frying in the heat of the oil. Once in the oven, this will produce a crisp surface to the outside of the potato while the heat from the oven will penetrate to the centre.

CHEF'S TIP Two methods to sear roast meats:

1 The meat is placed into a hot oven in which the heat from the oven immediately starts to sear the outside of the meat. The temperature would then be reduced to enable the heat to penetrate to the centre of the meat.

2 The meat is seared on the top of the stove by frying. It would then be placed into the oven to roast until cooked.

To prevent meat or poultry from frying through being in direct contact with hot oil or fat, whilst roasting in the oven, a trivet can be used to provide a gap between the base of the roasting tray and the item being cooked. A trivet could be in the form of a rack or vegetables. The vegetables, such as carrots, leeks, celery and onions, are normally sliced at an angle or into chunks to provide a large, flat cut, suitable to provide a 'bed' for the item to be placed on. The bed of vegetables is shown in the 'step-by-step' on page 130.

VIDEO CLIP Roasting a shoulder of lamb.

Temperature when roasting

When roasting foods it is important that the temperature of the oven is carefully controlled. Time is also important to ensure that the item is cooked to the degree required without drying or burning. The structure of the item must be taken into consideration. For example, a large item will require a

Step-by-step: Roast leg of lamb

STEP 1 The ingredients for roasting a leg of lamb – leg of lamb, garlic, rosemary, vegetable/olive oil, vegetables for the trivet (carrots, onions, leeks, garlic).

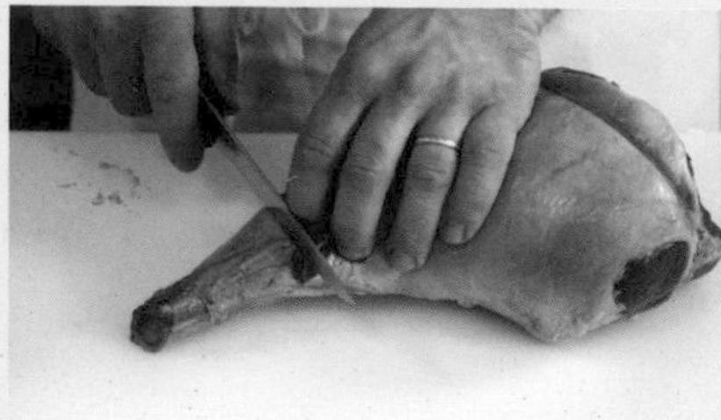

STEP 2 With a boning knife, cut around the shin bone in a circular motion.

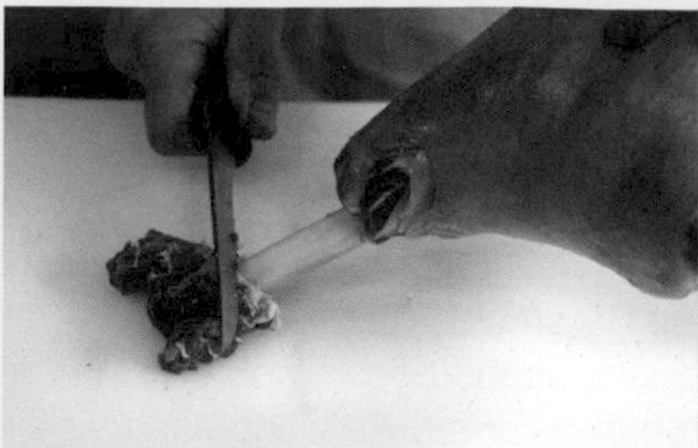

STEP 3 Scrape the skin and flesh back away from the bone to expose the clean bone.

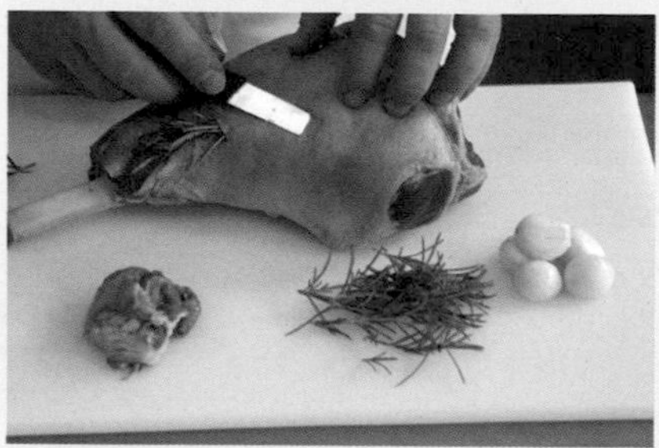

STEP 4 Using a small, sharp knife, make small incisions into the flesh of the joint. Place small sprigs of rosemary into the incisions.

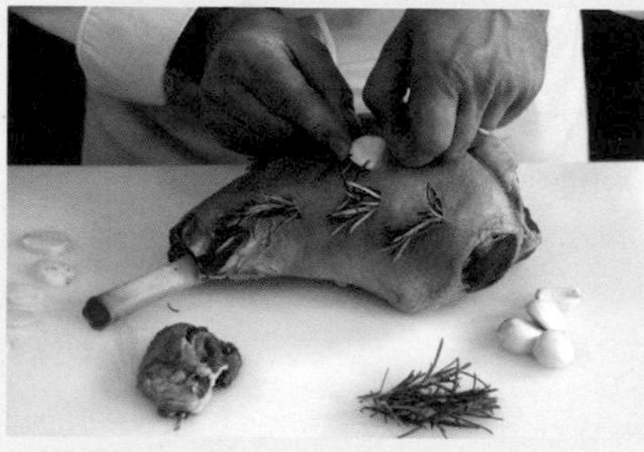

STEP 5 Cut fine slices from the peeled garlic cloves and place a slice next to each sprig of rosemary.

STEP 6 Wrap a piece of kitchen foil around the exposed bone to prevent it from burning during the roasting process.

STEP 7 Prepare the trivet by cutting the vegetables into fairly large pieces as shown (mirepoix).

STEP 8 Cut the bulb of garlic through the centre and place in the centre of the trivet. Place the prepared leg of lamb onto the trivet.

STEP 9 Brush the meat with oil and pour a small ladle of oil around the base of the roasting tray to prevent sticking. Season the lamb with salt and freshly ground black pepper and place in a pre-heated oven at 200°C.

STEP 10 Throughout the roasting process, **baste** the meat by pouring the oil and roasting juices from the roasting tray back over the lamb. Do this every 15 to 20 minutes.

STEP 11 Check the degree of cooking by inserting a temperature probe into the core of the meat.

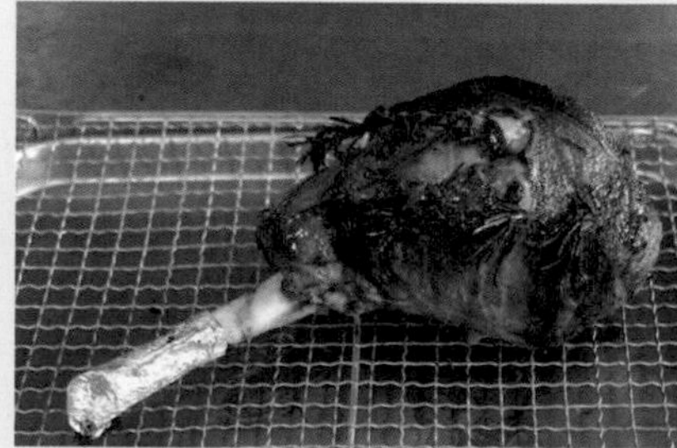

STEP 12 Once cooked, place the lamb onto a rack to relax in a warm environment for at least 10 to 20 minutes before carving. The core temperature of the meat will remain safe and this will allow the structure of the meat time to relax and become less tense (taut), making carving much easier and more efficient.

longer cooking time than a small item. In the case of meat, if the item is to be roasted on the bone, this will also have to be taken into consideration. In addition, red meats can be cooked to various degrees from underdone, where the flesh will be pink, to cooked through (more thoroughly cooked) where the meat will be a darker colour. To check the degree of cooking, a temperature probe can be inserted into the meat to determine the temperature in the centre of the meat and provide an indication as to the degree at which the item is cooked.

CHEF'S TIP The core temperature is the temperature in the centre of the item being cooked. To test the core temperature, a temperature testing device called a probe is inserted into the centre. The electronic reading then displays the temperature in the centre of the food, telling you if the item has reached a safe temperature to kill bacteria, making the food safe to eat. The photo in step 11 on page 130 shows this process in action.

When cooking is complete

Upon removing the tray from the oven, the roasted item will have to be removed from the tray. This should also be planned before undertaking the task. Clean and appropriate tools should be used, such as a carving fork and spoon. This does not mean that the item is pierced with the fork as it is preferable that the item retains its natural juices and flavours. Some of these would be lost if pierced, resulting in the potential loss of moisture and flavour.

Raw and cooked meats require different boards to avoid cross-contamination from the raw to cooked food.

Spit roasting

Spit roasting usually involves larger items, such as whole items (e.g. pig/hog roast), larger cuts of meat or birds (such as chickens) being placed onto a spit (large skewer) and rotated (continuously turned) over the heat source. This could be a radiant heat from electricity of gas bars or an open fire of wood or charcoal. Therefore, it can be an indoor or outdoor activity. This particular method of cookery is associated with a larger number of customers due to the size of the item being cooked; an outdoor celebration or festival, for example.

Techniques used when roasting foods

- *Stuffing* – This refers to stuffing the meat or poultry. Stuffings can be made from ingredients, such as sausage meat, vegetables, fruit, cereals and grains to provide a variety and contrast in flavours.

HEALTH & SAFETY It is important, particularly if using any meat products, that stuffing is thoroughly cooked before serving. A safe way to cook stuffings, particularly when serving with poultry (chicken), is to cook the stuffing separately. The stuffing can then be carved and served alongside the meat.

- *Trussing* – Trussing refers to the tying of birds, such as chickens to make them compact and retain their shape during the cooking process. This ensures that the bird will cook more evenly and presentation will be enhanced. Traditionally, poultry was tied with string using a trussing needle to pierce the chicken in key places to hold the bird tightly together. Poultry in current times is often trussed with oven-proof elastic bands, especially if it is purchased for the domestic (household) market.
- *Tying* – Joints of meat are often tied to retain their shape during the cooking process. Joints are also tied when they have been boned out (had the bone removed). Examples of this include a boned and rolled shoulder or leg of lamb or silverside of beef.
- *Basting* – Basting refers to the regular spooning of fat or oil and cooking juices over the outside surface of the food item during the cooking process. This helps to keep the item moist and will enhance the colour of the item as it cooks. Fat within the meat itself will melt and drain away from the meat during the roasting process. This will assist in keeping the meat moist but it is also beneficial because the fat content is reduced.
- *Relaxing before carving* – Meat and poultry is very difficult to carve straight from the oven, not only due to its extremely hot temperature but because of the contraction of the muscle structure. Relaxing on a board in a hygienic and safe environment for approximately 20 minutes will make the carving process much easier and therefore portion control and presentation are improved.

CHEF'S TIP Poultry refers to domestically reared birds for the purpose of eating. Examples include chicken, turkey and duck, which are often roasted.

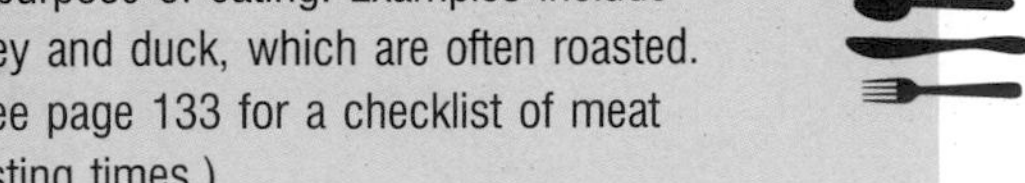

(Please see page 133 for a checklist of meat cuts and roasting times.)

Step-by-step: Roast chicken

STEP 1 Roughly crush a few cloves of garlic.

STEP 2 Peel the zest from a fresh lemon.

STEP 3 Remove the wishbone from the chicken and stuff the cavity of the chicken with the lemon and garlic.

STEP 4 Place a trivet of vegetables into a roasting tray. Place the prepared chicken on top of the trivet and baste with vegetable oil. Season the chicken with salt and freshly ground black pepper.

STEP 5 Roast the chicken in a pre-heated oven at 200°C, basting on a regular basis and turning the chicken throughout to ensure that the legs of the chicken are sufficiently roasted.

STEP 6 Once cooked, place the chicken onto a rack to relax in a warm environment for at least 10–15 minutes before carving. The core temperature of the chicken will remain safe and this will allow the structure of the chicken time to relax and become less tense (taut), making carving much easier and efficient.

VIDEO CLIP Roasting a chicken.

Step-by-step: Carving a roast chicken for service

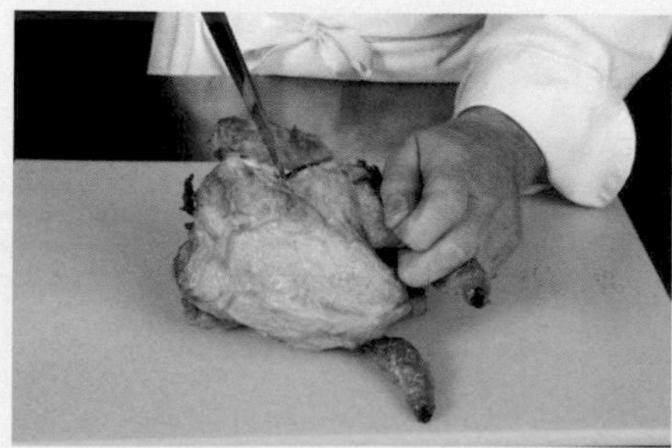

STEP 1 Cut through the skin between the leg and the breast and remove both legs.

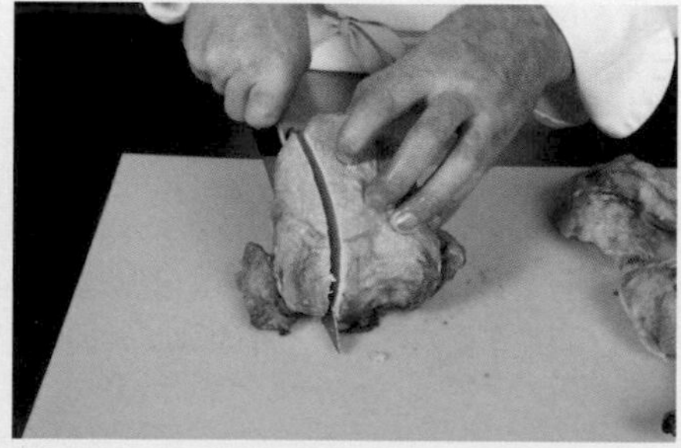

STEP 2 Cut halfway between the breast bone and the outside of the breast to remove the first cut from the breast.

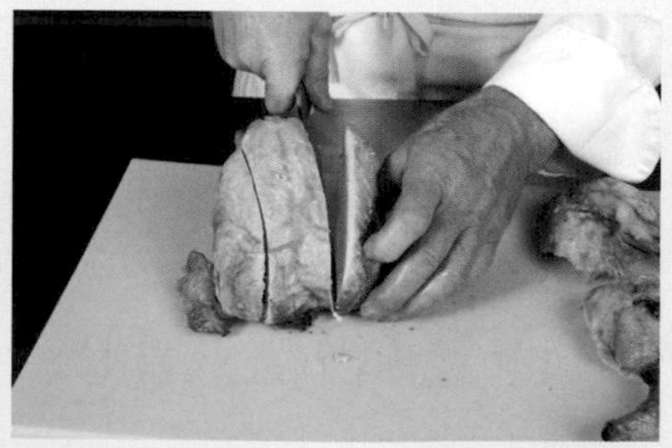

STEP 3 Repeat this on the other side to remove the second cut from the breast.

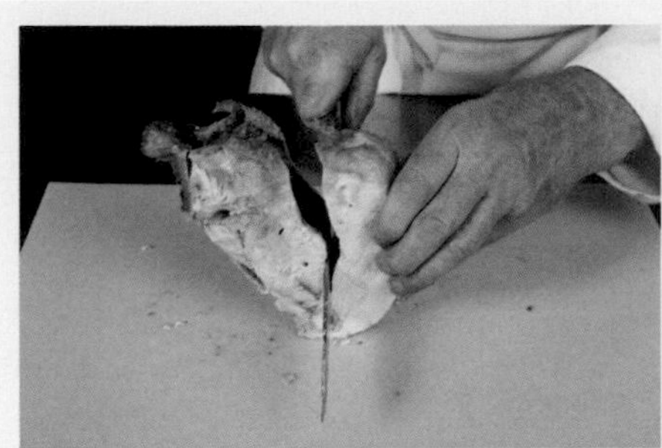

STEP 4 Cut the remaining breast meat from the carcass in one piece.

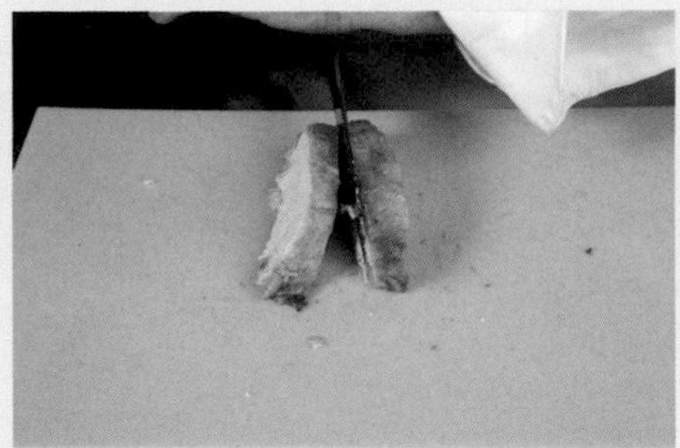

STEP 5 Split this into two pieces, either lengthways or across the width of the meat.

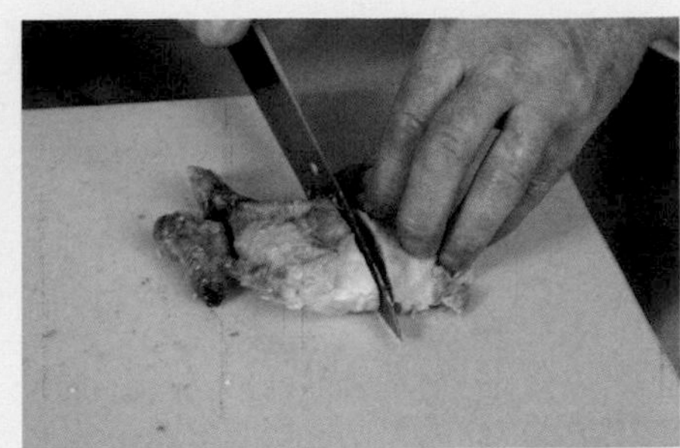

STEP 6 Cut the legs into two pieces by cutting between the ball and socket joint. This will provide cuts known as the thigh and drumstick.

A medium chicken will provide four portions if cut in this way, four cuts from the leg and four from the breast. When serving, it is important that each person receives one cut from the leg and one from the breast.

Points requiring consideration when roasting

There are many factors that will impact the way that roasted meats will turn out following the roasting process. Many meats can be cooked to different degrees, e.g. rare or well-done. The temperature of the oven, the cooking time and the size of the joint or bird to be roasted will affect the degree of cooking.

Joints of meat left on the bone tend to have enhanced flavour due to the natural flavours and aromas that are released during the cooking process. However, the presence of bone can lead to increased cooking time and also to uneven cooking due to the varying shape of the joint in question. It can also make carving more difficult. To overcome some of these issues, joints are often boned, rolled and tied before being roasted. Below is a table of temperatures to achieve the various degrees of cooking.

TABLE OF TEMPERATURES

	RARE	MEDIUM	WELL-DONE
Beef Sirloin, topside/top rump, rib, silverside, brisket	20 mins per 450 g approx before 1 lb x 7 (1 lb) + 20 mins Approximate internal temp: 60°C	25 mins per 450 g/½ kg (1 lb) + 25 mins Approximate internal temp: 70°C	30 mins per 450 g/½ kg (1 lb) + 30 mins Approximate internal temp: 80°C
Lamb Loin, shoulder, leg, rack, shanks, breast		25 mins per 450 g/½ kg (1 lb) + 25 mins Approximate internal temp: 70–75°C	30 mins per 450 g/½ kg (1 lb) + 30 mins Approximate internal temp: 75–80°C
Pork Loin, shoulder, leg, belly, hock		30 mins per 450 g/½ kg (1 lb) + 30 mins Approximate internal temp: 75–80°C	35 mins per 450 g/½ kg (1 lb) + 35 mins Approximate internal temp: 80–85°C

Associated products

Gravy or jus

During the roasting process, roasting juices and sediment (deposits) from meat and poultry will be captured in the roasting tray along with oils and fats. Once the meat or poultry is removed from the roasting tray to relax, the natural juices and sediment should be retained to enhance the flavour of the accompanying sauce. However, the fats and oils need to be removed or the sauce will become greasy and oily. These fats and oils naturally rise to the surface and will be found on top of any natural roasting juices. Therefore, if the roasting tray is tipped at an angle, all the liquid will slide to the lowest point in the tray. At this point it will be possible to carefully spoon off the oil and discard.

The tray is now ready to make a gravy or jus to accompany the roasted meat or poultry. This is usually achieved by the addition of a suitably flavoured stock and reduced. The liquid would then be strained to remove any sediment and adjusted in terms of seasoning, colour and consistency (thickness).

Accompaniments

Most roasted meats are enhanced by accompaniments such as mustards. However, certain roast meats are traditionally associated with a particular accompaniment which is thought to aid digestion or specifically enhance the meat. An example of this is roast beef and horseradish sauce.

Health and safety requirements

When roasting, the roasting tray should be of a suitable size for the job in hand. This will allow easy access to the food without causing difficulties that could lead to an accident. A roasting tray that is too large will burn in the empty spaces. This would impair and spoil the accompanying sauce if the roasting tray was used to produce the sauce by using the natural roasting juices and sediment. The meat itself may also get **tainted** by burnt fumes.

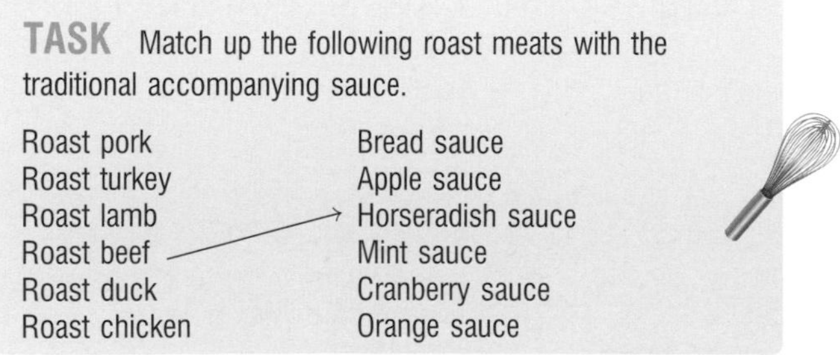

TASK Match up the following roast meats with the traditional accompanying sauce.

Roast pork	Bread sauce
Roast turkey	Apple sauce
Roast lamb	Horseradish sauce
Roast beef	Mint sauce
Roast duck	Cranberry sauce
Roast chicken	Orange sauce

Quality points

- Not all cuts of meat are suitable for roasting. Cuts that are particularly high in muscle and fat will toughen during the process and will be chewy and potentially unpleasant to eat. However, fat is a requirement during the roasting process in order for the meat or poultry to remain moist. This is why it is particularly important that regular basting takes place when cooking lean joints and poultry.
- When searing meat, it is recommended that external seasonings are added after the initial searing process has taken place. This will prevent a delay in the browning of the item. Once the item is coloured sufficiently, it should then be seasoned lightly with salt and pepper to enhance the flavour.

Grilling

What is grilling?

Grilling is the cooking of food items by radiant heat. This refers to the heat source transferring heat directly towards the food item being grilled.

The purpose of grilling

Grilling food helps to enhance the natural flavours in foods in a way that is unique to this process. This is particularly the case when grilling using a true grill, char-grill or barbeque. The initial high temperatures sear the outside of foods, helping to retain nutrients, natural flavours and moisture within the food. As natural fats and cooking juices fall from the food and onto the heat source they ignite producing a short burst of flames. If controlled so that the food is not fuel-charred, this helps to produce a very distinctive flavour. If this is achieved, grilled foods should remain tender as well as flavoursome when consumed.

The grilling process colours foods, making them attractive to the eye. The degree of cookery can also be judged according to the external appearance of the food. This can help to distinguish whether the item is cooking too quickly or slowly, providing the chef with the opportunity to move the item to a hotter or cooler part of the grill to complete the cooking process.

Grilling is also considered more healthy as it requires very little in terms of additional ingredients. Natural fats within the food items themselves also melt during the grilling process and fall from the food, naturally reducing the fat content of the finished item.

Foods suitable for grilling

Grilling is a particularly **intense method** of cooking in that items are usually cooked at high temperatures for a fairly short amount of time. Therefore, commodities such as meat have to be of high quality and low in muscle and connective tissue. These are referred to as the prime cuts of meat. Poultry, particularly breasts of poultry and cuts free from bone are most suitable for grilling as they are low in muscular structure. However, it is possible to grill a chicken on the bone if it has been prepared correctly (e.g. spatchcock). In this situation, it is important that the grilling process is closely monitored to ensure that the chicken is sufficiently cooked without drying out or burning.

A cut of meat high in muscular structure would retract (tighten) when exposed to the heat from the grill and become tough and unpleasant or difficult to eat.

Other suitable meat items include bacon, sausages and other mince-based meat products such as burgers and grill steaks. Certain offal are also suitable for grilling due to the structures of the items concerned.

Due to its delicate structure most types of fish are suitable for grilling. Obviously, larger fish, such as a tuna or salmon would have to be cut down into, for example, a darne (fish steak) or supreme (cut from the fillet), whereas it is possible to grill smaller fish such as sardines, mackerel and small trout from whole.

Many vegetables are also suitable for grilling, particularly tomatoes, mushrooms, courgettes, bell peppers and aubergines. Other vegetables, particularly ones with less water content would tend to dry and burn, so would be unsuitable for grilling as the initial method of cookery. Examples include French beans (haricots verts), cauliflower, broccoli, corn and potatoes. However, once these items are cooked, it is perfectly feasible that they could be sauced and placed under the grill to gratinate, cauliflower cheese (mornay) for example.

Associated techniques when grilling food

- *Batting out* – Batting out refers to the use of a meat bat to make the item of meat an even in thickness and also to breaks down connective tissue in the meat itself, making the item concerned more tender to eat. This process usually involves the item being placed between two sheets of cling film for protection. The bat is used in a firm motion until the item is of the shape and size required. In this situation, the item will naturally become wider and longer but thinner and this is dependent on the degree to which the bat is used.
- *Oiling, greasing and basting* – To prevent items from sticking to grill bars or racks they are often lightly oiled or greased before cooking. It is also advisable that the grill bars themselves are lightly oiled before and after use. If food sticks to a grill bar, the point of contact will rip the surface away from the food as it is lifted and remain stuck to the grill bar. Food that is low in natural fat can continue to be lightly oiled throughout the grilling process to ensure that it retains a moist external surface and does not dry out. This process is referred to as basting.
- *Traying up* – Food items, such as bacon, sausages and tomatoes, would usually be placed on lightly oiled or greased trays if they were being grilled under a salamander. This would be the case when preparing multiple breakfasts, for example. When traying up, it is important to consider space for turning items and making full use of the space at hand. Items that have been floured, such as fish fillets, or crumbed (**pané**) such as a chicken escalope, would also be placed on lightly oiled trays before being placed under the salamander.
- *Marinating* – To impart additional flavours to foods which are to be grilled, they can be soaked in what is referred to as a marinade. A marinade is usually a flavoured liquid into which food items, such as meat, poultry and fish, may be placed to absorb the flavours concerned. This process can take some time and will increase in strength the longer the food is left in the marinade. Marinades can be produced from bases of wine, vinegar, yoghurt and oils to name but a few possibilities. They can also be flavoured with herbs and spices to add another **dimension** to the flavour of the item being grilled. Chicken breast, for example, is quite commonly marinated as it absorbs flavours well and this can completely transform its flavour. A marinade can also help to break down the connective structure within meat, making it more tender to eat once cooked.

Considerations when grilling foods

Shelf position

Shelf position is particularly important when grilling foods. The closer food is to the heat source, the faster it will cook as the heat will be more intense. However, the thickness of the food item also has to be taken into consideration. If the food item was very thin, such as a fillet of plaice or an escalope of chicken, the time it would take to sear the outside of the food would usually be sufficient for heat to go through to the centre of the food. This would ensure that the item is cooked through whilst retaining moisture and a pleasant texture. If such items were placed towards the bottom shelf of the grill, where the heat would not be so intense, by the time the outside of the item was sealed, the item would, in all probability, be dry and much less pleasant to eat.

On the other hand, when cooking a thicker item, such as a fillet steak, consideration has to be taken as to where the steak would be placed within the salamander or grill. This is because red meats can be cooked to varying degrees and still remain safe to eat. For example, when ordering a fillet steak in a restaurant, it would be customary that you would be asked how you would like the item to be cooked.

DEGREE OF COOKING	APPEARANCE OF THE STEAK
Rare	The steak is well seared on the outside. Once the steak is cut open, the internal meat is not cooked through with almost raw meat towards the centre of the steak.
Medium-rare	The steak is well seared on the outside. Once the steak is cut open, the internal meat is under-cooked with meat that is red in colour towards the centre of the steak.
Medium	The steak is well seared on the outside. Once the steak is cut open, the internal meat is very slightly undercooked with meat that is pink towards the centre of the steak.
Well done	The steak is well seared seared on the outside. Once the steak is cut open, the internal meat is cooked through showing no signs of red or pink meat towards the centre of the steak.

Time and temperature are therefore key considerations when grilling foods. The structure, size and, in some cases, degree of cooking, has to be taken into account when grilling foods.

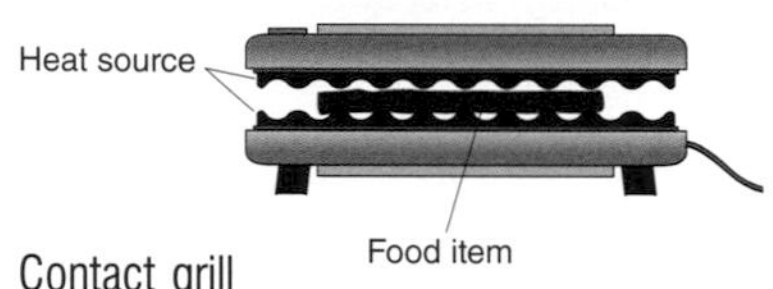

Contact grill

The methods and equipment used to grill foods

There are three main processes applied when grilling foods. The first is grilling where the heat source is above the food and is referred to as grilling by salamander.

The second method of grilling is where the heat comes from beneath the food item. Examples of this method include a barbeque, whether fuelled by charcoal, wood, gas or electricity, and char-grills which are often used in restaurant kitchens. These grills are sometimes referred to as 'true grills'.

True grill (flame/grill barbeque)

The third method of grilling is where the food item is placed between the sources of heat. Examples include a contact grill where an item such as a chicken breast could be placed between the plates of the grill. This type of grill is currently popular in the domestic market as it involves very little use of fat. In addition to this, any fats or oils that come away from the food during the cooking process are drained away leaving a very lean cooked product.

Grilling by salamander

As with most other cookery processes, it is important that the salamander is pre-heated before cooking commences. Salamanders are fitted with a **transferable shelf** usually consisting of a rack or grill bars and a tray. These can sometimes be in one contained unit or the shelf can be separate from the tray. In this situation, as an item is being grilled, any fats or liquids that come away from the food fall between the gaps in the rack or bars and are collected by the tray underneath.

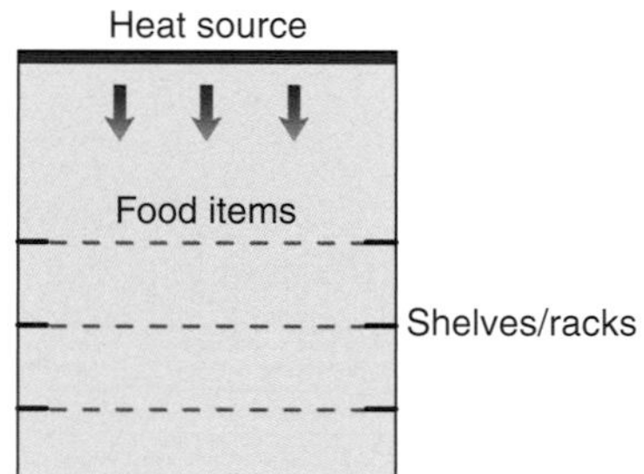

Salamander

With items such as kidneys or small fish, it may be more appropriate to place them on a tray to grill them, as these items could potentially fall between the bars. In this situation, it is important that such items are placed on a tray that is suitable for catching fats and other liquids as they will inevitably come out of the food during the cooking process, i.e. a tray with a lip.

CHEF'S TIP When making kebabs using wooden kebab skewers, it is recommended that they are soaked in water for a few hours to help prevent them from burning during the grilling process.

When cooking large but fairly delicate items, such as whole fish, the use of a double-wired cage is often used. This enables easy handling of the fish, particularly when turning, and will help to hold the shape of the fish, preventing it from curling under the heat and burning.

The radiant heat generated from a salamander is hotter towards the top of the grill, where it is closer to the source of the heat, becoming less hot the further away from the heat source. Therefore, if an item is to be cooked very quickly, it should be placed on a shelf close to the top of the salamander. On the other hand, if the item requires cooking for a longer period, it should be placed on a shelf nearer to the bottom of the salamander. The power of the heat source can also be controlled in a similar way to a control on a gas or electric hob, i.e. the size of the flame or the heat of the ring.

OTHER USES FOR SALAMANDERS

Salamanders are also used for 'flashing' food. This refers to a short, intense period where items can be placed under the salamander to raise the temperature of the item concerned. Great care is required in this situation as, if left too long, the food item could potentially burn, dry out and lose eating quality.

The second purpose would be to 'gratinate' foods. This is when food is placed under the salamander to brown, providing an attractive glaze to the dish, e.g. cheese lightly browned (gratinated) on the top of a dish of pasta.

HEALTH AND SAFETY CONSIDERATIONS WHEN USING A SALAMANDER

Moving items on a salamander

As food items are grilled, they will release fats and natural juices. These will fall onto the grilling tray and will become very hot. Therefore, it is essential that trays are moved carefully so that these liquids are not spilled causing injury. The tray itself will also become very hot so a clean, thick and dry oven cloth should be used to hold the tray and protect the hands.

Placing items on top of a salamander

When a salamander is in use, the top casing will become extremely hot. This is not always **visually clear** as there is no flame evident and the surface will not change colour to indicate a rise in temperature. Therefore, this space should not be used for storage and contact should be avoided.

VIDEO CLIP Cooking lamb cutlets under a salamander.

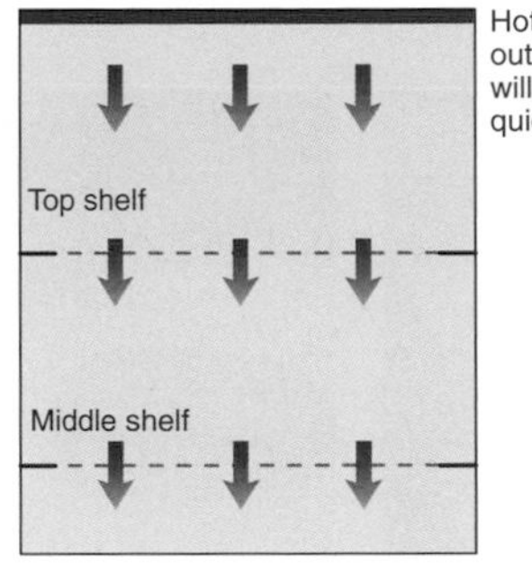

Grilling using a salamander

Grilling by true grill (char-grill)/ barbeque

Once again, it is very important that these types of grills are pre-heated so that food items begin to cook immediately on contact. When using these grills, food items are usually placed directly onto the bars above the source of the heat. Some grills, such as a barbeque may have shelving options to raise or lower the height of the food. Fixed grills, as found in many restaurant kitchens, will not have this option and it will require the skill, knowledge and experience of the chef to place the food item on the grill according to how it is to be cooked. Although different parts of the grill will be hotter than others, it is possible to reduce the source of power (gas or electricity) by reducing the input, although the bars will retain their heat for a long time.

These types of grills leave the distinctive 'grill lines' on food often in a crisscross pattern where the food has been turned 90° as it is being grilled. Food cooked in this way will also have the distinctive flavour of grilled food, particularly if barbecued as the charcoal or lumpwood produces a smoky flavour that is transferred into the food. The flavour is also enhanced as natural fats, oils and juices fall from the food and onto the heat source, resulting in a flame being produced and shortly catching the food (flame grilled). If this process is controlled, it produces a very pleasant and unique taste to the item being grilled.

When grilling in this manner, the bars on the grill (or the food itself) are usually lightly oiled to prevent the food items from sticking.

VIDEO CLIP Grilling steaks on a charcoal grill.

A true grill

Step-by-step: Preparing kidneys for grilling

STEP 1 A tray of lambs' kidneys.

STEP 2 From the side of the kidney, use a small, sharp knife to cut into the centre of the kidney.

STEP 3 Using a pair of kitchen scissors, cut away the fatty tissue in the centre of the kidney.

CHEF'S TIP Offal refers to the edible organs of an animal, e.g. liver, kidneys, heart, sweetbreads (pancreas and thymus glands).

STEP 4 Repeat this process with the remaining kidneys.

STEP 5 Using cocktail sticks, secure each kidney by inserting two cocktail sticks at 90° from one another across the kidney.

STEP 6 Place onto a lightly greased tray, brush the kidneys with melted butter and season with salt and freshly ground black pepper. Grill as required.

Step-by-step: Salmon and courgette kebabs

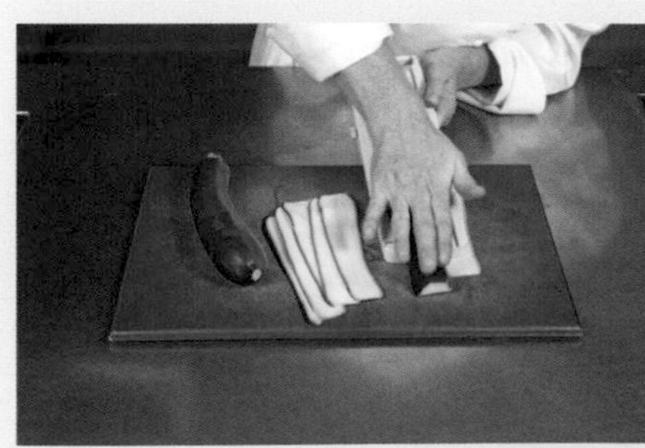

STEP 1 Top and tail a courgette and carefully slice lengthways into thin slices using a mandolin.

STEP 2 Cut the salmon across the fillet into approximately 2.5 cm slices.

STEP 3 Cut each slice into cubes of approximately 2.5 cm cubes.

STEP 4 Roll each cube of salmon in a ribbon of courgette allowing for 5 or 6 pieces per portion.

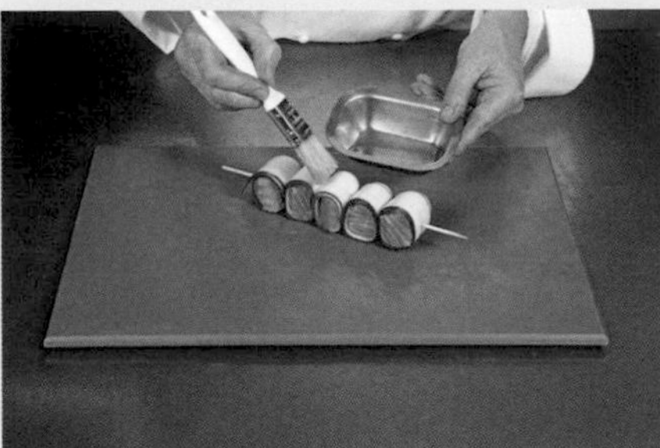

STEP 5 Carefully skewer each piece of wrapped salmon by securing with a wooden kebab skewer and brush lightly with olive oil before grilling under the salamander.

STEP 6 To make the dressing, squeeze lemon juice into olive oil (ratio of 1 to 4 or 5) and season with salt and freshly ground pepper.

STEP 7 Cut snippets of chives using a sharp knife.

STEP 8 Add the chives to the olive oil and lemon dressing along with the tomato concasser.

Note: The full recipe and a picture of the finished dish can be seen on page 148.

Step-by-step: Grilling a supreme of tuna

STEP 1 Brush the tuna with oil and season with salt and freshly ground white pepper.

STEP 2 Place onto the heated griddle pan.

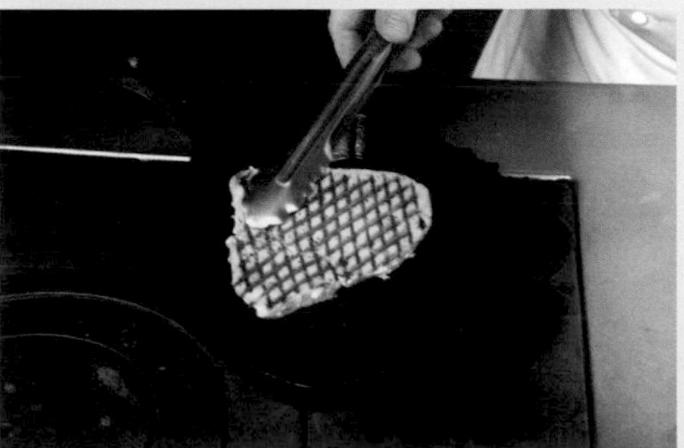

STEP 3 As the tuna is cooking, turn it by 90° and place back onto the griddle pan. This will produce the visually enhancing 'grill' lines as demonstrated in this picture.

STEP 4 A simply grilled but delicious supreme of tuna.

Grilling between radiant heat

Grilling in this form is less common in the professional kitchen. There are many specialist forms of contact grill where griddle plates are pressed onto the food item to be cooked. An example of this is provided in 'panini'. Paninis are grilled sandwiches that are pressed between specially designed griddle plates to compress the bread and heat the filling of the sandwich. There are also a number of similar types of contact grills designed to griddle small items such as steaks, chicken supremes, cuts of fish and vegetables such as onions, courgettes and bell peppers.

These grills are powered by electricity, and although fats and liquids will fall away from the food as the griddle bars in direct contact are raised, there is more direct contact with the heat supply than in the examples of grilling by salamander or barbeque/flame grill.

Step-by-step: Chicken supreme (breast) using a contact grill

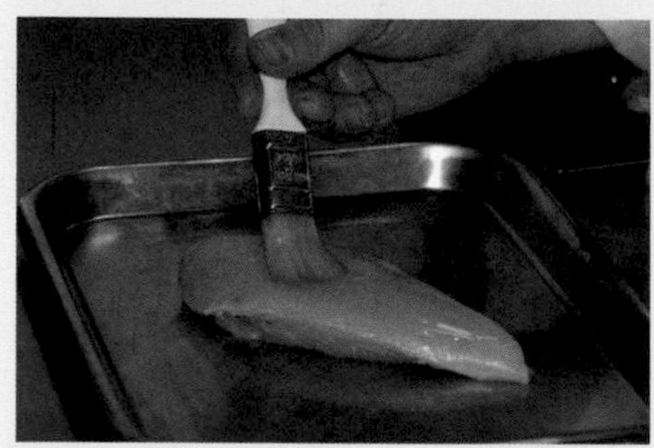

STEP 1 Brush the chicken supreme with oil and season with salt and freshly ground white pepper.

STEP 2 Place into the pre-heated contact grill and close the two grilling plates around the chicken.

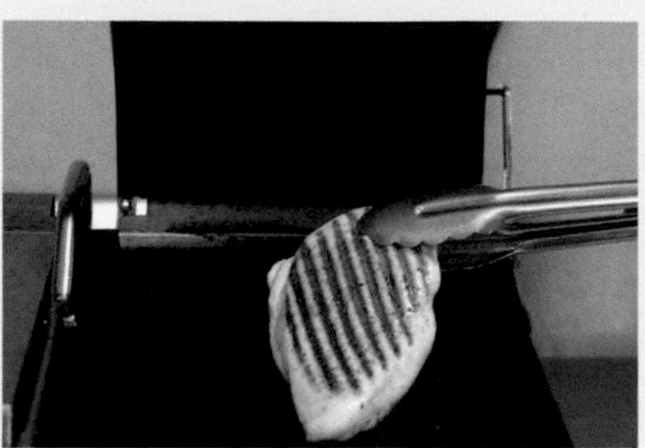

STEP 3 The chicken will develop the authentic grill lines as it cooks via this process.

STEP 4 A contact grilled chicken supreme served with a vegetable kebab.

Associated products with grilled foods

As grilling is a dry method of cookery, it is important to consider the sauces and accompaniments that can be served with grilled foods to make the eating experience as enjoyable as possible. The range of sauces that could accompany grilled dishes is vast and come in many formats such as hot sauces, cold sauces, dressings, salsas and mustards.

TASK Provide examples of suitable sauces and accompaniments for the following grilled foods:

- Flame grilled fillet steak
- Chicken breast
- Supreme of salmon
- Grilled field mushroom

Small equipment often used when grilling foods

The following items are often used when grilling foods:

Tongs – Used to turn items to ensure even cooking, for example, sausages, burgers, steaks or chicken.

Palette knives – Used to slide under items such as fillets of fish.

Slices – For larger items such as small whole fish or darnes (fish steaks).

Skewers – To secure food items when grilling kebabs.

Guest Chef

Smoked Goosnargh duck and beetroot risotto

Chef *Ian Corkhill*

Centre/College *St Helens College*

The smoked Goosnargh duck breast, has been locally sourced from Reg Johnson and Bud Swarbrick poultry suppliers who have been producing poultry in Goosnargh in the Ribble Valley for three decades. They supply hotels and restaurants throughout the United Kingdom.

Ingredients	*Serves 4*
Smoked Goosnargh duck breast	150 g (reserve 12 neat slices for presentation, finely dice the rest)
cooked beetroot, finely diced	150 g
Risotto rice	150 g
Finely chopped onion	40 g
Finely chopped garlic	25 g
Butter	50 g
Dry white wine	75 ml
White chicken stock	250 ml
Grated Parmesan	2 tblspn
Double cream	50 ml

METHOD OF WORK

1. Melt half the butter and sweat the onions and garlic until translucent.
2. Add the rice and cook for 2 minutes, stirring until all the grains are coated.
3. Add the white wine and reduce until the mixture begins to dry out.
4. Gradually add the hot stock, stirring regularly until the liquid is absorbed and the rice is al dente.
5. Fold in the diced beetroot and duck.
6. At the last minute stir in the remaining butter, Parmesan and adjust the consistency of the risotto with the cream.
7. Do not allow the risotto to boil again once the cheese, butter and cream have been added.
8. Arrange neatly on a warm plate and finish with the smoked duck slices, and a small dressed herb salad.

TEST YOURSELF

1 Link the following types of grill with the correct description

Char-grill/barbecue	Items are cooked under the heat source
Salamander	Items are cooked between the heat source
Contact grill	Items are cooked over the heat source

2 What type of heat is associated with grilling?

a. Convection ☐
b. Conduction ☐
c. Radiant ☐
d. Induction ☐

3 If you were asked to grill a steak rare, would you . . .

a. Cook the steak for a long time under intense heat ☐
b. Cook the steak for a short time under low heat ☐
c. Cook the steak for an intermediate time under medium heat ☐
d. Cook the steak for a short time under intense heat ☐

4 Name the degrees/stages to which a grilled steak may be requested by a customer.

a. ______________________
b. ______________________
c. ______________________
d. ______________________

5 Why is grilling considered to be a healthy cooking process?

____

6 Which type of grill would produce the 'char' lines on food items?

____

7 Name four vegetables that can be grilled successfully with menu examples.

i) ______________________
ii) ______________________
iii) ______________________
iv) ______________________

8 What steps could you take to ensure that a cut of chicken did not dry out during the grilling process?

____

9 What are the main reasons for marinating food items before grilling?

____

10 Name three pieces of small equipment that would commonly be used when grilling foods.

i) ______________________
ii) ______________________
iii) ______________________

Recipes

Apple tart

Ingredients

For the apple tart	
Sweet paste (see below)	200 g
Sugar	100 g
Apples (Granny Smith, Braeburn, Bramley's)	500 g
Apricot glaze	
For the sweet paste	
Unsalted butter – cut into small pieces	280 g
Icing sugar	70 g
Large egg yolks	2
Soft plain flour	350 g
Double cream	2 tbsp

energy	cal	fat	sat fat	carb	sugar	protein	fibre
864 kJ	205 kcal	8.2 g	5.0 g	32.6 g	24.8 g	1.5 g	1.4 g

METHOD OF WORK
For the sweet paste

1. Place the icing sugar into a food mixer.
2. Add the butter and toss.
3. Cream the butter and sugar mixture until the sugar is no longer visible, scraping down the sides of the bowl as you work.
4. Add the egg yolks gradually and blend again, scraping the bowl as before.
5. Add half the flour and mix until the paste becomes crumbly.
6. Stop the machine and add the remaining flour and mix until the dough forms into a ball.
7. Shape, wrap and chill until firm.

For the pastry case

1. Line a flan ring leaving excess pastry to overhang. Dock the base to prevent rising and leave to relax for 30 minutes.
2. Line with a cartouche or cling film and baking beans and bake at 200°C for 10 minutes. Take out, remove the baking beans and continue to bake for a further 5 minutes.
3. Take out, remove the cartouche and allow to cool.
4. Carefully slice off the overhanging pastry by cutting away from the tart along the line of the flan ring.

Apple puree

Reserve the two best-shaped apples and make the remainder into a puree by completing the following.

1. Peel, core and slice the apples.
2. Melt 25g of butter in a pan.
3. Add the apples and sugar. Stir well, place a lid on the pan and cook until the apples are soft.
4. Remove the lid and cook while stirring to evaporate any excess liquid and intensify the flavour.
5. Pass through a sieve or liquidizer.
6. Allow to cool.

To finish

1. Place the apple puree neatly into the flan case.
2. Peel and quarter the remaining apples.
3. Cut the apple quarters into neat thin slices and lay carefully on the apple puree overlapping each slice. Ensure that each slice points to the centre of the flan, joining the pattern up neatly.
4. Sprinkle a little sugar on the apple slices and bake the flan in a moderately hot oven (200°C/410°F/Gas 6) for 10–15 minutes.
5. When cooked, remove the ring and place carefully onto a cooling rack.
6. Brush all over with hot apricot glaze (including the sides of the pastry).

Bread rolls

Ingredients	32–40 rolls
White rolls	
Strong plain flour	1 kg
Butter	50 g
Yeast	35 g
Milk powder	25 g
Salt	20 g
Caster sugar	10 g
Water	1050 ml at 37°C
Wholemeal rolls	
Wholemeal flour	1 kg
Butter	50 g
Yeast	35 g
Salt	20 g
Sugar	10 g
Water	1300 ml at 37°C

energy	cal	fat	sat fat	carb	sugar	protein	fibre
471 kJ	111 kcal	1.8 g	0.6 g	21.6 g	1.0 g	3.6 g	1.9 g

energy	cal	fat	sat fat	carb	sugar	protein	fibre
424 kJ	100 kcal	2.0 g	0.7 g	18.1 g	0.9 g	3.6 g	2.6 g

Equipment

- large mixer machine with hook attachment
- proover
- baking sheet lined with silicone paper
- oven set: 230°C/450°F.

METHOD OF WORK

1. Sieve flour onto paper or a bowl.
2. Rub in fat.
3. Dissolve the yeast in half the water.
4. Dissolve milk powder, salt and sugar in other half of water.
5. Add BOTH liquids to the flour in one go.
6. Using a mixing machine, mix on speed No I for 5 minutes to achieve a smooth dough.
7. Cover with cling film and leave to prove for 1 hour (double in size).
8. Knockback to expel the carbon dioxide.
9. Scale into 50 g rolls, keeping covered at all times.
10. Roll, shape and place on silicone covered baking sheet in neatly spaced staggered rows.
11. Egg wash carefully and prove until double in size.
12. Bake at 230°C/450°F) for 8 to 10 minutes (with steam).

Alternatives (suitable for white bread dough)

Tomato and basil bread – Replace half the water with tomato juice, add fine chopped sun-dried tomatoes and dried basil after the 'knockback'.

Olive and walnut bread – Replace butter with olive oil (add to salt, sugar, etc), add chopped walnuts and sliced olives after the 'knockback'.

Caramel creams Crème caramels

Ingredients	4–6 Caramel creams	10–12 Caramel creams
For the caramel		
Granulated or cube sugar	200 g	400 g
Water	10 ml	20 ml
For the cream		
Eggs	4	8
Caster sugar	100 g	200 g
Milk	600 ml	1200 ml
Vanilla pod (or drop of good quality vanilla essence)	1 pod	2 pods

energy	cal	fat	sat fat	carb	sugar	protein	fibre
1479 kJ	349 kcal	6.2 g	2.5 g	68.7 g	68.6 g	9.1 g	0.0 g

METHOD OF WORK

For the caramel

1. Using a solid based, small saucepan (e.g. a lined copper pan), dissolve the sugar in the water and bring to the boil.
2. Cook quickly until a light caramel colour is achieved, cleaning the sides of the pan with a pastry brush soaked with clean water.
3. Remove from the heat and add a few drops of water and shake thoroughly. This will help to prevent the caramel from setting to a hard texture.
4. Pour the prepared caramel into the base of the dariole moulds and allow to set.

VIDEO CLIP Making caramel creams. 

For the cream

1. Mix the eggs and sugar in a bowl.
2. Bring the milk and split vanilla pod or essence carefully to the boil.
3. Strain and whisk onto the egg and sugar mixture.

To cook

1. Place the prepared moulds in deep trays.
2. Fill to just below the brim with the egg custard mixture.
3. Pour warm water into the tray about half way up the height of the dariole moulds.
4. Carefully place into the oven, set at 150°C and bake until set (approximately 30 minutes).
5. Once set, carefully remove from the oven and remove the dariole moulds from the tray.
6. Once cool, turn out onto plates and serve. The caramel will naturally run down the set custard to provide its own caramel sauce.

Plain scones

Ingredients	*12 scones*
Medium strength flour	450 g
Baking powder	30 g
Pinch of salt	
Butter	115 g
Caster sugar	100 g
Milk	150 ml
Sour cream	150 ml
Vanilla essence (to taste)	

energy	cal	fat	sat fat	carb	sugar	protein	fibre
1125 kJ	268 kcal	11.1 g	6.8 g	40.0 g	10.5 g	4.5 g	1.2 g

Oven temperature: 190°C/375°F.

METHOD OF WORK

1 Sieve the flour, baking powder and salt into a bowl.

2 Cut the butter into small cubes and rub into the flour mixture as finely as possible.

3 Make a bay in the centre and dissolve the sugar using milk and sour cream. Add a few drops of vanilla essence to taste.

4 Gradually mix the flour mixture into the milk.

5 Continue mixing until equally blended, but avoid over-mixing.

6 Place the mix onto a lightly dusted surface and form into a ball.

7 Gently roll out until half an inch thick and cut into individual scones using a scone cutter.

8 Place on a lightly greased baking tray and egg wash.

9 Rest for 15–20 minutes before baking until the tops of the scones are golden brown (approximately 15–20 minutes).

10 Once cooked, place onto a wire rack and allow to cool.

Roast chicken with bread sauce and roast gravy

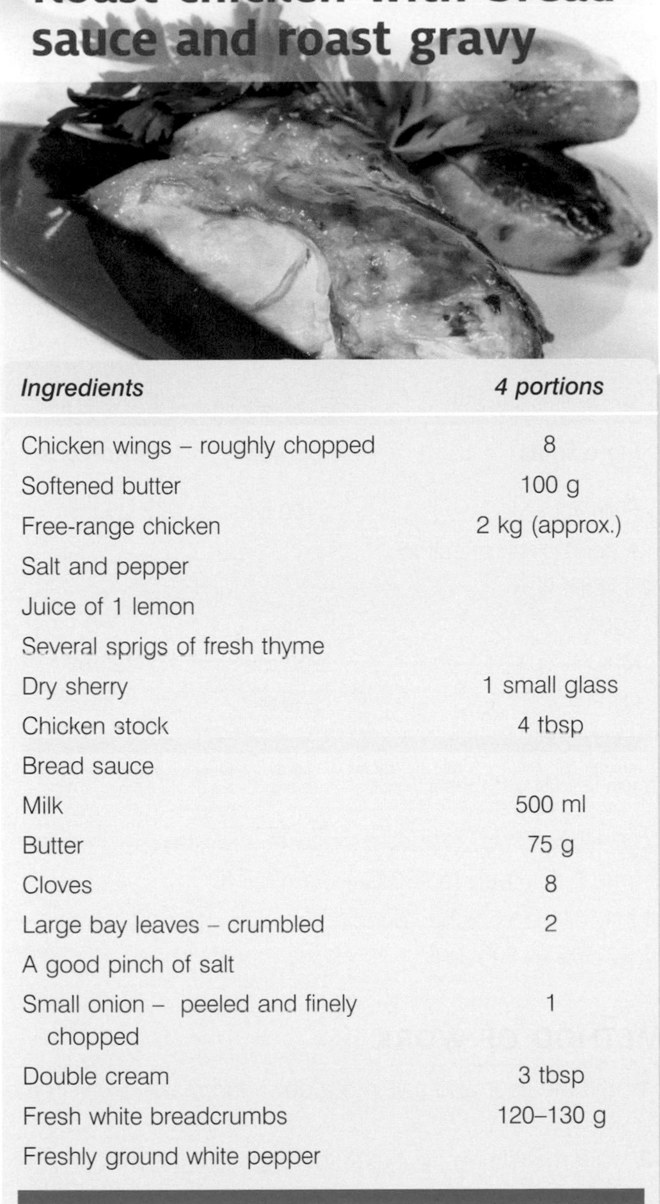

Ingredients	*4 portions*
Chicken wings – roughly chopped	8
Softened butter	100 g
Free-range chicken	2 kg (approx.)
Salt and pepper	
Juice of 1 lemon	
Several sprigs of fresh thyme	
Dry sherry	1 small glass
Chicken stock	4 tbsp
Bread sauce	
Milk	500 ml
Butter	75 g
Cloves	8
Large bay leaves – crumbled	2
A good pinch of salt	
Small onion – peeled and finely chopped	1
Double cream	3 tbsp
Fresh white breadcrumbs	120–130 g
Freshly ground white pepper	

energy	cal	fat	sat fat	carb	sugar	protein	fibre
4734 kJ	1134 kcal	71.3 g	35.3 g	36.4 g	8.9 g	86.6 g	3.9 g

METHOD OF WORK

1. Pre-heat the oven to 450°F/230°C/Gas 8.
2. Place the chicken wings over the base of a solid-bottomed roasting tray.
3. Rub the butter all over the chicken, season well and position on top of the wings.
4. Squeeze the lemon all over the chicken, then push the exhausted halves and the thyme inside the chicken cavity.
5. Pour in the sherry and stock.
6. Roast in the oven for about 10–15 minutes, then turn the temperature down to 350°F/180°C/Gas 4.
7. Continue roasting for a further one to 1¼ hours.
8. Baste the chicken every 20 minutes.
9. When the skin is crisp and a rich golden colour, skewer the thigh and look for the clear juices that show it's done.
10. Lift out the chicken and tip out its interior juices, thyme and lemon halves into the roasting dish. Put the chicken onto a suitable tray and relax in a warm place (e.g. in an oven that has been switched off).
11. Allow to rest for at least 10 minutes before carving.

Bread sauce

1. Infuse the milk with the cloves, bay leaves, salt and pepper.
2. Heat together the milk (with spices), butter and chopped onion. Bring to the boil and reduce to a simmer.
3. Simmer for 5 minutes and turn off letting the flavours continue to infuse off the heat.
4. Strain through a fine sieve into a clean pan.
5. Add the cream and re-heat to just below boiling point.
6. Whisk in the breadcrumbs gradually until the desired consistency is achieved.
7. Season and pour into a bowl.
8. Keep covered and warm using a bain-marie.

Roast gravy

1. Squash the lemon halves around the roasting dish to extract any remaining flavour, then throw away.
2. Put the roasting tray directly on the heat and stir vigorously with a wooden spoon to displace the roasted sediment (bits).
3. Add more stock, if required, and simmer for 10 minutes, skimming away any fat or impurities that rise to the surface.
4. Strain through a sieve into a small pan.
5. Bring back to the boil and season with salt and freshly ground white pepper.
6. Adjust the consistency using a little diluted arrowroot, if necessary.

Bread sauce

Salmon and courgette kebab with tomato vinaigrette

Ingredients	*4 portions*	*10 portions*
Salmon fillet	500 g	1250 g
Medium courgettes	2	5
Olive oil for greasing and soaked wooden kebab skewers		
For the vinaigrette		
Tomatoes – skinned, deseeded and diced neatly	4	10
Chopped fresh basil	50 g	125 g
Olive oil	100 ml	250 ml
Lemon juice	20 ml	50 ml
Seasoning (freshly cracked Maldon salt and pepper)		

energy	cal	fat	sat fat	carb	sugar	protein	fibre
2572 kJ	620 kcal	51.5 g	8.6 g	5.7 g	4.9 g	33.8 g	2.3 g

METHOD OF WORK

1. Cut the salmon fillet into 1 inch (2.5 cm) dice.
2. Peel, or use a mandolin, to produce thin ribbons (lengths) from the courgette.
3. Wrap each piece of salmon in a ribbon of courgette and place onto the skewer (five or six in total).
4. Season and brush with olive oil.
5. Cook on the grill for about 5 minutes turning once.
6. Mix all the ingredients for the vinaigrette in a mixing bowl.
7. Carefully remove the kebabs from the skewer and serve neatly with a few spoonfuls of the tomato vinaigrette.

Yorkshire pudding

Ingredients	*4 portions*	*10 portions*
Plain flour	100 g	250 g
A good pinch of salt to season		
Eggs	3	7/8
Milk	290 ml	725 ml
Oil	2 tbsp	5 tbsp

energy	cal	fat	sat fat	carb	sugar	protein	fibre
1001 kJ	239 kcal	12.9 g	2.5 g	22.8 g	3.8 g	9.5 g	0.8 g

Pre-heat the oven to 230°C/450°F/Gas 8.

Lightly oil the Yorkshire pudding moulds and heat in the oven to get the oil very hot.

METHOD OF WORK

1. Sift the flour and salt into a bowl and make a well in the centre.
2. In a measuring jar, break the eggs into the milk and mix well.
3. Pour half of the liquid into the well of the flour, gradually drawing in more flour to the centre.
4. Beat until the batter is smooth before adding the remainder of the liquid while continuously whisking.
5. Strain and leave to rest for 30 minutes before use.
6. *To cook*: Pour the batter into the pre-heated and oiled Yorkshire pudding moulds. Roast in the pre-heated oven for 25 to 30 minutes, or until risen and golden brown.

Served as a traditional accompaniment to roast beef.

Roasting beef

Ingredients	*1 portion*
First class cuts – fillet, sirloin, wing and fore ribs Second class cuts – topside and middle rib	150 g off the bone 200 g on the bone

energy	cal	fat	sat fat	carb	sugar	protein	fibre
1104 kJ	263 kcal	7.7 g	3.2 g	0.0 g	0.0 g	48.3 g	0.0 g

METHOD OF WORK

1. Season joints with salt and pepper before placing on a trivet of vegetables or bones in a roasting tray.
2. Place a little dripping or oil on top and initially cook in a hot oven at 230–250°C for 20 minutes to sear the meat and develop colour.
3. Reduce the heat, referring to the tables of temperatures on page 133 for the time and temperature requirements and the degree of cooking required. Note: Beef is usually cooked underdone (rare).
4. Baste frequently throughout the cooking process.
5. On removing the joint from the oven, rest for 15 minutes to allow the meat to relax before carving.
6. Carve the meat by cutting against the grain of the meat.
7. Serve with pan juices or gravy, Yorkshire pudding, watercress and horseradish sauce.

Roast leg of lamb with mint sauce and roast gravy. Follow stepped instructions on page 130.

Sardines with tomato sauce

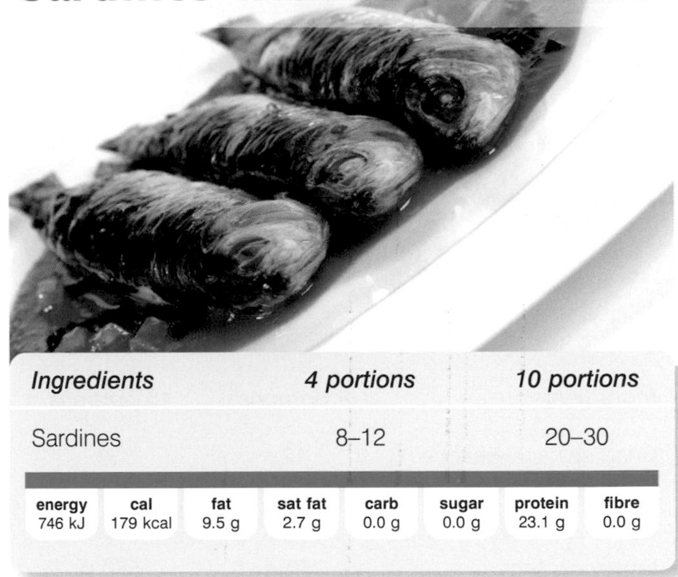

Ingredients	*4 portions*	*10 portions*
Sardines	8–12	20–30

energy	cal	fat	sat fat	carb	sugar	protein	fibre
746 kJ	179 kcal	9.5 g	2.7 g	0.0 g	0.0 g	23.1 g	0.0 g

METHOD OF WORK

Allow two to three sardines per portion depending on size.

1. Clean the sardines and trim the fins using kitchen scissors
2. Grill the sardines on both sides, either on an open flame grill or under the salamander for approximately 5 minutes or until cooked through. Larger sardines can be turned once during the grilling process.
3. Serve with tomato sauce (see page 93) and some finely chopped black olives.

Ricotta and spinach cannelloni with tomato and basil sauce

Ingredients	4 portions	10 portions
Dried spinach lasagne sheets	12	30
Ricotta cheese	200 g	500 g
Fresh spinach	350 g	850 g
Tomato sauce (page 93)	200 ml	500 ml
Basil – shredded	1 tbsp	2 tbsp
Parmesan cheese – grated	50 g	125 g

energy	cal	fat	sat fat	carb	sugar	protein	fibre
2963 kJ	702 kcal	17.0 g	8.4 g	104.0 g	5.8 g	33.3 g	6.1 g

METHOD OF WORK

1. Pre-heat oven to 190°C.
2. Cook the lasagne sheets in a large pan of boiling salted water for the stated time as shown on the packaging. Refresh immediately in ice-cold water.
3. Pick the spinach to de-branch and blanch by plunging it into rapidly boiling water for 20 seconds before refreshing it in ice-cold water.
4. Strain the spinach and squeeze out the excess water before chopping roughly.
5. Beat the ricotta with a spoon until soft, stir in the spinach and season well with salt and pepper.
6. Using a piping bag, pipe the ricotta mixture down one side of each lasagne sheet and roll them up to form a filled tube. Cover and chill in a refrigerator.
7. Place the cannelloni into a lightly oiled baking dish.
8. Pour the sauce over the prepared cannelloni, sprinkle with freshly sliced basil and the Parmesan.
9. Bake at 190°C for 20 minutes and serve.

Baked cod with a cheese and herb crust

Ingredients	4 portions	10 portions
Cod fillet portions, 100 g each	4	10
Fresh white breadcrumbs	100 g	250 g
Butter – melted	100 g	250 g
Fresh herbs – chopped (e.g. basil, tarragon, parsley)	1 tbsp	2.5 tbsp
Salt		

energy	cal	fat	sat fat	carb	sugar	protein	fibre
1588 kJ	381 kcal	21.9 g	13.2 g	19.7 g	0.8 g	26.0 g	0.7 g

METHOD OF WORK

1. Place the fillets on a greased tray or ovenproof dish.
2. Combine all the other ingredients thoroughly. Season lightly with salt and press an even layer onto the fish.
3. Bake in an oven at 180°C for approximately 10–15 minutes until cooked and the crust is a light golden brown.
4. Serve with a suitable sauce – e.g. white wine butter sauce.

Cottage pie

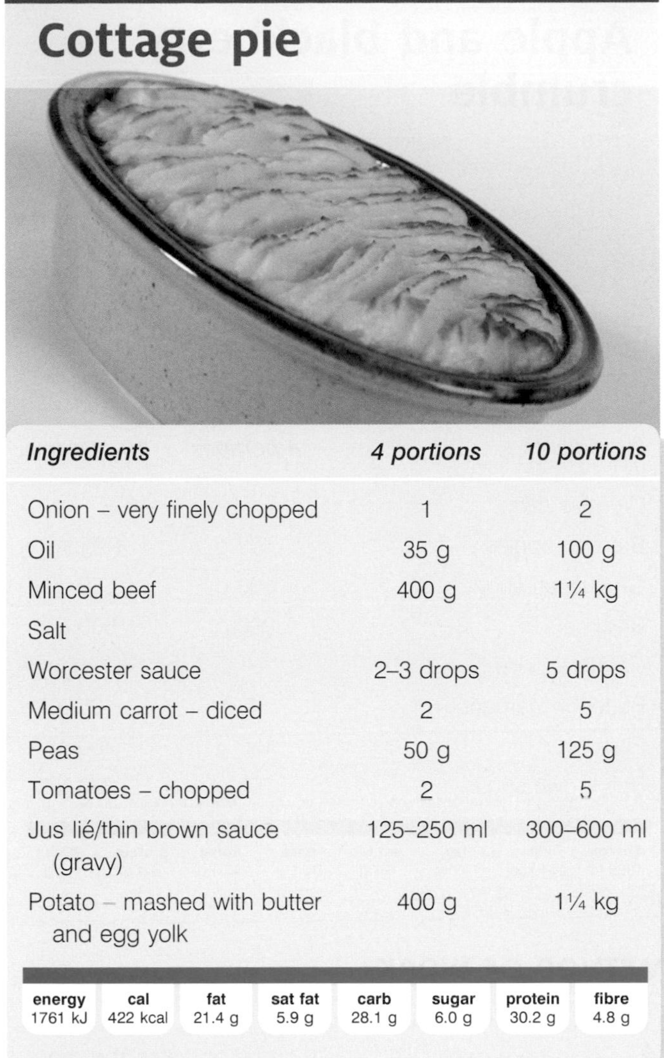

Ingredients	4 portions	10 portions
Onion – very finely chopped	1	2
Oil	35 g	100 g
Minced beef	400 g	1¼ kg
Salt		
Worcester sauce	2–3 drops	5 drops
Medium carrot – diced	2	5
Peas	50 g	125 g
Tomatoes – chopped	2	5
Jus lié/thin brown sauce (gravy)	125–250 ml	300–600 ml
Potato – mashed with butter and egg yolk	400 g	1¼ kg

energy	cal	fat	sat fat	carb	sugar	protein	fibre
1761 kJ	422 kcal	21.4 g	5.9 g	28.1 g	6.0 g	30.2 g	4.8 g

METHOD OF WORK

1. Gently cook the onion in the oil in a thick-bottomed pan, without colouring, until soft.
2. Add the minced beef and continue to cook through.
3. Add the vegetables and mix in to the mince.
4. Add Worcester sauce and sufficient sauce to bind the mince and vegetables.
5. Bring to the boil, stirring frequently, and reduce to simmer for 10–15 minutes.
6. Place into an ovenproof dish.
7. Pipe or neatly arrange the mashed potato on top.
8. Bake in the oven at 190°C for 30 minutes until the potato is golden brown.

Roast loin of pork and apple sauce

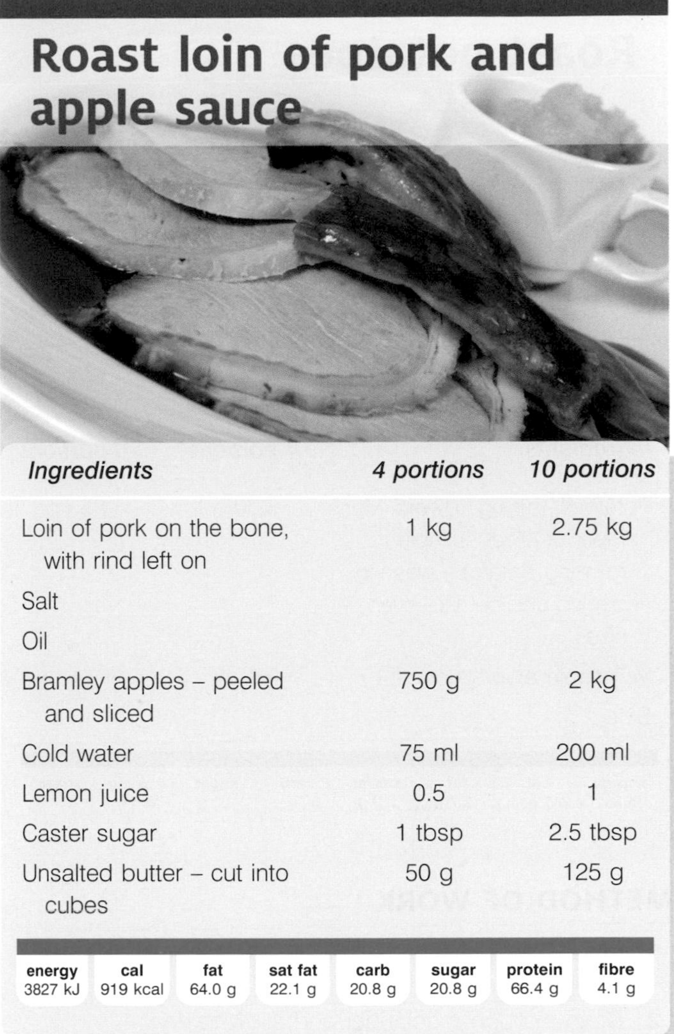

Ingredients	4 portions	10 portions
Loin of pork on the bone, with rind left on	1 kg	2.75 kg
Salt		
Oil		
Bramley apples – peeled and sliced	750 g	2 kg
Cold water	75 ml	200 ml
Lemon juice	0.5	1
Caster sugar	1 tbsp	2.5 tbsp
Unsalted butter – cut into cubes	50 g	125 g

energy	cal	fat	sat fat	carb	sugar	protein	fibre
3827 kJ	919 kcal	64.0 g	22.1 g	20.8 g	20.8 g	66.4 g	4.1 g

METHOD OF WORK

1. Lightly score the pork rind with the tip of a sharp knife.
2. Drizzle the oil over the pork and rub the salt generously into the rind.
3. Place the meat in a roasting tin. Roast at 220°C for 25 minutes, then reduce the temperature to 190°C and continue to cook until done (refer to table of temperatures on page 133).
4. Remove the joint from the tray and put on a plate or dish.
5. Cover the joint loosely with foil and allow it to rest for 10-15 minutes before carving.

To make the apple sauce

1. Place the sliced apple in a saucepan with the water and lemon juice and cook over low heat, stirring occasionally for about 12–15 minutes until the apples have softened.
2. Beat with a wooden spoon to break down the apple into a rough puree.
3. Stir in the sugar and whisk in the cubes of butter and keep warm. If cold apple sauce required, cold water leave out the butter.

Roast potatoes

Ingredients	4 portions	10 portions
Potatoes – (King Edward, Maris Piper or other suitable roasting potato) – washed, peeled and cut into even sizes	600 g	1.5 kg
Vegetable oil or goose fat	50 ml	125 ml
Salt		

energy	cal	fat	sat fat	carb	sugar	protein	fibre
1002 kJ	241 kcal	12.7 g	0.9 g	30.0 g	1.3 g	2.6 g	2.7 g

METHOD OF WORK

1. Blanch the potatoes in boiling, salted water for 5 minutes.
2. Drain through a colander and allow to dry.
3. Heat a good measure of oil or dripping in a roasting tray.
4. Add the well-dried potatoes and lightly brown on all sides.
5. Season lightly with salt and cook for 45 minutes to 1 hour in a reasonably hot oven (190°C to 200°C).
6. Turn the potatoes through the cooking process to ensure even cooking and colouring.
7. Cook to a crisp, golden brown. Drain off the fat and serve.

Mixed roast vegetables consisting of large dice of courgette, butternut squash, bell peppers and cloves of garlic. Coated in olive oil and roasted in a roasting tray.

Apple and blackberry crumble

Ingredients	4 portions	10 portions
Crumble filling		
Bramley apples	500 g	1.25 kg
Granulated sugar	100 g	250 g
Blackberries	200 g	500 g
Crumble topping		
Butter or margarine	50 g	125 g
Plain flour	150 g	400 g
Soft brown sugar	100 g	250 g

energy	cal	fat	sat fat	carb	sugar	protein	fibre
1965 kJ	464 kcal	11.0 g	6.6 g	94.1 g	65.5 g	4.4 g	4.5 g

METHOD OF WORK

1. Peel, core and slice the apples.
2. Cook them gently with a few drops of water and the sugar in a covered saucepan.
3. Mix the blackberries with the cooked apple and place in a baking dish or in individual moulds.
4. Make the topping by lightly rubbing the fat into the flour. Combine this with the sugar.
5. When the fruit is cool, sprinkle on the topping and bake at 190°C for about 15 to 20 minutes until lightly browned.
6. Serve with suitable sauce – e.g. custard or crème anglaise.

10 Deep frying and shallow frying

Unit 110 Deep frying and shallow frying

Recipes

ONLINE RECIPES

LEARNER SUPPORT

Escalope of salmon with basil

Vegetable stirfry

LEARNING OBJECTIVES

On completion of this chapter you will be able to:

- **Describe the methods of shallow and deep frying.**
- **Identify foods that can be shallow and deep fried.**
- **Identify the fats and oils that are used to shallow and deep fry.**
- **Select suitable techniques to shallow and deep fry.**
- **List the quality points to look for in food that has been shallow or deep fried.**
- **List the general safety points to follow when shallow or deep frying food.**

Shallow frying

What is shallow frying?

Shallow frying is described as the cooking of food in a small amount of pre-heated fat or oil. This can be achieved by using a variety of different pans or surfaces.

Methods and equipment used to shallow fry

Frying pan

FRYING PAN

A frying pan has shallow sides. This is because the food is cooked by heat being transferred from the base of the pan and into the fat or oil. This is in direct contact with the food and heat is then passed through the food until it is cooked.

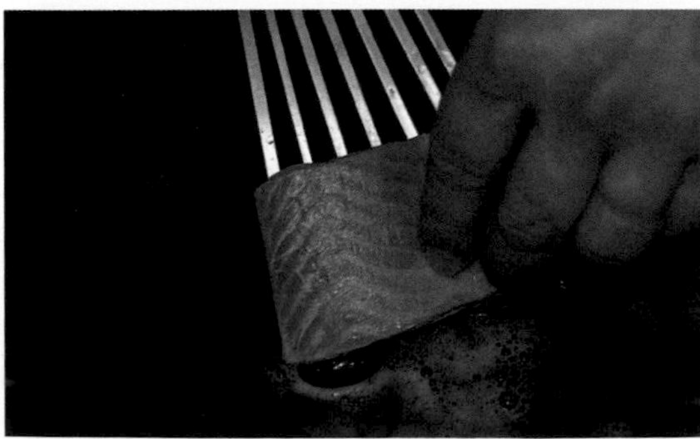

During the frying process, we usually have to turn the food over. This is important to ensure that the food is cooked evenly and also to provide an even colour to the food. As the pan is shallow, this is much easier to do than in a pan that has deep sides. To turn food over, we normally use a palette knife or slice.

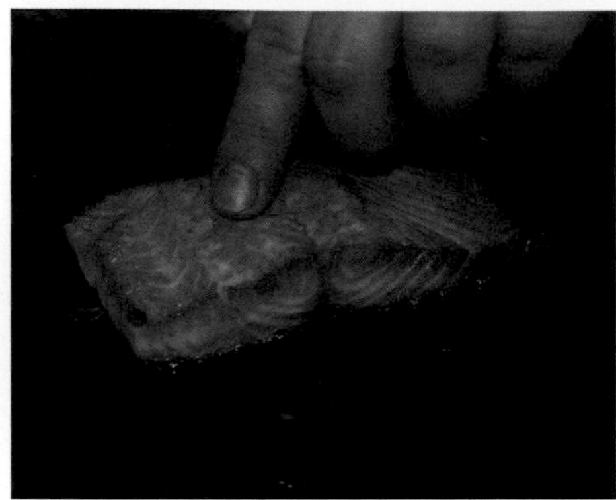

It is important that a frying pan is well looked after and clean before you use it. Many modern frying pans are lined with a coating to prevent foods from sticking. An example of this is Teflon™. It is very important that when using and cleaning a frying pan with such a coating that the surface is not scratched or damaged as this will remove the non-stick properties.

WOK (STIR-FRY)

Woks have become a very common piece of equipment in today's kitchens with the increase in Chinese and far-eastern foods consumed in the UK. Stir frying in a wok is a fast method of cookery, where the food is continuously stirred or tossed to ensure that the food is cooked evenly without burning. A wok can also be used to deep fry food but extreme care has to be taken to ensure that the oil or fat does not get too hot and ignite!

CHEF'S TIP Certain vegetables are also suitable to be cooked by sauté, the most common being sauté potatoes. In this case, the potatoes are usually blanched, sliced and cooked in hot oil or fat until cooked through to a light golden brown colour.

Sauté pan

SAUTÉ PAN

The term 'sauté' means to jump or to toss. In this case, the food is cooked quickly in hot fat or oil and usually to a light golden brown colour. When cooking food by sauté, the tossing of the food does not happen as rapidly or as often as it would when stir-frying. As this is a quick cookery method, the food must be tender (i.e. without a lot of sinew/muscle). Examples of food that can be sautéed include chicken, which has been cut into portions (thighs, drum-sticks, and breast pieces), leaner cuts of meat and offal such as liver and kidneys as well as vegetables such as potatoes.

Griddle

GRIDDLE

A griddle is a heated, solid metal plate which is lightly oiled to produce a frying surface. Griddles are very common pieces of equipment in mobile catering vans that you see at outdoor shows and events. As the surface area is usually quite large, griddles are good for cooking multiple items such as burgers, sausages, eggs, as well as pancakes, scones and potato cakes, etc. Griddles are also made into pans as well as large plates. A griddle pan is shown in the picture to the left of the page.

SPECIAL PANS (OMELETTES, CRÊPES/ PANCAKES, BLINIS, TAVA)

There are a number of pans that have been designed with a specific purpose. Examples of such pans include an omelette pan, a blinis pan and a tava. Each of these examples has been designed to cook certain types of food. For example, the omelette pan is usually smaller than a standard frying pan as it is designed to cook a single item. The blinis pan is smaller again as this is designed to cook blinis, which are small buckwheat pancakes usually served with caviar.

A tava is a flat pan, which is usually used to cook Indian flat breads such as chapatti and paratha. Tortillas are cooked in a similar way. Oil or fat is not always used to cook on these pans. For example, chapattis are cooked on a dry surface.

Step-by-step: Fish Meuniére

STEP 1 Fillets of lemon sole.

STEP 2 Place the skinless fillets into sieved seasoned flour.

STEP 3 Tap to remove any excess flour and the fillets are then coated and ready to shallow fry. The ingredients for the beurre noisette (hazelnut butter) are also ready – chilled slices of butter, chopped parsley and fresh lemon for lemon juice.

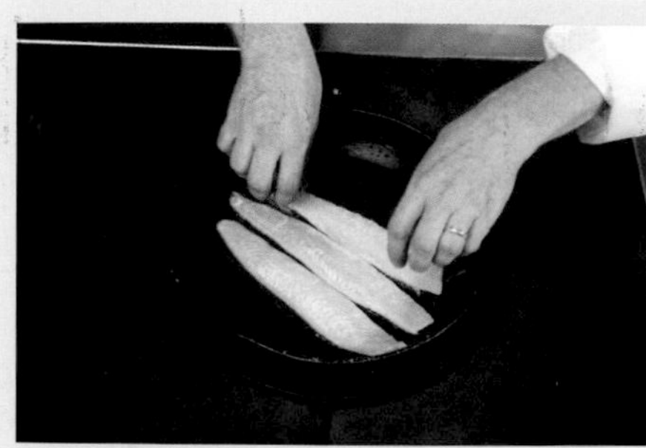

STEP 4 Fillets are placed, skin-side down, into a hot frying pan lined with oil and/or clarified butter.

STEP 5 After 1 minute or so, when the fillets gain a little colour, carefully turn the fillets over to cook on the other side. Remove the fillets from the pan and place onto a warm plate.

STEP 6 Heat a dry pan until it is very hot before adding the slices of cold butter.

STEP 7 When the butter turns a light golden brown (hazelnut) colour, squeeze in the lemon juice followed by the chopped parsley.

STEP 8 Pour the beurre noisette (hazelnut butter) over the fish and serve immediately.

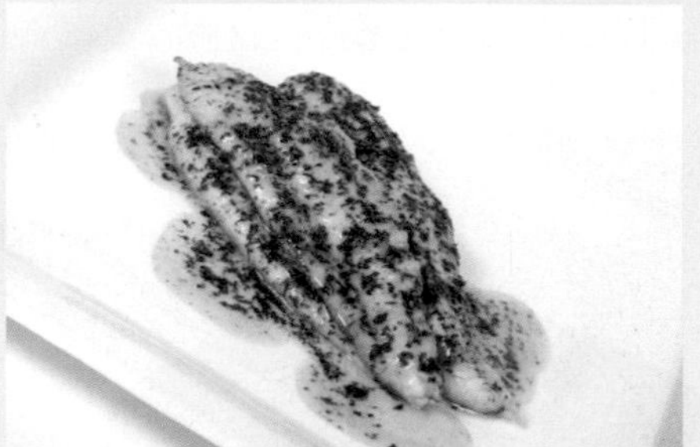

STEP 9 The finished dish, Lemon Sole Meuniére

The preparation of equipment for shallow frying

With the exception of sauté pans and pans that are lined with a non-stick coating such as Teflon^{TM}, traditional frying pans must go through a process known as 'proving'. This process creates a good frying surface and, if used correctly, the food should not stick to the pan.

CHEF'S TIP The two ways to prove a frying pan:

1. In the first method, the pan is lightly oiled, placed on the stove at a low to medium heat and heated for about 10 minutes. After this time, the oil is carefully tipped out into a suitable container and the pan is wiped clean. It is now ready for use.
2. The pan is filled with salt. This is heated as in example 1. The salt is then tipped out of the pan and the pan is wiped clean. The pan would then be lightly oiled and is ready for use. This is often used to prepare crêpe/pancake pans.

Step-by-step: Chicken stir-fry

STEP 1 Ingredients for the stir-fry – sliced onions, chopped ginger and garlic, spring onions, carrots, peppers, courgette, broccoli, blanched noodles, marinated chicken.

STEP 2 Heat oil in a wok or frying pan and stir-fry the chicken.

STEP 3 Add the onions, carrots, spring onion and the chopped garlic and ginger.

STEP 4 Add the remaining vegetables.

STEP 5 Add the noodles and mix carefully into the other ingredients.

STEP 6 Add a dash of sweet chilli sauce or other sauce of your choice – e.g. hoisin or plum sauce.

STEP 7 Using tongs, carefully place the stir-fry into a bowl to serve.

STEP 8 Chicken and vegetable stir-fry.

The effects of shallow frying on food

It is very important that the fat or oil is heated to the correct degree before adding foods to be shallow fried. If the temperature is too hot, the food will cook too quickly on the outside and even burn. If the temperature is not hot enough, the food will absorb the fat or oil, making the food greasy and increasing the fat content. There is more guidance provided on this subject in the practical examples of foods being prepared and cooked throughout the chapter.

The high temperature of the fat or oil helps to seal foods that are shallow fried. This also helps to retain nutrients and make some foods, such as chicken, more tender and moist. Fried food does, however, naturally absorb some of the fat or oil, increasing the fat content of the finished foods. This is reduced greatly if the process of frying is carried out correctly.

Foods suitable for shallow frying

Shallow frying is a quick method of cookery and therefore the foods to be fried need to be suitable. For example, it would be hard to shallow fry large commodities such as a joint of meat, a chicken or a whole vegetable. This could also be dangerous as the core temperature of the meat would not be high enough to kill bacteria by the time that the outside of the meat is cooked. To make food suitable for shallow frying, it usually has to be cut quite thinly or the texture of the food has to be such that it allows heat to penetrate through the food quickly without making it tough. Fish provides a good example of such a food, as the flesh of the fish is very delicate and easily digested. This enables the heat to penetrate through the food quickly.

CHEF'S TIP A bratt-pan is a versatile piece of equipment that can be used to boil, braise, stew or even poach. As most bratt-pans have a flat base, they can also be used to griddle (fry) food.

If using meat or poultry, it must be cut appropriately to ensure that shallow frying can be used successfully as a cookery method. Examples include a steak or a chicken escalope. It is also important to note that the structure of the food is suitable for shallow frying. For example, a piece of meat taken from an area that is high in connective tissue will require a long cookery process to tenderize the muscle and sinew. Lean cuts without such a muscular structure can be cooked by much quicker cookery methods and still remain tender. Finally, when shallow frying, it is important that when the outside of the food appears to be cooked, usually to a light golden brown colour, the centre is also cooked through. You can test this using a probe as described in Chapter 9 (pages 130 and 131).

VIDEO CLIP Shallow frying salmon.

Step-by-step: Shallow-fried supreme of salmon

STEP 1 Cut diagonally into the tail end of the fillet to expose a little of the skin. Holding the skin firmly, run a sharp knife almost horizontally (with the blade pointing slightly towards the skin) along the inside of the skin of the fish to separate the fillet from the skin.

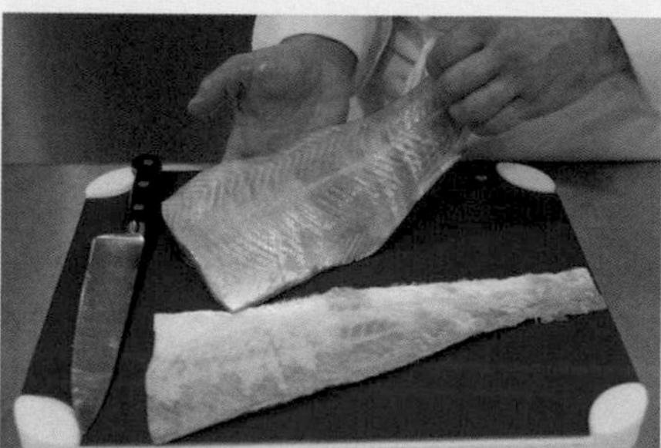

STEP 2 If this procedure is performed well, there will be very little flesh left on the skin.

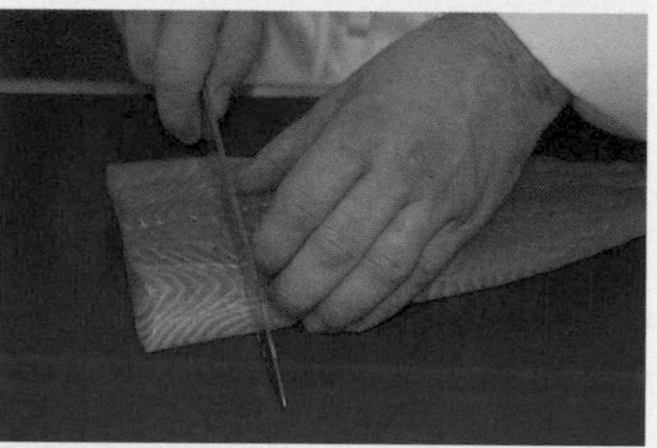

STEP 3 Cut the fillet into evenly sized/weighted supremes.

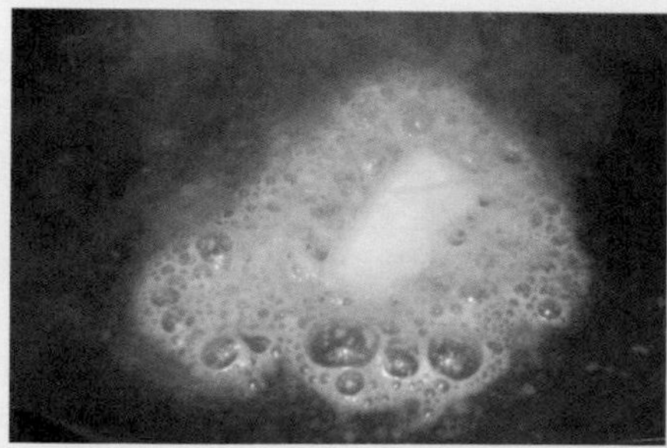

STEP 4 Heat some oil and butter in a frying pan and place the lightly seasoned supreme, service-side (skin-side) down, into the pan.

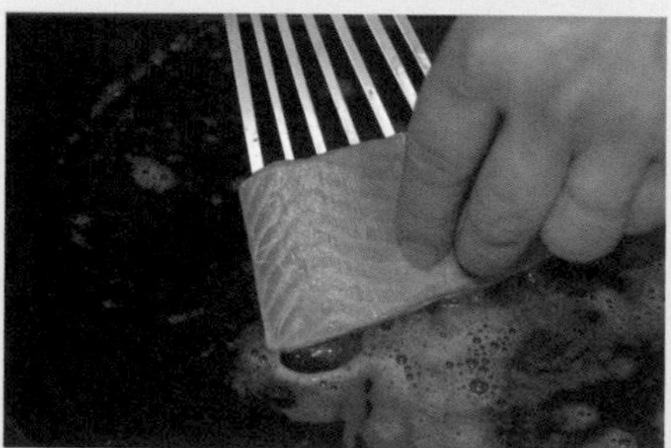

STEP 5 When the salmon is ready to be turned, gently press the top of the supreme and place a fish slice underneath.

STEP 6 When cooked, place the supreme onto a plate. In this example the salmon is served with a slice of herb butter and seasonal vegetables.

TASK In the categories below, name two products that would be suitable to shallow fry. Indicate the type of oil or fat most suitable to use.

FOOD	EXAMPLE	OIL/FAT
Vegetables	1.	
	2.	
Dairy products	1.	
	2.	
Fish	1.	
	2.	
Meat and poultry	1.	
	2.	
Fruit	1.	
	2.	
Ready prepared products (convenience products)	1.	
	2.	

HEALTH & SAFETY Food should never be thrown into hot oil or fat or dropped from a height.

Working safely

It is important to follow safe working practices when shallow frying food. The following points should be considered:

- **Use the right pan for the job**
  Make sure that the pan is the right size to fit the amount of food to be cooked. This will also make the job of **monitoring** and turning food much easier.
- **Be very careful when moving a pan when it is hot**
  This could be during the cooking process when the pan is on the stove or on top of a flame. You also have to be careful after you have finished cooking the food as the pan and the oil or fat will remain hot for quite a long time.
- **Take care when placing food into hot oil or fat**
  It is important that the oil or fat is heated to the right temperature before placing the item of food to be cooked into the pan. This ensures that the food starts to seal on impact and doesn't absorb excess oil or fat making the food greasy. It is also important that the food is placed carefully and in an action away from the body. Food should be lowered gently into the oil or fat to avoid splashes.
- **Monitor the temperature of the oil or fat**
  Never walk away from food that is being shallow fried. Oil can catch fire if it gets too hot and this could lead to a serious incident. It is also important to make sure that the item of food is cooking at the right speed to ensure it is cooked through whilst getting a light golden brown colour on the outside.
- **Take care when handling hot oil or fat**
  Occasionally, there may be circumstances when you have to handle hot oil and fat. Ideally, oil or fat should be cooled before it is handled or moved. If oil or fat has to be handled when it is hot, extreme care should be applied. You should also ensure that access is clear and that your work colleagues are informed of your actions.
- **Ensure that appropriate clothing and equipment is worn and used**
  Protective clothing is designed to protect you in the event of hot oil or fat being spilled or coming into contact with the body. Safety shoes will also protect your feet from such spillages and reduce the likelihood of a serious burn. It is also very important that the right equipment is used to handle food when shallow frying. This reduces the need for direct contact and helps to provide a safe distance between the skin and the hot oil or fat.

The use of fats and oils when frying foods

Shallow and, particularly, deep frying are not considered to be healthy methods to cook foods due to the high fat content. However, within a sensible and balanced diet, fried foods produce an appetizing and nutritious meal. Fats, such as butter or lard have unique flavours but are high in saturated fat, making them unpopular choices with many people. Lard is also an animal product and would be unsuitable for vegans, vegetarians and those offended by the use of animal products in this way. An un-clarified fat such as butter (butter containing buttermilk) will also burn at a lower temperature than oils. Butter is also an expensive product to use in comparison to vegetable oil, for example.

Therefore, it is much more usual to use oils for frying, particularly when deep frying. As cooking oils come from many sources, their flavours and properties differ. Oils from nuts, such as peanut, hazlenut and walnut oil have strong flavours, making them unsuitable (overpowering) when frying certain foods. They are more commonly used for their flavouring properties and in salad dressings.

CHEF'S TIP Peanut and sesame oils are associated with Chinese and Asian cookery but must be used carefully as they have a strong and overpowering flavour. For example, peanut oil is often blended with vegetable oil so that its flavour is not so intense when using it as a frying medium.

Vegetable, corn, sunflower and olive oils are the most commonly used oils throughout Europe. Vegetable oils have a very delicate flavour and are the most **economical**. Olive oil is considered one of the healthiest oils due to its make-up of unsaturated fats. However, olive oil is generally more expensive to purchase, particularly virgin (first pressed) olive oil. It also has a stronger flavour than vegetable oil, which will affect the flavour of the food being cooked. Mediterranean and fish dishes are considered to benefit from the flavour passed on through the use of olive oil.

Deep frying

Deep frying is described as the cooking of food in pre-heated deep fat or oil.

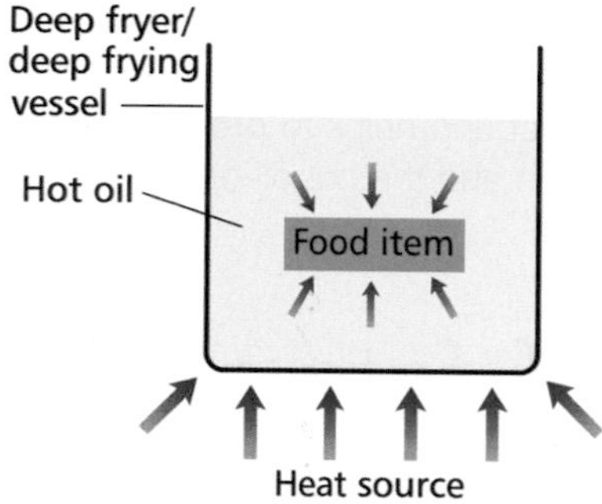

Deep frying

Thermostatically controlled deep fryer

Methods and equipment used to deep fry

Deep frying can be achieved by using a variety of different pieces of equipment. Here are some examples.

THERMOSTATICALLY CONTROLLED DEEP FRYER

This is the most common type of deep fryer. This is the type of fryer that you would normally see in use in a fish and chip shop. The energy used to heat a deep fryer can be electricity or gas.

In this type of fryer, the oil or fat is held within a deep container. This container heats up the oil or fat to the required temperature. The temperature is monitored and held at the required temperature by a device called a thermostatic control.

Underneath the source of heat is what is referred to as a cool zone. This is designed to catch all the bits of food that may come away from the item of food that is being deep fried. Examples of this include breadcrumbs coming away from a breaded chicken breast or excess batter separating from a piece of battered fish.

PRESSURE FRYER

Pressure fryers seal the air in an airtight container. This retains the heat within the unit, cooking the food more quickly and at a lower oil temperature. Pressure fryers are common in the home due to their safety features and ease of use.

COMPUTERIZED FRYERS

Computerized fryers are controlled by circuits of temperature probes, sensors and timers. They can be programmed to control the heat of oil or fat at different stages of the cooking process. They have the capacity to control the food at all stages, lowering the basket of food into the oil for a specific time and raising the food from the oil when it is ready. Some fryers even have programmes to clean themselves.

Computerized fryers are commonly used in the fast-food industry. Using pre-programmed equipment minimizes the training required to operate the equipment, while achieving a good quality and consistent finished product.

The effects of deep frying food

When food is being deep fried, it is submerged into a pool of very hot oil or fat. Therefore, it is important that the food being fried can stand up to being exposed to such high temperatures. To protect items of food, they can be coated so that the food is not directly exposed to the very hot oil or fat. The most common coatings are breadcrumbs and batters.

HEALTH & SAFETY Never throw or drop items into a deep fryer. The hot oil will splash and could cause a serious burn if it comes into direct contact with the skin.

In this example, it is the coating that is in direct contact with the oil or fat, which, if cooked at the correct temperature, will go crisp offering a contrast in texture with the item of food. The coating will also help to prevent the item of food becoming oily as it is not in direct contact with the oil or fat. There are exceptions to this where the item of food can form the crisp outside coating without the addition of a coating.

Chips provide a good example of this process. Normally the potatoes would be cut to an even size of chip. They would then be blanched, this time in the oil, but at a reduced temperature to cook the chip but without colour. The blanched chips can then be stored until required. At this point, the temperature of the oil is raised to finish the cooking of the chips, but also to add the crispy outside coating that you would expect with a good quality chip!

As with shallow frying, it is very important that the fat or oil is heated to the correct degree before adding foods to be deep fried.

Suitable food for deep frying

Deep frying is a quick method of cookery and therefore the foods to be fried need to be suitable and often have to go through a stage of preparation. This can vary quite a lot depending on the type of food. Fish, for example, is very delicate in structure and therefore does not necessarily need to be cut down to speed up the cookery process. An example of this is deep-fried sole. Other fish dishes are more suitable when the fish is filleted or cut into goujons.

Meat and poultry have to be prepared to deep-fry, normally by cutting into slices, strips or dice. This enables the heat to penetrate through the food quickly.

When deep frying, it is important that when the outside of the food is cooked, usually to a light golden brown colour, the centre is also cooked. Therefore, if the meat or chicken is cut appropriately, deep frying can be used successfully as a suitable cookery method. Examples include strips of beef or a chicken escalope. It is also important to note that the structure of the food is suitable for deep frying. Meats that are made up of a lot of muscle, such as the cuts for the leg of beef (e.g. shin, silverside, top rump) need slower methods of cooking like stewing, braising and roasting.

Step-by-step: Cod in beer batter

STEP 1 Ingredients – cod fillet, beer, seasoned self-raising flour.

STEP 2 Coat the cod in self-raising flour and tap to remove any excess.

STEP 3 Place the floured cod into the beer batter (made from self-raising flour and beer whisked together).

STEP 4 Scrape off the excess batter.

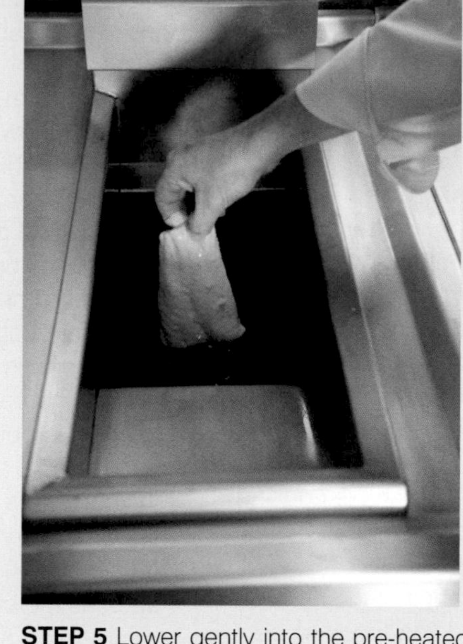

STEP 5 Lower gently into the pre-heated deep-fat fryer.

STEP 6 Fry until cooked through. The batter should be a crisp and a light golden brown colour.

STEP 7 Drain using a spider and place onto a tray lined with kitchen paper to absorb the oil before serving.

CHEF'S TIP Potatoes will begin to discolour once they are peeled. A way to prevent this from happening is to place them in a bowl of cold water. However, it is essential that potatoes, or any other foods kept in water prior to cooking, are dried thoroughly before placing into hot oil. This also applies to defrosted frozen food that may have a wet surface.

HEALTH & SAFETY Water will cause hot fat to spit and will burn if it comes into contact with your skin. The level of oil will also increase, causing a possible overspill and a potentially very dangerous situation.

Step-by-step: Goujons of plaice

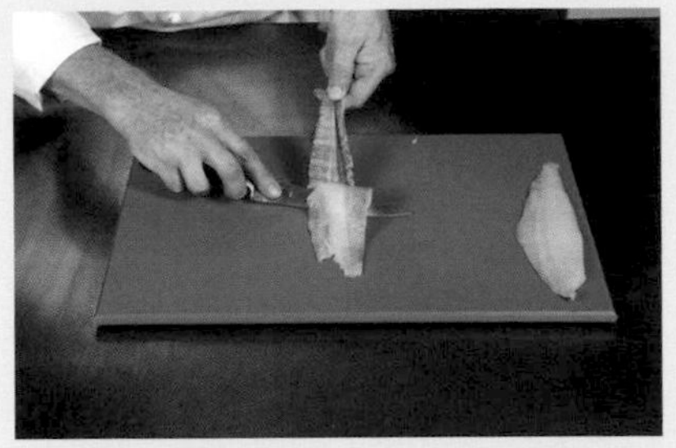

STEP 1 Using a sharp filleting knife, cut diagonally into the tail of the fillet to expose a little of the skin. Holding the skin firmly, run the knife almost horizontally (with the blade pointing slightly towards the skin) along the inside of the skin of the fish to separate the fillet from the skin.

STEP 2 Cut the fillet diagonally into strips (goujons).

STEP 3 Ingredients – goujons coated in oil and herbs, eggs for egg wash, seasoned flour, fresh breadcrumbs.

STEP 4 Place the goujons into seasoned flour, shaking off any excess.

STEP 5 Place the floured goujons into the egg wash to coat, draining off any excess.

STEP 6 Finally, place the goujons into the fresh breadcrumbs.

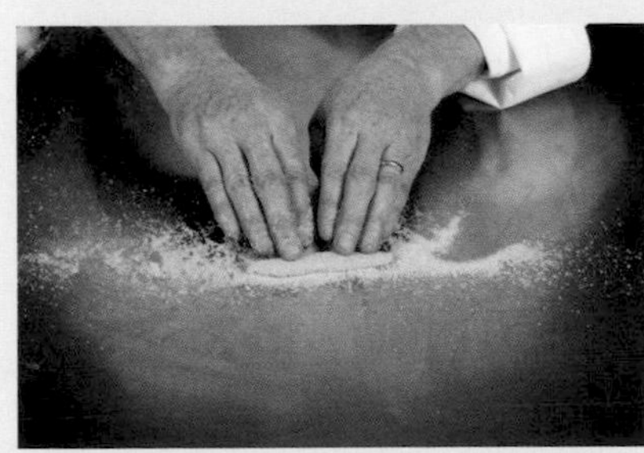

STEP 7 Roll the goujons to secure the breadcrumbs.

STEP 8 Place the breaded (panéd) goujons into a frying basket.

STEP 9 Lower the basket into the heated oil and deep fry until lightly golden brown.

STEP 10 Lift the basket from the oil and drain the goujons on absorbent paper.

Step-by-step: Spring rolls

STEP 1 Ingredients for the spring roll filling – beansprouts, julienne (strips) of carrot, sliced red onion, chilli, ginger and green pepper.

STEP 2 Heat the oil in a wok and toss the ingredients to soften.

STEP 3 Cool and season before placing in the centre of the spring roll wrapper.

STEP 4 Enclose two sides of the wrapper.

STEP 5 Brush the edges with a paste made from a mix of flour and water.

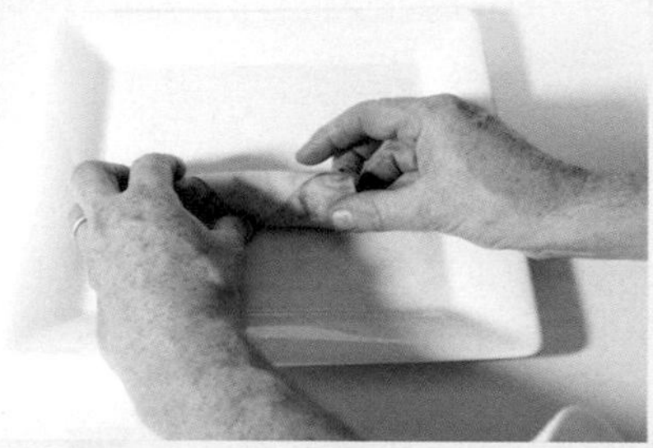

STEP 6 Roll the wrapper tightly.

STEP 7 Carefully lower into pre-heated oil.

STEP 8 Drain onto a tray lined with kitchen paper to absorb the oil.

Step-by-step: Apple fritters

STEP 1 Carefully peel the apples.

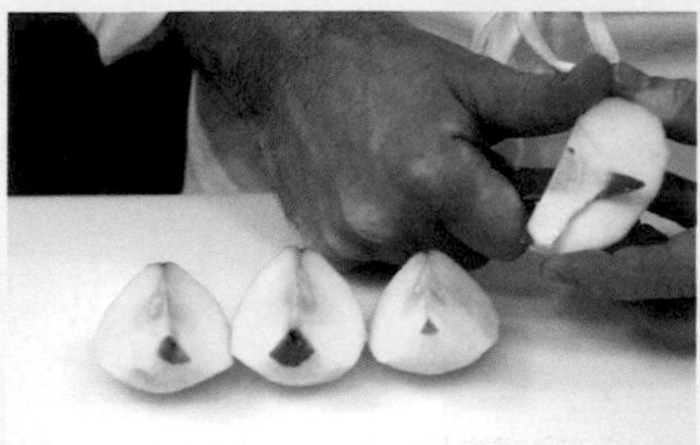

STEP 2 Cut the apple into quarters and cut out the core from each piece of apple.

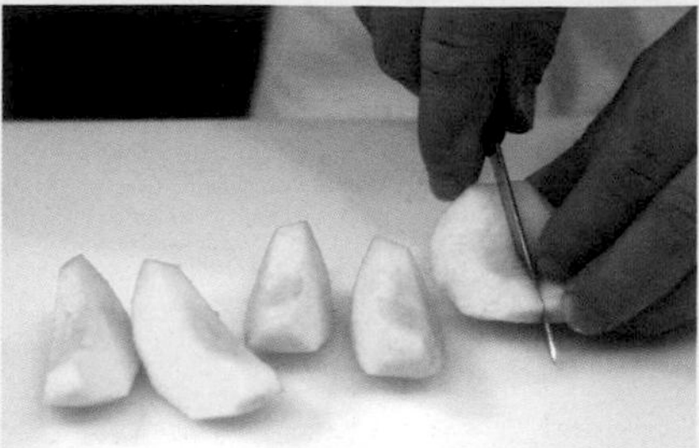

STEP 3 Cut each piece of apple in half to make eight segments in total.

STEP 4 Place the apple segments into water mixed with lemon juice. This will prevent the apple from discolouring.

STEP 5 When ready to fry, drain the apple segments on absorbent paper and then coat in flour.

STEP 6 Drop the apple segments into the frying batter.

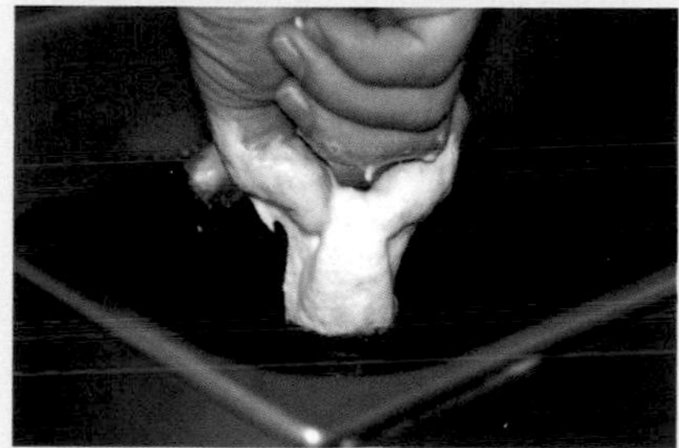

STEP 7 Drain off any excess batter and carefully place each segment into the deep fryer.

STEP 8 Once the batter has turned light golden brown, remove the fritters with a spider and drain on absorbent paper.

STEP 9 Roll each fritter in sugar and serve as required.

STEP 10 Finished dish.

CHEF'S TIP A little ground cinnamon mixed with the sugar produces a great combination with apples.

TASK In the categories below, name a product that would be suitable to deep fry alongside a suitable coating.

TYPE OF FOOD	EXAMPLE AND SUITABLE COATING	
Vegetables	1. ______	2. ______
Dairy products	1. ______	2. ______
Fish	1. ______	2. ______
Meat and poultry	1. ______	2. ______
Fruit	1. ______	2. ______
Ready prepared products	1. ______	2. ______

Guest Chef

Chicken breast with ham and cheese sauce

Chef *Robert Strachan*

Centre *Eastleigh College, Hampshire*

A slightly different take on the classic 'chicken cordon bleu' dish found on many menus in the 1970s and 1980s. Juicy chicken together with succulent cured ham and a full-flavoured cheddar cheese sauce.

Ingredients	*4 portions*
Chicken breasts trimmed	4 and skin removed
Wiltshire ham	4 slices
Mornay sauce	500 ml (made with cheddar)
Fresh breadcrumbs	160 g
Seasoned flour	
Grated parmesan cheese	40 g
knob of butter	
Olive oil	

METHOD OF WORK

1. Heat oven to 180°C.
2. Lightly batten the chicken breasts and cut each into three even-sized pieces.
3. Cut the ham slices into three pieces.
4. Heat a frying pan with a little olive oil.
5. Pass the chicken through seasoned flour, dust off any excess.
6. Add a knob of butter to the pan and when frothing slowly place in the chicken breasts and lightly colour on both sides.
7. Remove from the pan.
8. Place one piece of chicken onto a clean non-stick tray and place a piece of ham on top. (a cutter or ring can be used to give a more precise shape) and spoon over some of the cheese sauce.
9. Repeat this process three times, finishing with a layer of cheese sauce and top with breadcrumbs and Parmesan.
10. Bake in oven for 10 minutes until piping hot.
11. Gently using a step palette knife or slice to place onto a hot serving plate.

TEST YOURSELF

1 In your own words, describe the process of deep frying.

2 List three coatings that can be added to foods before deep frying.

3 Why is it important to heat the oil or fat before adding the food to be deep fried?

4 Describe the process of adding foods to be deep fried, explaining the reasons for these actions.

5 List the quality points you would look for in food that has been deep fried.

6 List five food items, (other than potatoes) suitable for shallow frying.

7 Name three types of pan that can be used to shallow fry foods.

8 What is the correct name for the dish where sliced potatoes have been tossed in a pan of hot oil/fat until they are cooked through with a light golden brown crisp surface?.

9 Name four types of oil or fat suitable for use when shallow frying.

10 What will happen to food items to be shallow fried if

i) the oil/fat is too hot?
ii) the oil/fat is not hot enough?

Recipes

Crêpes (pancakes)

Ingredients	*10–12 crêpes*
Plain flour	125 g
Salt	2 good pinches (for savoury pancakes only)
Medium eggs	2
Melted butter	1 tbsp
Milk	300 ml
Vegetable oil – to grease the crêpe pan	

energy	cal	fat	sat fat	carb	sugar	protein	fibre
397 kJ	95 kcal	4.9 g	1.5 g	10.1 g	1.5 g	3.1 g	0.4 g

METHOD OF WORK

1 Sieve the flour and salt (if using) in a bowl and add the eggs, butter and half of the milk and whisk until smooth.
2 Gradually add the remaining milk while continuously whisking.
3 Leave the batter to rest for 20 minutes.

Cooking the crêpes (pancakes)

1 Pour the batter into a jug or bowl and have a small ladle ready for ladling into the crêpe pan.
2 Pour a small amount of vegetable oil into a small measuring jug or cup.
3 Start to heat the empty crêpe pan until you can feel a good heat coming through.
4 Add a few drops of oil, tilt to grease the base of the pan and then tip out any excess.
5 Pour in a small amount of batter from the ladle and immediately swirl the pan so the batter thinly coats the entire base.
6 Put the pan back on the heat and cook until the batter is set and little holes appear in the surface.
7 Slide a palette knife carefully under the crêpe and turn it over.
8 Cook the other side for about 30 seconds.
9 Slide the cooked crêpe out onto a cooling rack lined with a small square of greaseproof paper. Place another square of greaseproof paper on top and repeat until all the crêpes are cooked.
10 Serve hot or cold.

Deep-fried cod in beer batter with chips

Ingredients	4 portions	10 portions
Plain flour (to dust the fish)	200 g	500 g
Cod fillet (boned, 200–225g pieces)	4	10
Squeeze of lemon juice		
Salt and pepper		
Self-raising flour – sieved	400 g	1 kg
Lager	550 ml	1350 ml
For the chips		
Large floury potatoes	800 g	2 kg
Oil for frying		
Sea salt – flaked or milled	2 tbsp	5 tbsp

energy	cal	fat	sat fat	carb	sugar	protein	fibre
3644 kJ	867 kcal	32.1 g	6.5 g	112.6 g	2.3 g	32.9 g	7.4 g

METHOD OF WORK

Pre-heat the fat-fryer oil to 180°/350°F.

Pre-preparation

1 Leaving the skin on the cod fillets holds the fillet together when it's passed through the batter and placed in the oil.
2 Squeeze a little lemon juice over each fillet and season with salt and pepper and lightly dust with the plain flour.

To make the batter

1 Sieve the flour into a large bowl and whisk in ¾ of the lager (the consistency of the batter should be very thick). Adjust as necessary using the remainder of the lager.
2 Season with a pinch of salt.
3 Pass the cod fillets, one at a time, through the batter mix, holding the fillet at the thin end, in one corner, between thumb and forefinger.
4 Coat the fish in batter and lift from the bowl. (Some of the batter will begin to fall away slowly.) If the batter falls away too quickly, it means it's too thin, in which case add a teaspoon or two more of flour.

To cook

1 Don't allow too much of the batter to fall off before placing in the deep hot oil.
2 Submerge only an inch at a time and, once ¾ of the fish is in, the batter will lift the fillet, floating the fish.
3 Submerge the remaining fillet in the same way, being careful not to burn your fingers.
4 Cook for 2 to 3 minutes before turning the fish over. At this point the fish will not be golden brown but the batter will have sealed and puffed out.
5 Cook until golden brown all around. (A thick slice of cod will take up to 12 minutes to cook, an average fillet 9 to 10 minutes.)
6 Once cooked, remove from the oil and drain onto kitchen paper. Sprinkle with salt and serve.

For the chips

1 Peel the potatoes and cut them into half inch slices.
2 Cut the slices lengthways into half inch chips.
3 Rinse in a bowl under a running cold tap until the water is clear to remove excess starch.
4 Drain and pat dry.

To blanch

1 Heat the oil in a deep fryer to 150°C and add the potatoes, not filling the basket more than half-full. If you do you risk the oil overflowing and you will also reduce the temperature of the oil.
2 Fry the chips for 5 to 6 minutes, stirring occasionally.
3 Check the degree of cooking by removing a chip and inserting a small knife into the centre of the chip. The chips should be soft right through but without colour at this stage. Lift the basket and set aside.

To finish

1 Increase the temperature of the oil to 190°C and replace the chips, frying for 2–3 minutes until golden and crisp.
2 Remove from the fryer, shake dry and then tip onto a tray lined with absorbent paper.
3 Season the chips with the sea salt.
4 Serve immediately.

Note: Thinner cut chips may not need to be blanched before finishing, depending on their size. This involves cooking the chips at a higher temperature (between 175–180°C) to cook the potatoes through whilst achieving the desired colour and a crisp finish.

Goujons of plaice

Ingredients	4 portions	10 portions
Whole plaice (approximately 300–325 g)	2	5
Eggs – beaten	2	5
Flour – sieved and seasoned with salt and white pepper		
Fresh breadcrumbs		

energy	cal	fat	sat fat	carb	sugar	protein	fibre
1501 kJ	355 kcal	6.0 g	1.2 g	38.9 g	1.2 g	38.7 g	1.4 g

METHOD OF WORK

1. Wash, fillet, skin and trim the plaice.
2. Slice into goujons (approx. 4cm × ½ cm strips).
3. Pass through the flour, egg and breadcrumbs.
4. Deep fry in hot fat at 170°C until golden brown.
5. Serve with appropriate sauce (e.g. Tartare sauce – page 204).

Chicken Kiev

Ingredients	4 portions	10 portions
Chicken supremes	4	10
Butter	200 g	500 g
Lemon juice	½ lemon	2 lemons
Chopped parsley	1 tsp	1tbs
Crushed garlic	2 cloves	5 cloves
Good quality salt and black pepper	To taste	To taste
Flour		
Egg wash		
Fresh breadcrumbs		

energy	cal	fat	sat fat	carb	sugar	protein	fibre
3320 kJ	921 kcal	47.3 g	27.7 g	41.0 g	3.1 g	59.7 g	1.5 g

METHOD OF WORK

1. Beat the butter, lemon juice, parsley and garlic to form a smooth paste. Put to one side.
2. Remove the fillet from the chicken supreme and gently bat out in a clear plastic bag or between two pieces of cling film.
3. From the side of the supreme, make a horizontal cut three-quarters of the way through the flesh.
4. Open the supreme from the cuts and carefully bat out as per step 2.
5. Mould the chilled butter to shape (without melting) and place into the centre of the supreme.
6. Place the batted fillet to the side of the butter and carefully wrap the supreme to conceal the butter. Chill the wrapped supreme to firm before proceeding to the next stage.
7. Pass through seasoned flour, egg wash and breadcrumbs (pané) and allow to set in a refrigerator for at least 20 minutes.
8. Deep or shallow fry until golden brown and with a core temperature of 75°C.
9. Place onto clean kitchen paper to drain from excess fat and then serve with watercress.

Sauté potatoes with onions

Ingredients	*1 portion*
Potatoes	125 g
Onion	60 g

METHOD OF WORK

1. Select evenly sized, medium potatoes and scrub well.
2. Boil the potatoes in their jackets or steam until the potato is just cooked through but still firm.
3. Cool and peel the potatoes before cutting into slices of approximate 3 to 4 mm.
4. Place the slices into a hot frying/sauté pan lined with oil and fry until the potatoes turn a light golden brown colour on each side.
5. Slice the onions and shallow fry separately over a medium heat in oil, turning frequently, until tender and browned.
6. Combine the onions and potatoes and toss together.
7. Season lightly with salt and serve sprinkled with finely chopped parsley.

Macaire/Byron potatoes

Ingredients	*2–3 portions*
Potatoes	½ kg
Butter	25 g

METHOD OF WORK

1. Prepare and cook as for baked jacket potatoes (page 121).
2. Cut the potatoes in half and remove the centre with a spoon and place in a bowl.
3. Add butter and season with salt and milled pepper.
4. Mash and mix as lightly as possible with a fork.
5. Using a little flour, mould into a roll, then slice into round pieces (approximately 2 cm deep and 5 to 6 cm wide), allowing one or two per portion.
6. Mould neatly into round cakes and flour lightly.
7. Shallow-fry on both sides very gently and serve.

Note: To make 'Byron' potatoes, make a small indentation to the top of the finished dish (as described in steps 1 to 7). Add a little grated cheese and sour cream and gratinate under a salamander. An example is show in the picture above.

Steak in red wine sauce

Ingredients	4 portions	10 portions
Steak	4 steaks	10 steaks
For red wine sauce		
Red Wine	10 ml	25 ml
Demi-glace (Basic brown meat sauce)	200 ml	500 ml
Chilled diced better	20 g	50 g
Freshly ground salt and white pepper	To taste	To taste

METHOD OF WORK

Fry the steaks to your liking. The example above uses a 'minute steak', a cut from the sirloin which is very thin and literally fried for one minute, hence its name.

For the red wine sauce

1. Bring the demi-glace to the boil then add the alcohol and re-boil for 5 minutes.
2. Whisk the diced butter into the sauce*, check seasoning and serve.

*Do not re-boil the sauce once the butter has been added as it will split from the sauce.

Fried eggs

Ingredients	1 portion
Butter or oil	25 g per egg
Eggs	2 eggs

METHOD OF WORK

1. Melt the butter or oil in a small non-stick frying pan.
2. Crack the eggs and remove from their shells, adding them carefully and gently to the pan, without breaking the yolks.
3. Cook slowly over a moderate heat.
4. Once cooked, remove carefully with a slice letting the butter or oil drain from the egg.
5. Serve on a warmed plate.

Escalope of pork cordon blue

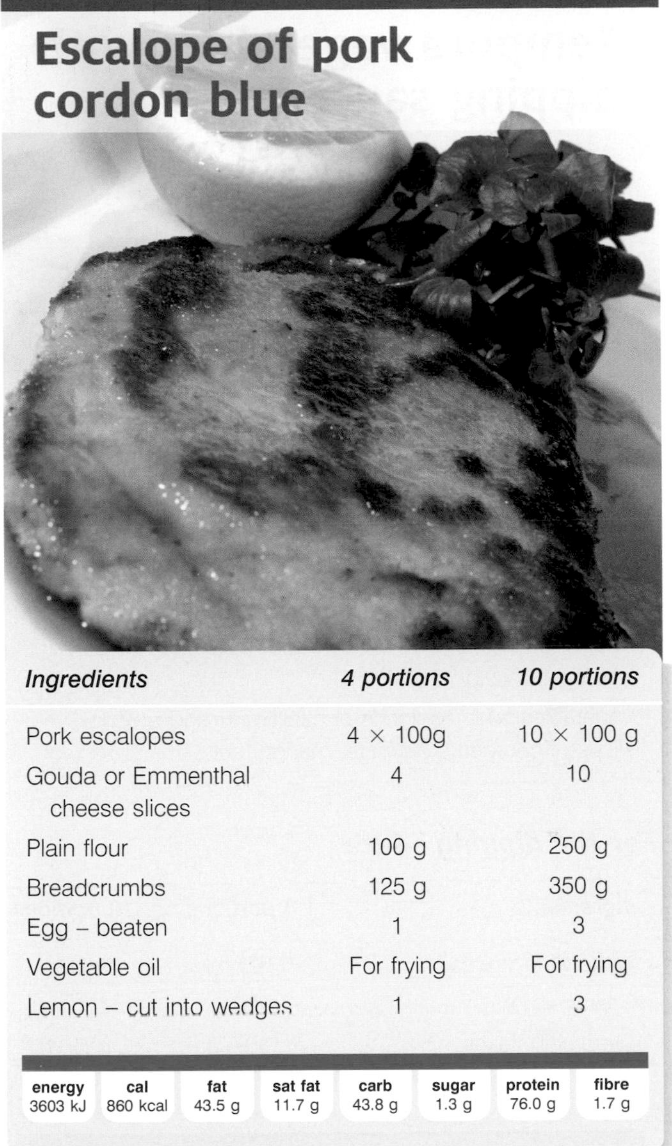

Ingredients	*4 portions*	*10 portions*
Pork escalopes	4 × 100g	10 × 100 g
Gouda or Emmenthal cheese slices	4	10
Plain flour	100 g	250 g
Breadcrumbs	125 g	350 g
Egg – beaten	1	3
Vegetable oil	For frying	For frying
Lemon – cut into wedges	1	3

energy	cal	fat	sat fat	carb	sugar	protein	fibre
3603 kJ	860 kcal	43.5 g	11.7 g	43.8 g	1.3 g	76.0 g	1.7 g

METHOD OF WORK

1 If cutting from the tenderloin of pork, flatten 100 g slices into escalopes using a meat bat using a clear plastic bag or cling film to protect the meat.
2 Take the escalopes, and lay them on a board, place a slice of ham and cheese on top of each and fold over to make a parcel, press the edges together well.
3 Take three different trays, sieve the flour on one, bread-crumbs on another and egg on the last. Coat each parcel in the crumbs, then flour, followed by the egg, then coat in the crumbs again.
4 Heat a little oil in a large heavy-based ovenproof pan and then carefully add the crumbed escalopes.
5 Cook on one side until golden, approximately 4 minutes before turning to cook on the other side.
6 Serve with lemon wedges and seasonal vegetables.

Omelette with tomato sauce

Ingredients	*1 portion*
Eggs	2–3 per portion
Small pinch of slat	
Butter or oil	

METHOD OF WORK

1 Break the eggs into a bowl and season lightly with salt and pepper.
2 Mix thoroughly with a fork or whisk until whites and yolks are thoroughly combined.
3 Heat a non-stick omelette pan and wipe thoroughly clean with a dry cloth.
4 Add the butter or oil and heat until the butter/oil begins to foam and bubble.
5 Add the eggs and cook quickly, stirring continuously with a fork until lightly set. Remove from the heat.
6 Using the fork, carefully fold the mixture in half at a right angle to the handle of the pan.
7 Pointing the pan slightly downwards, sharply tap the pan handle with the other hand to bring the edge of the omelette up to the bottom of the pan.
8 Carefully, using a fork, bring up the opposite edge of the omelette as near to the first edge as possible.
9 Take a warm plate in one hand and, holding the pan under the handle, carefully tip the folded omelette onto the plate. The omelette should be cigar shaped.
10 Neaten the shape if necessary and serve immediately accompanied with fresh tomato sauce.

Deep fried spring greens seaweed

Ingredients	4 portions	10 portions
Spring greens	200 g	50 g

energy	cal	fat	sat fat	carb	sugar	protein	fibre
1269 kJ	308 kcal	30.1 g	2.0 g	4.4 g	0.4 g	4.8 g	5.5 g

METHOD OF WORK

1. Chiffonade (shred) the spring greens very finely.
2. Carefully lower into hot fat (190°C) and deep fry for 10 to 15 seconds.
3. Remove with a spider onto a tray lined with kitchen paper and dry immediately.
4. Sprinkle with a little salt and sugar before serving.

Tempura vegetables with dipping sauce

For the tempura

Ingredients	4 portions	10 portions
Self-raising flour	200 g	500 g
Sparkling mineral water – ice-cold	50 ml	125 ml
Vegetables such as florets of cauliflower and broccoli, slices of courgette, peppers, mange tout		

For the dipping sauce

Ingredients	4 portions	10 portions
White wine vinegar	100 ml	250 ml
Caster sugar	100 g	250 ml
Dried chilli flakes	0.5 tsp	1.25 tsp
Fresh ginger – finely chopped	1 tbsp	2.5 tbsp

energy	cal	fat	sat fat	carb	sugar	protein	fibre
1332 kJ	313 kcal	3.0 g	0.4 g	67.3 g	29.6 g	7.3 g	3.7 g

METHOD OF WORK

1. Heat the oil in a deep, heavy-bottomed pan or deep fryer. The oil is ready when a breadcrumb dropped into it will sizzle gently.
2. Place the flour and the sparkling water into a large bowl and whisk until a smooth batter is formed.
3. Dip the vegetables into the batter and carefully place into the oil and deep fry for 2 minutes, or until crisp and golden. Carefully remove with a slotted spoon and drain on kitchen towels.
4. To make the sauce, place all the ingredients into a small saucepan over a medium heat. Bring to the boil and reduce the heat to simmer for 3 minutes.
5. Place into a food processor and blend until smooth. Transfer to a serving bowl.
6. To serve, place the tempura vegetables into a bowl and serve the sauce alongside.

Onion bhajis

Ingredients	15–20 bhajis
150 g gram flour	
4 tsp ground cumin	
4 tsp ground coriander	
2 tsp turmeric	
1 tsp salt	
1 tsp mixed spice	
1 tsp curry powder	
1-2 tbsp chopped fresh coriander	
8 tbsp water	
4 finely sliced onions	
50 g grated potato	

energy	cal	fat	sat fat	carb	sugar	protein	fibre
224 kJ	53 kcal	1.2 g	0.1 g	8.5 g	2.0 g	2.6 g	2.5 g

METHOD OF WORK

1. Mix together the gram flour and all the spices.
2. Add the water, mix well to make a smooth batter.
3. Add the sliced onions and grated potato and mix well.
4. Heat oil to 170°C. Mould mixture into balls the size of large walnuts.
5. Deep fry the onion bhajis until golden brown on all sides.
6. Drain well before serving.

Vegetable spring rolls

Ingredients	4 portions	10 portions
Medium carrot – cut into julienne/fine strips	1	2.5
Chilli – cut into julienne/fine strips	1	2
Medium leeks – cut into julienne/fine strips	0.5	1.5
Pepper – sliced	1	2
Medium onion – sliced	1	2
Ginger– chopped	10 g	25 g
Garlic – chopped	10 g	25 g
Bean sprouts	20 g	50 g
Oil		
Spring roll wrappers	4	10
Flour and water paste for sticking		

energy	cal	fat	sat fat	carb	sugar	protein	fibre
458 kJ	109 kcal	3.6 g	0.3 g	16.8 g	5.1 g	3.1 g	3.0 g

METHOD OF WORK

1. Prepare all ingredients into the required cuts.
2. Heat the oil in a wok and toss the ingredients to soften.
3. Cool and season before placing in the centre of the spring roll wrapper.
4. Enclose two sides of the wrapper.
5. Brush the edges with a paste made from a mix of flour and water.
6. Roll the wrapper tightly.
7. Carefully lower into oil pre-heated to 175°C in the deep-fat fryer.
8. Drain onto a tray lined with kitchen paper to absorb the oil.
9. Serve with an appropriate dipping sauce (e.g. sweet chilli sauce or chilli jam).

Sweet and sour pork

Ingredients	4 portions	10 portions
Pork fillet	400 g	1 kg
Sake	1 tbsp	3 tbsp
Plain flour – sifted	50 g	125 g
Medium egg – lightly beaten	1	3
Red peppers – quartered and deseeded	2	4
Spring onions (bunch) – trimmed	1	2.5
Bamboo shoots (tinned) – drained	225 g	675 g
Pineapple chunks (tinned) in juice	225 g	675 g
Cornflour (+ extra for dusting the pork before frying)	1 tbsp	2.5 tbsp
Soy sauce	1 tbsp	2.5 tbsp
Sunflower oil for deep frying		

Sweet and sour sauce

Ingredients	4 portions	10 portions
Cornflour	2 tbsp	5 tbsp
Water	100 ml	250 ml
Soft brown sugar	60 ml	150 ml
Soy sauce	30 ml	75 ml
Rice or white wine vinegar	90 ml	225 ml
Tomato ketchup	30 ml	75 ml

energy	cal	fat	sat fat	carb	sugar	protein	fibre
2263 kJ	539 kcal	20.4 g	3.4 g	53.0 g	32.2 g	37.6 g	3.0 g

METHOD OF WORK

Pre-heat the deep-fat fryer to 180°C.

1. Cut the pork into 2.5 cm cubes and place in a bowl and mix in the sake and soy sauce to marinate.
2. To make the batter, sift the flour into a medium-sized bowl, drop the egg into the centre and beat until the mixture is smooth.
3. Cut the peppers and spring onions into 2.5 cm pieces. Drain and rinse the bamboo shoots and also drain the pineapple chunks.
4. Prepare the sweet and sour sauce by placing the corn-flour in a small saucepan and mixing in the water, sugar soy sauce, vinegar and ketchup.
5. Place over a low heat and simmer gently until it has thickened, stirring, which should take about 3 minutes.
6. Meanwhile, remove the pork from its marinade. Place on a plate, dust with one tbsp cornflour then mix into the batter.
7. Deep or shallow fry the batter-coated pork (in batches if necessary).
8. Once the pork is a deep gold colour, remove and drain on kitchen paper.
9. Heat the sunflower oil in a non-stick frying pan or work. Once sizzling hot, add the red pepper and spring onions, stir-fry for 1 minute, then add the bamboo shoots and pineapple chunks and the pork.
10. Add the sauce and bring up to a simmer.
11. Once all the ingredients are coated in the sauce, serve with rice (e.g. egg-fried rice).

Chips

Ingredients	4 portions	10 portions
Good frying potatoes (for example King Edwards/ Maris piper)	600 g	1.5 kg

energy	cal	fat	sat fat	carb	sugar	protein	fibre
1002 kJ	241 kcal	12.7 g	0.9 g	30.0 g	1.3 g	2.6 g	2.7 g

METHOD OF WORK

1. Wash, peel and re-wash potatoes.
2. Trim the potatoes to give straight sides.
3. Cut into neat batons measuring 5cm long by 1 cm × 1 cm.
4. Wash well and dry in a clean kitchen cloth.
5. Deep fry at 160°C to blanch until soft without colour.
6. Drain and place on tray and store in a refrigerator until required.
7. When required for service, deep fry at 180°C until golden in colour and crisp.
8. Remove from the fryer, drain and season with salt.

Fish cakes

Ingredients	4 portions	10 portions
Cooked white fish and or salmon	200 g	500 g
Potato – mashed	200 g	500 g
Flour	25 g	60 g
Eggs – beaten	1	2
Fresh white breadcrumbs	50 g	125 g

energy	cal	fat	sat fat	carb	sugar	protein	fibre
735 kJ	174 kcal	2.5 g	0.5 g	24.6 g	0.8 g	14.5 g	1.4 g

METHOD OF WORK

1. Combine the fish and potatoes. Taste and correct the seasoning.
2. Using a little flour, form the mixture into a long roll on a clean work surface.
3. Divide the mixture into 4, 8, 10 or 12 pieces and mould into balls.
4. Pass the balls through flour, beaten egg and breadcrumbs.
5. Using a palette knife, flatten each shape firmly. Neaten the shapes and shake off surplus crumbs.
6. Deep fry in hot oil at 185°C for 2 to 3 minutes until golden brown. The fish cakes can also be shallow fried.
7. Serve with an appropriate sauce – e.g. a white wine butter sauce or tomato sauce.

Note: Additional ingredients, such as chopped spring onions, can be added to the fish and potato mix for an additional dimension.

11

Regeneration of pre-prepared food

Unit 111 Regeneration of pre-prepared food

LEARNING OBJECTIVES

By the end of this chapter you will be able to:

- **Identify the different types of pre-prepared foods suitable for regeneration.**
- **Describe the differences between regenerated, pre-prepared products and other food types.**
- **Describe the purpose of regenerated, pre-prepared foods in the food industry.**
- **State the possible limitations and potential implications of using regenerated pre-prepared foods.**
- **Identify the correct methods for regenerating a range of pre-prepared foods.**
- **Explain the possible effects on health if too much regenerated, pre-prepared food is eaten.**
- **List the general quality points and associated products when regenerating pre-prepared foods.**

Types of pre-prepared foods suitable for regeneration

The term **regeneration** or regenerated refers to the fact that a process has to take place to bring pre-prepared food back from an unedible state (e.g. dried or frozen) to a safe and enjoyable condition to eat.

Dried foods

Drying refers to the removal of liquid from food. Examples of foods that are dried include stock cubes, powdered sauces and soups as well as batter and scone mixes.

Fresh foods

Many fresh products can be cooked, chilled and then reheated. In the professional kitchen, it is good practice to have food items cooked (blanched) and rapidly chilled. The items can then be quickly re-heated and served. Suitable foods include boiled vegetables and certain soups and sauces.

Boiled potatoes

Ready-made products

Some ready-made products require no further processing to make them edible. Examples of this include cakes, biscuits, cold savoury products (e.g. sausage rolls, quiches, etc.) as well as a whole range of dough products (breads, buns, croissants, etc.).

Other ready-made products have to be heated before they are safe to eat. Examples include ready-made meals, soups, sauces and part-baked rolls.

Frozen foods

There are endless products that can be regenerated from frozen. Care has to be taken when regenerating from frozen as some foods have to be fully defrosted before cooking, whereas others may require the products to be strictly reheated from frozen. Manufacturers should produce very clear instructions on the handling of their products.

Some frozen foods, such as cakes and desserts, are ready to eat once defrosted. Such products, particularly the ones which are served cold are ready to eat once thoroughly defrosted.

Freezing is a readily available process for the chef to use to **preserve** foods for use at a later date. In most cases, foods frozen in this way will require defrosting before use or being re-heated. Certain items, such as soups and sauces, may be safely re-heated from frozen, although this will depend on the way they have been produced and the ingredients they contain.

Frozen green beans

HEALTH & SAFETY It is essential that defrosting follows the instructions of the manufacturer as many products can take a long time to defrost. If food isn't defrosted properly it may be dangerous to eat.

CHEF'S TIP It is very important that food items are labelled and dated and that good **stock control and rotation** practices are followed.

Pre-prepared foods

Pre-prepared products can save the chef a great deal of time during the service period. However, quality must also be taken into consideration as certain products are more suited to being pre-prepared and re-heated than others.

Dishes that are sauced and cooked using a long cookery process, such as stewing and braising are generally suited to being pre-prepared, cooled and then re-heated. Quality is not adversely affected, although additional liquid may be required to re-hydrate the sauce slightly. Pies are another example of a product that can be pre-prepared and re-heated at a later time.

Items that are cooked by the faster cookery methods, such as frying and grilling will lose quality if pre-cooked for use at a later time. They may tend to lose moisture and shrink or, in the case of fish for example, break up.

Tinned foods

There is an enormous range of foods available in cans/tins. This includes a whole variety of vegetables, soups and sauces as well as ready-to-eat dishes such as stews.

Differences between regenerated, pre-prepared products and other food types

As pre-prepared products have been through a process that affects their natural state, their nutritional value will be affected as a result. This may be through cooking, freezing or drying, for example. The quality of food will also be affected and usually will not be as high in quality as fresh food.

The taste of pre-prepared foods normally differs in comparison to a fresh version. For example, a piece of freshly grilled tuna looks and tastes different to tuna from a can/tin. Many pre-prepared foods will contain **additives and preservatives** to increase the shelf-life and flavour of the food concerned. Others such as dried stock cubes contain high levels of salt, making them unsuitable for reducing to intensify flavour when making a sauce.

Pre-prepared products generally require fewer skills than when working with fresh food items. Preparation skills are not required as this part of the process has already taken place. Skills required usually involve the heating and finishing of the food (boiling, baking, etc.) although not all pre-prepared foods require further cooking, frozen gâteaux for example.

Many pre-prepared foods are easy to identify by the trained eye. For example, tinned vegetables have a different appearance to fresh vegetables.

Tinned and fresh carrots

The purpose of regenerated, pre-prepared foods in the food industry

Pre-prepared foods have positive points to consider.

- Pre-prepared foods require fewer skills in preparation and this helps to reduce costs. Foods that are out of season can also be used as the pre-preparation can involve a form of preservation, tinned strawberries for example. This helps to keep the cost of such ingredients down. Once preserved, their shelf-life is extended massively beyond their fresh equivalent.
- Strawberries are a seasonal fruit and at their prime during the summer months in the UK. Now that rapid exporting of food is much more economical than in previous years, it is possible to purchase fresh strawberries all year round. However, imported strawberries can still be expensive and not always high quality in terms of flavour. Another thing to consider is that fresh fruits and vegetables have a limited storage life, and as such, must be used within a short space of time. Pre-prepared foods,

particularly those that have been tinned, frozen or dried will have a much longer 'use-by' period.

- The use of pre-prepared foods can also save on the necessity to have the equipment to produce foods from the beginning of the preparation and cookery process. This can range from basic equipment such as a board and knife, through to utensils (saucepans, mixers, etc.) and larger equipment such as ovens, steamers and bratt pans.
- Pre-prepared foods also offer a consistent standard as many have been through a standardized mass production line, following very precise procedures.

It is generally accepted that lifestyles have become a lot faster during recent years and the growth in pre-prepared foods has run alongside this trend. There is a view that many people are too busy to spend time cooking, preparing dishes from fresh ingredients using conventional cookery methods. It is now possible to have a ready-made meal within a few minutes by simply popping a dish into a microwave. There are also many sauces and mixes available, reducing the amount of preparation needed to prepare a meal. The idea is to simply cut open the packet, mix and cook!

Microwave meals

However, there have been many **criticisms** of this trend. This includes the reduction in time that families spend together enjoying a meal, the rise in obesity in the western world, where fast food and ready-made meals are most highly consumed, as well as the reducing numbers of people actually spending time preparing and cooking using fresh ingredients.

TASK Using the Internet, find recipes for a main course that you could prepare, cook and finish within 30 minutes as an alternative to 'fast food'.

HEALTH & SAFETY Fast food outlets have had to take action to counteract declining sales of their products. There are now more fresh foods available, such as salads and sandwiches and more emphasis on reduced fat, sugar and salt intake. **Marketing potential** is therefore increased when catering and hospitality outlets can promote the fact that they are producing meals from fresh ingredients.

The possible limitations and potential implications of using regenerated, pre-prepared foods

There is mixed success in the regeneration of pre-prepared foods. This depends on the type of food and the method of processing it has been through. Soft fruits, for example, are not particularly successful when regenerated from any processed form, particularly if it is intended that the fruit is to be used as if it were fresh. During the process, the composition (structure) of the fruit changes and it is impossible for such fruits to re-form into their original state. A strawberry or raspberry, for example, will never return to its fresh firm state once it has been tinned, frozen or dried. Fish also tends to lose its firmness once it has been frozen and then defrosted, making it very difficult to work with if defrosting back into a raw state.

With certain, high risk ingredients, a great deal of care has to be taken to ensure that the product retains quality but also that it remains safe to eat. Eggs provide a very good example of a food item where such measures are necessary.

With nearly all foods that are regenerated, certain changes, whether in appearance, texture or nutritional value, unavoidably take place. This can make them much less appealing than their fresh equivalent. People are also now becoming much more aware of the consequences of diet and the links this has to health and well-being.

The hospitality and catering industry has an important role in providing good quality, healthy options for its consumers. The re-introduction of fresh foods in school meals is starting to happen through various projects and there is a great deal of coverage about eating fresh foods in the media (television, newspapers, magazines, etc.). Eating five portions of fresh fruit and vegetables daily (5 A Day!) is a good example of this type of promotion. However, everything comes at a cost! It is rarely the cheaper option to use fresh, high quality ingredients in place of pre-prepared foods. Other issues, such as the skill requirements in preparation and cooking, the life span of the food and the spending power of the customer often outweigh the use of fresh ingredients in favour or in place of pre-prepared foods.

Possible effects of eating pre-prepared or regenerated foods on health

Some pre-prepared foods are high in fats, carbohydrates and have high levels of added salt and sugar. Furthermore, many pre-prepared foods are often adjusted by the addition of preservatives, additives and flavour enhancers to prolong their shelf-life alongside taste, flavour and texture.

Eating products of this nature on a regular basis is likely to have an impact on health. Many pre-prepared products have been designed for economy and convenience but with maximum enjoyment for the consumer. However, they are often quite neutral in taste making them easy to eat and appealing to a wide audience.

People should consider the consumption of such pre-prepared products and be aware of exactly what they are eating. Pre-prepared foods should be considered alongside other foods as part of a healthy and well balanced diet as described in 'The eatwell plate' in Chapter 4 (Introduction to healthier foods and special diets). Consumers also need to consider the content of pre-prepared foods as they may contain ingredients that are allergenic as well as being high in calories, fats, sugars and/or salt. An over-consumption of such ingredients is linked to health problems such as heart disease, high blood pressure and obesity, as well as links to many other potentially related illnesses.

It is important to state that this is not the case for all pre-prepared foods. Some have very little in the way of added fat, sugar and salt or none at all. In fact, some pre-prepared foods such as frozen peas (petit pois) and some dried pasta are considered to be enhanced by the preservation process.

The methods used to regenerate pre-prepared foods

The methods used to regenerate pre-prepared foods differs according to the food type (dried, fresh, ready-made, frozen, pre-prepared, tinned) and the processing the food has undertaken. The methods used include the following regeneration processes.

Re-heating

Reheating refers to food that has already been cooked, chilled and frozen. This may be a dish that has been produced from fresh, to use at a later date, such as vegetable garnishes and accompaniments, or items made externally by another company, such as ready-made meals or sauces.

Step-by-step: Celery being prepared, refreshed and re-heated

STEP 1 Tying sticks of celery together.

STEP 2 Celery is tied into batches for initial cookery.

STEP 3 Celery being blanched in boiling water.

STEP 4 Refreshing the blanched celery.

STEP 5 Braised celery that has been regenerated by reheating in stock or water.

STEP 6 Testing the core temperature to ensure that the celery is re-heated properly.

CHEF'S TIP Certain foods will need additional cookery after rehydration. Examples include pancake mixes, where the mixture will be shallow fried, and scone mixes, where the mixture will be baked.

Re-hydrating

Re-hydrating refers to foods that have had their water content removed to make them dry. Drying foods extends their life span as the scope for bacterial growth is reduced significantly. As with the majority of life forms, water is essential for survival, growth and reproduction.

To re-hydrate dry foods, the liquid content is placed back into the food. Examples of foods that require re-hydration include dried sauces and soups, dried beans, cereals and grains, such as couscous.

Cooking

Other pre-prepared foods will require cooking to ensure they are safe and digestible. Pre-prepared pasta provides an example of a pre-prepared food that can be sold fresh or dried, which requires cooking (boiling, baking) before it is ready to eat. Some ready-made meals may also have raw ingredients that require to be cooked through before they are ready and safe to eat.

Other products, such as part-baked bread rolls require a degree of cooking before they are ready to eat. In this example, the item is partially cooked and then the cookery process is stopped. At this point, the roll will have a firm structure (shape) but will not be suitable to eat. The roll will normally be packed in a suitable way (e.g. vacuum packed) to prevent any bacterial growth or spoilage. When the roll is required, it is cooked again, but this time to complete the cooking process making it safe and enjoyable to eat.

Defrosting

Defrosting can be a complete regeneration process (i.e. no further cooking process is required), and refers to products that simply require defrosting to make them safe and enjoyable to eat. The most obvious examples are the defrost-only varieties of frozen pastries, cakes and desserts.

TASK Provide four examples of dishes that could benefit from the use of a pre-prepared ingredient. An example is provide in the first row.

DISH	PRE-PREPARED INGREDIENT(S)	USE	BENEFIT	SEASON/TIME TO USE (IF RELEVANT)
Peach melba	Tinned peaches/ frozen raspberries	Peach halves – use as they are. Frozen raspberries pureed and **passed** to make the coulis (sauce)	Saves time poaching and preparing peaches. Raspberries will be **liquidized** and passed. Cheaper than using the fresh variety.	Winter months as the fresh variety of these ingredients will be out of season and expensive to source

HEALTH & SAFETY Always follow the manufacturer's instructions when handling frozen foods. Some foods are processed to be cooked from frozen and should not be defrosted whereas others may require complete defrosting before being cooked.

The general quality points when regenerating pre-prepared foods

The quality points to look for when selecting, preparing and regenerating pre-prepared foods are very similar to those to look for in any other food items and are described below.

In selection

When buying pre-prepared food items, the following points should be taken into consideration.

Quality points

- *Quantity* – Is there a sufficient amount of the food item required?
- *Type* – Is the food of the type required? Does it meet the specifications for the recipe/dish concerned?
- *Appearance* – Does the food look as it should? Is it the right colour, size and shape?
- *Smell* – Is there any odour coming from the food? There are very few pre-prepared foods that will have any noticeable smell. The exception to this would be fresh foods that are cooked, chilled and stored to be re-heated at a later time. A fresh fish pie, for example, might have a very slight fishy smell, although this should be very subtle and not at all rancid.
- *Temperature* – Is the food at the correct temperature depending on its type? – (i.e. fresh, frozen, dried, etc.). This is extremely important as commodities of this nature, stored at an incorrect temperature could be dangerous as they may have developed unsafe levels of bacterial growth.
- *Condition* – Is the food in good condition with no blemishes, bruises or breaks?
- *In-date* – Is the food within its use-by or sell-by date? This may have an effect on the food's quality and could also contain potentially unsafe levels of harmful bacteria.

During regeneration

During the regeneration of pre-prepared products, it is essential that correct procedures and instructions are followed to ensure that the product is of the highest possible quality once it has been regenerated.

Quality points

- *When re-hydrating* – The correct amount of liquid has been used. The temperature of the liquid is appropriate for the type of food being regenerated (e.g. cold, boiling, etc.).
- *Temperature control* – The food items are placed into, and monitored at, the correct temperatures throughout the cooking process. The temperature is checked to ensure that food items are sufficiently cooked (to a safe level for consumption – i.e. the core temperature).
- *Time* – The food is cooked for the correct amount of time.
- *Taste* – The food has good flavours and is well seasoned.
- *Consistency* – Food items are consistent across all the quality points (size, temperature, appearance, taste, etc.).
- *Texture* – The texture of the food is appropriate to expectations (i.e. crisp, soft, short, etc.).

In finishing

Completing the quality checks in finishing and presenting food items is equally important.

Quality Points

- *Consistency* – Food items should be the same in colour, flavour and temperature. Food items should also be of a consistent portion size and seasoned and sauced in a consistent manner.
- *Presentation* – Presentation is a vital element within professional cookery. Service equipment, whether using silver salvers or plates, should be spotlessly clean. Dishes should be garnished consistently and presented in a uniform manner.

The associated products served with regenerated foods

As with all foods, regenerated foods can be enhanced with the addition of further products. This includes the inclusion of appropriate sauces, accompaniments and garnishes.

Guest Chef

Gypsy tart with Kentish plum compote and tuile biscuit

Chef *Calvin Gear*

Centre *Mid Kent College*

We source our ingredients from local suppliers in Kent and encourage our students to do the same at home. We are fortunate to have an abundance of farms around us and our suppliers from Detling, Biddenden and Ashford do their best for us in sourcing directly from them.

For the tart

12 oz evaporated milk (must be refrigerated for 24 hours)

1 lb dark soft brown sugar

1 × 10 inch sweet pastry case which has been baked blind

Plum compote

500 g plums – washed, stoned and chopped roughly

25 g brown sugar

1 cinnamon stick

Tuile mix

100 g melted butter

100 g egg whites

100 g sugar

100 g plain flour

METHOD OF WORK

Tart

1. Whip evaporated milk in the mixer until maximum volume has been reached and it forms firm peaks.
2. Put the sugar in a bowl and rub through with your fingers to make sure there are no lumps in it.
3. Fold the sugar into the milk until well mixed and there are no lumps.
4. Put into sweet pastry case and cook at 170°C for 10 minutes.

Plum compote

1. Put the plums, sugar and cinnamon into a heavy-based pan.
2. Cook over a medium to low heat stirring occasionally for 1½ hours until thickened.
3. Leave to cool before refrigerating.

Tuile mix

1. Mix the sugar well into the egg, then the flour and finally the butter. Chill well before using.
2. Spread thinly onto a baking sheet into desired shape
3. Bake at 180°C for 5 to 6 minutes.
4. Twist or mould whilst still hot and leave to cool.

TEST YOURSELF

1 Provide one example of a food that can be regenerated from each of the following categories.

Dried ____
Fresh ____
Ready-made ____
Frozen ____
Pre-prepared ____
Tinned ____

2 List three advantages associated with the use of pre-prepared foods.

i) ____
ii) ____
iii) ____

3 List three possible health considerations associated with the regular consumption of pre-prepared or processed foods.

i) ____
ii) ____
iii) ____

4 Other than health considerations, name three other disadvantages associated with the use of pre-prepared foods.

i) ____
ii) ____
iii) ____

5 How would you ensure that a gâteau was ready to eat if you were regenerating it from frozen?

____

____

____

6 Why do soft fruits change in structure and appearance when processed and regenerated?

____

____

____

7 Provide one example of a food that is regenerated by each of the following methods.

Re-heated ____
Re-hydrated ____
Cooked ____
Defrosted ____

8 Why do products that have been dried have a longer shelf-life (use-by date) than their fresh equivalent?

____

____

____

9 After dried foods have been re-hydrated, they may require further cooking. Can you provide two examples of food items and the cookery methods required?

i) ____
ii) ____

10 List four points that you would check to ensure that regenerated dishes were cooked and presented to requirements.

i) ____
ii) ____
iii) ____
iv) ____

12 Cold food preparation

Unit 112 Cold food preparation

Recipes

LEARNING OBJECTIVES

On completion of this chapter you will be able to:

- **Identify foods used in cold preparation.**
- **Identify the quality points when preparing cold foods.**
- **Describe a range of hors d'œuvres, salads and sandwiches.**
- **List the techniques used to present cold foods.**
- **List the general safety points to follow when preparing and presenting foods for cold presentation.**

Introduction

Cold food preparation is about using skills and techniques to put cold food items together in an appetizing and appealing way. Cold food can be made from raw ingredients, for example lettuces, carrots and melons; pre-prepared ingredients, such as smoked fish, hams, rolls; or items that have been cooked and then cooled like potatoes, roast meats, asparagus.

It is important to state that food items can come prepared in a variety of formats. This includes frozen (e.g. prawns), tinned (e.g. tuna) or as a convenience product (e.g. ready-made pastry cases). This is not limited to any particular type of food.

Styles of service

Cold food can be presented and served using a variety of service styles. Whatever the style of service, it is important that the food is presented very well to make the food as attractive as possible to diners. This provides chefs with an opportunity to show their creative skills.

The type of service selected largely depends on the occasion. For example, plated service would normally be used in a restaurant scenario where a guest orders a particular dish, a platter of smoked fish or a terrine for example. It is also possible that cold food items could be silver served, although this is not seen as often as it would have been in the past.

Cold food is also commonly served at buffets, where food items are displayed on a service table. Depending on the type of food, this may be offered as a finger buffet or a fork buffet. In the case of a finger buffet, it is essential that the food items prepared are appropriate for this style of service and that they can be eaten easily using only the fingers to handle the food items. If food cannot be eaten easily using this method, the appropriate cutlery should be offered alongside.

Cold food can form part of a takeaway option. It is common practice to see chilled cold food display areas with take-away containers. Often, such containers will come in two or more sizes so that customers can decide how much they wish to purchase and this can then be priced accordingly.

Equipment to present cold food

The type of equipment required for the presentation of cold food is largely dependent on the type of service. It is vitally important that cold food is served safely at the temperature it is required to be served at. In the case of food that is going to be displayed for any length of time, this must be kept under chilled conditions, for example in a chilled display cabinet.

Food that is going to be served directly to customers is offered in many different formats, from silver salvers to a wide range of plates and bowls. Cold food designed for the takeaway market must be thoughtfully packaged and clearly labelled with any handling instructions necessary.

Safety points to consider when preparing and presenting foods for cold presentation

- Hygiene should be maintained at the highest level. Preparing cold food items involves raw and cooked items, both of which must be handled properly to ensure that the foods do not become contaminated.
- Cold food items whether served raw or previously cooked will not be cooked again to kill harmful bacteria as with hot items. This is one reason why hygiene standards must be very high when working with cold foods.
- All equipment and utensils should be clean and well maintained so they do not contaminate the food. Clothing and personal hygiene standards should also be extremely high and food items should be handled as little as possible.
- All cold food items should be stored in appropriate conditions, which would normally be in a refrigerator between 1°C and 5°C. Food items should always be covered, clearly labelled and dated. When serving cold foods, they should be unwrapped as late as possible and ideally served from refrigerated equipment. The time food is left out for service should be limited to the minimum possible to avoid any form of contamination. Food items should also be served from clean utensils.
- It is a legal requirement that ambient food is served within 4 hours from being presented. Beyond this time, the risk of food becoming unsafe to eat gets higher and therefore should not be offered for consumption.

The meal occasions when cold food may be presented

Cold food items can appear at just about any meal occasion. Sometimes cold food items are served exclusively whereas on other occasions they may form part of a meal where hot and cold items will both be served. Here are some examples of cold food items being served at a variety of meals.

Breakfast

Throughout most of continental Europe, breakfast usually consists of cold items such as croissant with preserves (jams, marmalade), yoghurt with fresh fruits and selections of cold meats with various styles of bread.

Lunch

Lunch could consist of entirely cold items, a cold buffet for example, with a range of salad items, cold meats, smoked fish, pasta and rice. There are no set rules about the items that can be offered other than that they should be fresh (within use-by date), served at the appropriate temperature and safe to eat.

CHEF'S TIP Cold dishes are often offered as part of a menu. In fact, it is good practice to offer a variety of options for the customer to choose from.

Afternoon tea

A traditional meal providing a range of items to enjoy alongside a cup of tea. Examples of items that would commonly be served for afternoon tea include sandwiches, pastries (e.g. Danish, fruit tartlets, etc.) and scones served with fresh cream and sliced strawberries.

Special receptions

A special reception provides the opportunity for chefs to show off their creativity and presentation skills. Examples of special receptions include the launch of a new product for a business, a celebration to mark a special occasion or a cocktail party hosted by the captain on a cruise ship.

CHEF'S TIP The chef planning the menu for the special event has to take the nature of an event into consideration. If guests are standing, for example, they will not be able to use cutlery. Therefore, the food items have to be easily managed by guests and fairly small, maybe even designed to be eaten in one mouthful.

Dinner

Dinner is usually a more formal occasion and less likely to offer entirely cold items. Cold dishes, offered as part of a dinner menu are acceptable as it provides a range of options for the diner. Many hotels, especially in hot climates, and cruise ships offer a cold buffet service in evenings for dinner.

Portion sizes are generally larger and the quality of food items used are of higher quality. Comparing lunch menus to dinner menus in most restaurants and hotels would confirm this, even by the price difference to customers.

However, similar to lunch, there is scope for cold dishes to be offered as part of a dinner menu and this is acceptable as it provides a range of options for the diner.

Step-by-step: Smoked salmon and prawn platter

STEP 1 The salad ingredients (mixed salad leaves, spring onions, cherry tomatoes, peeled cucumber, fine asparagus tips which have been blanched and refreshed, fresh dill, lemon wedge) and cooked prawns to be prepared for a smoked salmon and prawn platter.

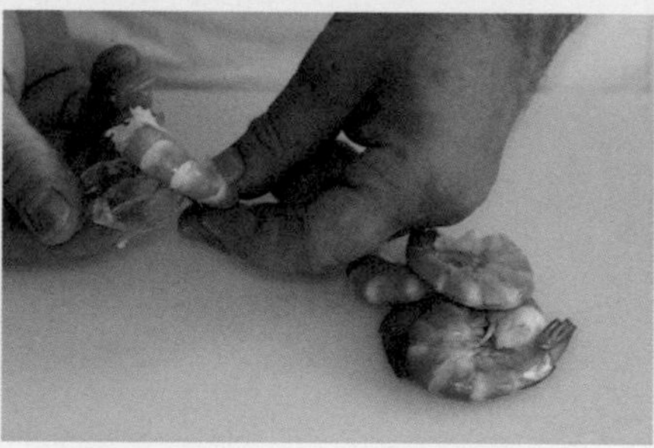

STEP 2 Peel away the shells from the prawns.

STEP 3 Place a prawn flat onto a chopping board. Using a small, sharp knife, make an incision into the top of the prawn tail.

STEP 4 Using the tip of the knife, remove the intestine (tract from the prawn tail. This is visible as a small black thread.

STEP 5 Begin to dress the plate by placing some smoked salmon on a plate. To enhance the presentation, this can be curled and raised to provide the dish with height and dimension.

STEP 6 Cut the cucumber into a small neat dice and mix with chopped dill.

STEP 7 Quarter the cherry tomatoes.

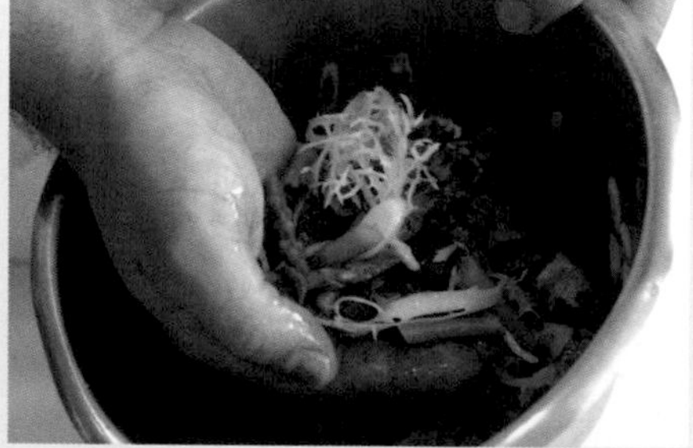

STEP 8 Mix the salad leaves with the neatly cut asparagus tips, the quartered cherry tomatoes and sliced spring onions. Put a little vinaigrette into a mixing bowl and toss the salad ingredients to take on the flavour and seasoning from the vinaigrette.

STEP 9 Place the salad leaves neatly onto the plate with the smoked salmon. Continue to dress with the cucumber, the de-veined prawns, brown bread and butter and a wedge of lemon. Spoon over a little more vinaigrette mixed with chopped dill.

Foods used in cold preparation

The range of foods that can be used in cold preparation is huge. There are many classic combinations such as prawn cocktail or Waldorf salad as well as many other possible combinations.

The following table provides examples of food types that are commonly used in cold food preparation.

TYPE OF FOOD	EXAMPLES
Fruit	Melon, grapefruit, avocado, orange, strawberry, kiwi, grapes, apple, pear, plum, peach, etc.
Vegetables	Onion, garlic, mushrooms, cauliflower, carrot, cabbage, peppers, celery, beetroot, etc.
Meat and meat products	Roast meats and poultry (beef, lamb, pork, chicken, turkey, etc.) hams, pâtés and terrines, pies, etc.
Fish, shellfish and fish products	Smoked fish (salmon, mackerel, trout), tinned fish (sardines, tuna, salmon), pickled fish (herrings), shellfish (prawns, crab, lobster), fresh cooked fish (salmon, seabass, cod), etc.
Salad items (also part of the vegetable food group)	Lettuce (lollo rosso, frisée, oakleaf, little gem), cucumber, tomatoes, spring onions, mustard cress, radish, fresh herbs, etc.
Dairy	Cream (sour/acidulated/crème fraiche, fresh cream – single/whipping/double), yoghurt, cheese, milk, etc.

TYPE OF FOOD	EXAMPLES
Breads and pastries	Bread rolls/loaves (wholemeal, white, wholegrain) speciality breads – ciabatta, foccacia, chapatti, naan, pastry products (ragout shells, barquettes, vol-au-vents/bouchées), etc.
Cold sauces, oils, vinegars and dressings	Cold sauces (mustard, Cumberland, horseradish), oils (olive, vegetable, walnut), vinegars (malt, raspberry, white wine), dressings (vinaigrette, mayonnaise), etc.

Identifying the quality points when preparing cold foods

The quality points to look for in foods will vary between the stages of preparation and cooking. However, it is essential to work with the best quality products available from the offset.

CHEF'S TIP If you start work with high quality ingredients, you have more chance of making a high quality finished dish. If your ingredients are of poor quality it is much more difficult to produce a finished dish of high quality.

Quality points to look for in raw ingredients

- *Freshness* – Ingredients should be as fresh as possible, particularly items such as ripe fruit, vegetables and fish, which are at their peak when only just picked or caught.
- *Appearance* – Appearance plays a big part in the presentation of cold food. Therefore, it is essential that your ingredients have a high-quality appearance in line with the specification for the dish. Appearance covers aspects such as colour, shape and checks are required for blemishes, breaks or bruising.
- *Smell* – Our sense of smell can inform us if food is off or beginning to turn. Some foods, such as fish have a natural smell, even a very slight one when fresh, but this is a natural smell from the environment in which they live and should not be too strong. A fish that is off will produce a much stronger and far more unpleasant smell.
- *Temperature* – The temperature at which food is stored is vital to maintain its freshness and appearance, as well as ensuring that it is safe to eat. Checks for temperature should always take place when receiving food items from suppliers.

Quality points to look for in the preparation of ingredients

- *When handling and preparing* – Food items need to be handled and prepared carefully to produce a high quality finished product. Food items should be prepared to the specification required for the dish being produced. This requires knife work to be performed carefully and accurately throughout all the preparation stages.

- *Peeling* – Following the washing of food items such as vegetables and fruits, it may be necessary to peel them. This can range from a potato, turnip, an apple or pear, for example. It should be noted that peeling is a technique, and as such, a skill.
- *Cutting and chopping* – Accurate cutting of food into a variety of shapes and sizes can enhance dishes, making them very appealing for the customer. Consideration of the size ingredients are cut and the amount used will also influence the flavour of the dish. For example, if onions were going to be used in a potato salad and they were chopped very finely, their flavour would be delicate and not overpowering. However, if large chunks of onion were used, the flavour would be stronger and the texture much coarser.
- *Carving* – Carving refers to the slicing of cold meats. Carving is quite a difficult skill to master. As meat is an expensive commodity, accurate carving is very important so that waste is minimized. Well carved meat also looks very appealing when presented carefully.
- *Slicing* – Slicing is a similar skill but performed on different food items. Smoked fish, such as smoked salmon, is often sliced very thinly. Vegetables, such as tomatoes and cucumber are also often cut into slices when presented as cold food.
- *Shredding* – Many vegetables are shredded when used in cold dishes. For example, to make fresh coleslaw, onion and white cabbage are shredded into very fine strips. Carrots can also be shredded, although many chefs would choose to grate the carrot rather than use a knife. Lettuces, such as iceberg and little gems, are also often shredded in a similar way when being used in dishes for cold presentation.

Step-by-step: Finely chopping an onion

Finely chopped onion is a basic ingredient of many cold food dishes.

STEP 1 Cut off the tip of the root at the top of the onion and trim the base. Peel the onion and cut in half through the root. (The root can be identified by a small light brown circle.)

STEP 2 With the root pointing away from you, cut thin slices three-quarters of the way up towards the root across the onion. The onion should stay intact as there should be no slices that go right the way through the onion.

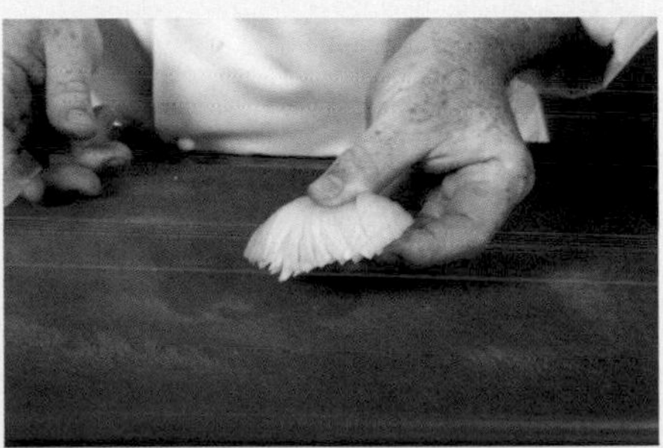

STEP 3 Turn the onion 90°.

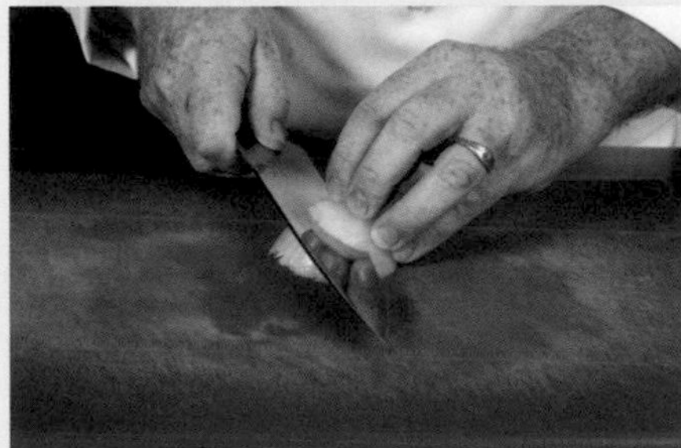

STEP 4 Holding the knife horizontally, make a cut half way up into the slices of onion. If using a large onion, two cuts can be made across the slices.

STEP 5 Cut down the slices to produce finely chopped onion.

STEP 6 A finely chopped onion.

Step-by-step: Blanching a tomato

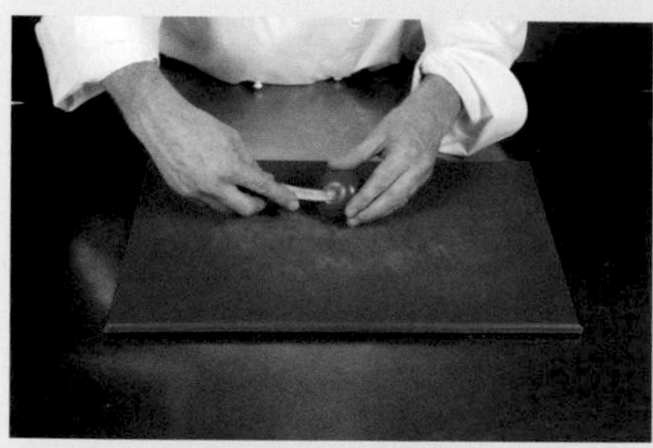

STEP 1 Using the point of a sharp paring knife, remove the core from the tomato.

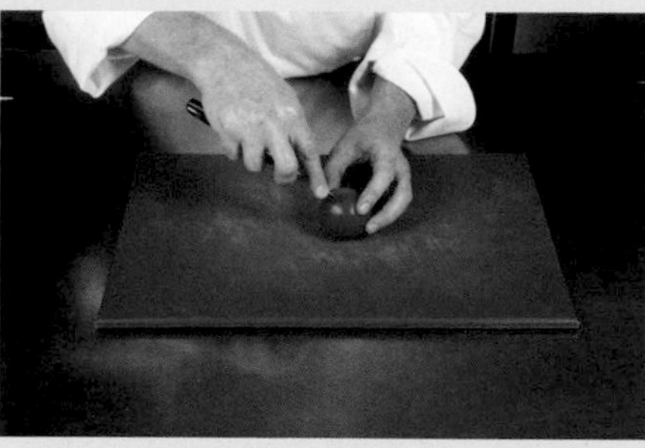

STEP 2 At the top of the tomato, score a cross to just break through the skin.

STEP 3 Lower the tomato into boiling water for 10 to 15 seconds (depending on how ripe the tomato is, an unripe tomato will take slightly longer than a ripe one).

STEP 4 Place the tomato into ice-cold water to cease the cooking process. The skin of the tomato should then peel off very easily with the flesh remaining firm.

Step-by-step: Fresh fruit salad

STEP 1 Cut a slice from the top and bottom of an orange so that the segments can be seen. Carve around the shape of the orange to remove the peel.

STEP 2 Cut in between the white pith, dividing the segments to remove the segments.

STEP 3 Prepare the kiwi using the same process as described in step 1.

STEP 4 Cut the kiwi in half lengthways and then cut into slices.

STEP 5 Cut around the stone of a plum in one slice.

STEP 6 Using the tip of a paring knife, carefully remove the stone of the plum.

STEP 7 Cut the plum halves into slices.

STEP 8 Cut a slice of a mango lengthways.

STEP 9 Score the flesh by cutting lengthways and then across the mango without breaking the skin.

STEP 10 Invert the flesh to show cubes of mango flesh. Cut these along the skin to remove.

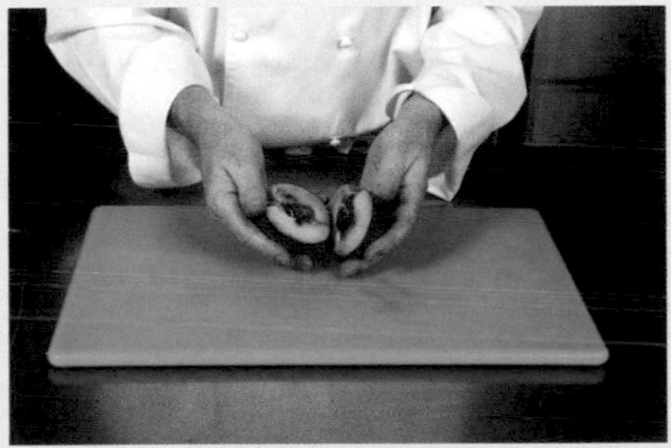

STEP 11 Prepare slices of peach following the same method as the plum (steps 5, 6 and 7).

STEP 12 Remove the stem (hull) from a strawberry and cut in half (depending on size).

STEP 13 Cut a pear into 4 lengthways and remove the core by slicing at an angle.

STEP 14 Apples are prepared in the same way as the pear before cutting both into slices.

STEP 15 The finished fruit salad, soaked in stock syrup (equal quantities of sugar and water, brought to the boil and cooled). Some sliced banana and soft fruits (raspberries, blackcurrants and blueberries) can be added just before serving.

- *Proportion/amount of ingredients* – Many cold dishes consist of more than one ingredient. As such, it is very important to gain an understanding of the quantities (ratios) in which ingredients are mixed together. Flavours should complement (balance) one another and the combinations of foods need to be considered when menu planning.
- *Dressing* – Cold foods, particularly salads, are usually dressed with a cold sauce to provide additional flavours and bind ingredients together. A plain mixed leaf salad without any dressing can be fairly uninspiring to eat. The addition of a well-made, flavoursome vinaigrette completely changes the eating quality of such a dish.

Other dressings regularly used in cold preparations include:

- *Mayonnaise* – Egg mayonnaise, potato salad.
- *Yoghurt* – Raita (yoghurt mixed with diced cucumber and mint).
- *Sour/acidulated cream* (cream with lemon juice) – Used on a range of salads including Mimosa salad and Japanese salad.

- *Seasoning* – Cold food is greatly enhanced by seasoning. For example, sliced tomato is transformed by the addition of salt and pepper, although salt intake should be monitored for health reasons.
- *Garnishing and presenting* – Garnishes are used to make dishes appealing and can range from simple effective garnishes to elaborate, artistic pieces. Cold food is lifted by its presentation and it is therefore very important that care and thought is put into producing an attractive range of food items.

CHEF'S TIP When using vinaigrette, it is good practice to mix the salad with the dressing at the last possible moment before being served. If the salad was mixed and then left to sit, the leaves would soak up the dressing and become limp and soggy. By mixing just before service, the flavours are fresh and the leaves will be in good, crisp condition.

Step-by-step: Vinaigrette

STEP 1 The ingredients required to make vinaigrette – vinegar (e.g. white wine vinegar, cider vinegar, etc.), oil (e.g. vegetable, olive), mustard (e.g. English, Dijon, whole-grain, etc.), salt and freshly ground black pepper.

STEP 2 Place the mustard into a mixing bowl.

STEP 3 Mix in the vinegar and season with the salt and freshly ground black pepper.

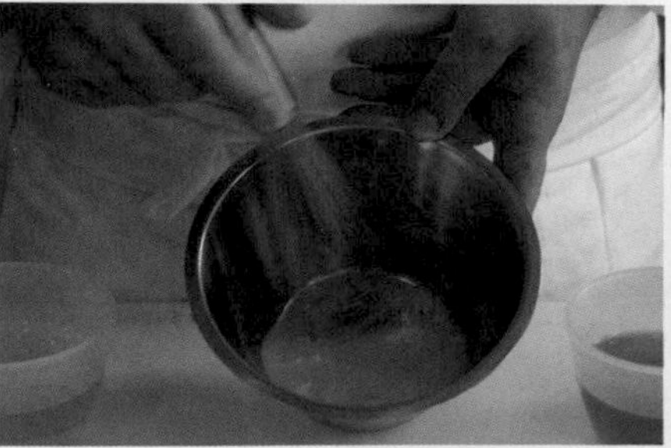

STEP 4 Whisk all the ingredients together.

STEP 5 Gradually, pour the oil slowly whilst whisking continuously to form an emulsion. (In this example, a mixture of olive and vegetable oils are being used.)

STEP 6 Continue to add the oil while whisking until all the oil has been added. A typical vinaigrette is made up of four to six parts oil to one part vinegar. The liquid should thicken slightly as more oil is added.

Hors d'œuvres

Hors d'œuvres is a French term used to describe foods served before or outside (hors) the main dishes of a meal (d'œuvres). The term is often replaced in English with terms such as 'starter' or 'first course'.

Traditionally, hors d'œuvres were served in two styles. These were:

- hors d'œuvres variés (an assortment of dishes)
- hors d'œuvres single (a single main food item).

Assorted hors d'œuvres consist of a range of dishes whereby the guest will receive or have the choice of a variety of items. Assorted hors d'œuvres consist of a range of food items including meat, fish, vegetable, fruit and dairy based dishes. The customer then has a choice as to which dishes they would like and in the quantities they prefer. A selection of hors d'œuvres can be plated, with a selection of each item being placed neatly onto the plate. Alternatively, the individual dishes could be served separately in ravier dishes, flats, trays or even bowls, giving the customer a choice of preferred items.

A single hors d'œuvre focuses on one main food item being the main part of the dish. For example, smoked salmon or pâté could be offered as the principle food item, although other food items would often be used to garnish and/or complement the dish – e.g. a baby leaf salad and chutney for the pâté or neatly diced marinated cucumber with the smoked salmon.

Salads

Salads also fall into two main categories:

- *Simple salads* – As the title suggests, these are basic salads containing one or a small number of ingredients such as a mixed leaf salad or a tomato salad.
- *Composite salads* – Contain a number of different ingredients and are usually bound together with a suitable dressing (vinaigrette, mayonnaise, etc.). Examples of composite salads include mixed vegetable salad, meat salad and Niçoise salad.

Sandwiches

Sandwiches are very popular and nutritious cold food items enjoyed by millions of people on a daily basis. In professional cookery, there are many ways in which sandwiches are prepared and presented. Sandwiches can appear as hot as well as cold items, although in this chapter we will be focusing on cold sandwiches only.

Sandwiches can be made using any form of bread, of which there are many varieties made from a wide range of flours. Breads in styles from around the world are now readily available from artisan bakers and suppliers.

A standard sandwich is made up of two slices of bread which is filled with a filling. The range of possible fillings and combinations is endless and is very much dictated by the customer. In many modern sandwich shops sandwiches are made to the customers' exact requirements. This ranges from the type of bread they would like to the type and number of fillings they require. The sandwich is then priced accordingly. Sandwich shops are one of the fastest growing areas of the fast food sector in the UK.

In the hotel environment, sandwiches are often available as room service or as part of an afternoon tea service. It is quite normal practice for the sandwiches to have the crusts removed and be cut into small triangular shapes. From a standard sized loaf, two slices would normally make four small triangular sandwiches.

Sandwich fillings

Sandwich fillings are almost unlimited. However, there are classic fillings and combinations that have become favourites and have stood up to the test of time.
Examples of fillings:

- Egg mayonnaise
- Ham and tomato
- Beef and horseradish
- Smoked salmon
- Cheese and pickle
- Tuna and sweetcorn
- Cream cheese and chive
- Cucumber

Examples of breads include:

- White
- Wholemeal
- Whole-grain
- Rye
- Granary

Styles of bread include:

- French sticks
- Ciabatta
- Cottage loaves
- Foccacia
- Rolls
- Soda

A platter of mixed sandwiches

Step-by-step: A range of sandwiches

STEP 1 Using an egg slicer, slice a boiled and refreshed egg.

STEP 2 Place the egg into a bowl, season with salt and a little freshly ground white pepper and bind with mayonnaise.

STEP 3 Place the egg mixture into the centre of a slice of buttered bread.

STEP 4 Using a palette knife, spread the mixture evenly across the slice of bread.

STEP 5 Sprinkle with some fresh mustard cress.

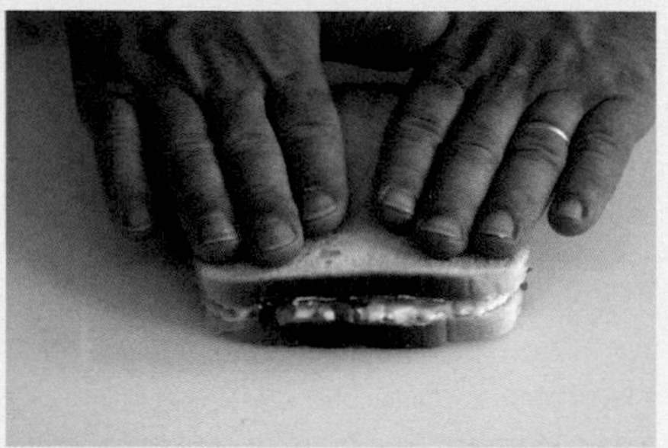

STEP 6 Place another slice of buttered bread on top of the egg and cress to form a sandwich.

STEP 7 Using a serrated slicing knife, neatly cut the crusts from the sandwich.

STEP 8 Sandwiches can be cut into many shapes and sizes. In this example, cucumber sandwiches are being cut into finger slices.

STEP 9 In this example, a round cutter is being used to produced circular smoked salmon sandwiches.

STEP 10 Circular shaped smoked salmon sandwiches.

STEP 11 In this example, some pâté filled sandwiches are being cut into squares.

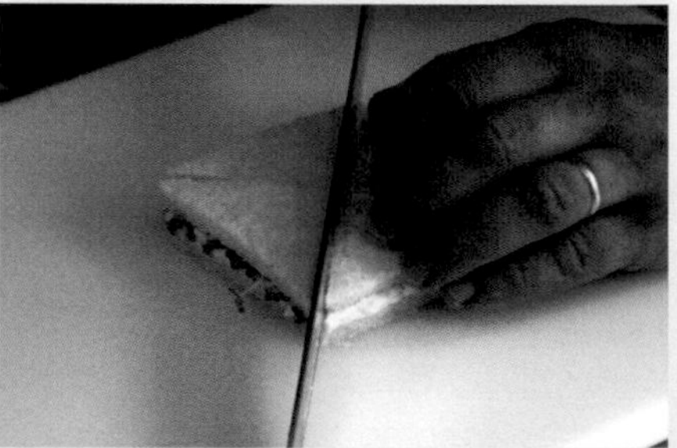

STEP 12 And finally, the egg and cress sandwiches are cut from corner to corner (diagonally) to produce triangular shaped sandwiches.

Open sandwiches

Not all sandwiches are made with two slices of bread. The open sandwich is associated with Scandinavia (Denmark, Sweden, Finland and Norway) and forms part of the tradition of the smorgasbord, a buffet style event. This type of sandwich uses a single piece of bread to which a hot or cold topping is added. Open sandwiches are usually carefully garnished with small cuts of various items to enhance their presentation. Examples of open sandwiches include:

- roast beef with tomato
- smoked salmon with dill
- scrambled egg with pancetta
- asparagus, baby plum tomato and Serrano ham.

Once again, the possibilities are endless. However, it is good practice for open sandwiches to be served neatly, with care taken over their presentation. Small garnishes, such as chopped herbs, sliced radishes, brunoise of vegetables, capers and gherkins are often used to enhance the dish.

Canapés

Canapés are small, bite-size items usually served at cocktail parties, promotional events or alongside pre-dinner drinks. Canapés can be made from a variety of bases and topped with a variety of toppings. They can be savoury or sweet and served cold or hot.

Canapé bases can be made of fresh bread or bread that has been fried or toasted. Bases can also be made of pastry, such as short, sweet and puff pastry. Occasionally, food items will not require a base. A cherry tomato stuffed with cream cheese, for example, would not require a base as the tomato itself provides a sufficient shell to allow for easy pick up.

As with sandwiches, there are no restrictions on the possibilities of food items used in the production of canapés. It is important, however, that a variety of food items are used in order to satisfy a wide range of tastes.

As canapés are so small, the decorative work involved can be quite fiddly. Therefore, good knife skills are required to ensure that garnishes are of the same shape and size. Other garnishes may require the chef to pipe a garnish onto the canapé. Once again, this will require a steady hand and precise handling to ensure that the product is neat and well presented. Finally, it is common practice for canapés to be served on flats or trays. In these circumstances, canapés are laid in uniform lines and should look identical. Canapés laid in such lines form a very effective presentation despite being relatively simple. Once again, a variety of food items, such as:

- meat
- dairy products (e.g. eggs, cheese)
- fish
- fruit
- vegetables

across a range of shapes:

- round
- triangular
- square
- barquette (boat shaped)
- rectangular

with the use of various bases:

- choux pastry
- puff pastry
- speciality breads (e.g. Pumpernickel, pitta, naan, etc.)
- short pastry
- toasted, fried bread
- sweet pastry
- crackers.

This will provide an effective range of food items, textures, colours and flavours to produce a good quality selection of well-presented canapés.

A selection of canapés

Guest Chef

Baked Christmas cheesecake

Chef *Maureen Dempsey*
Centre/College *Leeds City College*

Ingredients and quantities

For the sponge base	
Margarine	200 g
Caster sugar	200 g
Self-raising flour	180 g
Cocoa powder	20 g
Eggs	4
For the filling	
Butter	150 g
Caster sugar	100 g
Rum essence	1 tsp
Large eggs	3 separated, you need 3 yolks and 2 whites
Double cream	150 ml
Full-fat cream cheese	600 g
Sweet mincemeat	200 g
Large orange	1 finely grated

Decorate with icing sugar and a relevant Christmas decoration.

METHOD OF WORK

For the sponge base:
Grease and line a 20 cm cake tin.
Pre-heat the oven to 190°C.

1. Cream the sugar and margarine in a bowl.
2. Add the eggs one at a time.
3. Sieve the flour and cocoa powder together and add to eggs, sugar and margarine mixture by gently folding in.
4. Place the mixture into the cake tin and bake in the oven for 20 minutes.
5. Allow to cool.

For the filling
Lower the oven to 170°C.

1. Grease the sides of a 20 cm loose-bottom cake tin and line the base with non-stick baking paper.
2. Cut the chocolate cake into even discs approximately ½ cm deep, you will need two of these.
3. Cover the sponge discs with the sweet mincemeat and leave to the side.
4. Cream the butter and caster sugar together, add the rum essence and the grated orange peel and cream until fluffy.
5. Separate the yolks from the whites.
6. Beat in the egg yolks and add the cream and the softened cream cheese. Beat in. Whisk two of the egg whites until just stiff and fold into the mixture.
7. Place one of the sponge discs in the cake tin with the mincemeat to the top and pour half of the cheese cake mix over it, cover with the second sponge disc once again with the mincemeat to the top and pour the remaining cheese cake mix over it.
8. Bake in the oven pre-heated to 170°C for 1½ hours until set to the touch.
9. Leave the cheese cake to cool and continue setting.
10. Carefully remove from the tin very carefully; turn onto a cooling wire to give a crisscross finish and gently dredge with icing sugar before placing a nice Christmas decoration onto the top.

TEST YOURSELF

1 What is the difference between a simple salad and a composite salad?

2 Why is it important to cut foods into regular shapes and sizes for cold presentation?

3 List four sauces that are regularly used with cold dishes.

i)
ii)
iii)
iv)

4 What size should a canapé be served and why?

5 Name four possible bases for a canapé.

i)
ii)
iii)
iv)

6 What factors would you take into consideration when producing an assortment of hors d'œurves (hors d'œurves variés).

7 Name four items that could be used as single hors d'œurves.

i)
ii)
iii)
iv)

8 What is the purpose of seasoning and dressing cold food items?

9 Name four types of lettuce.

i)
ii)
iii)
iv)

10 What is the difference between shredding and chopping?

11 Why should you dress a salad just before it is served?

12 Name four pieces of equipment that could be used to serve an assortment of buffet items.

i)
ii)
iii)
iv)

13 Why is it important to have the correct proportions of mixed cold food items when binding them together?

Recipes

Chicken Caesar salad

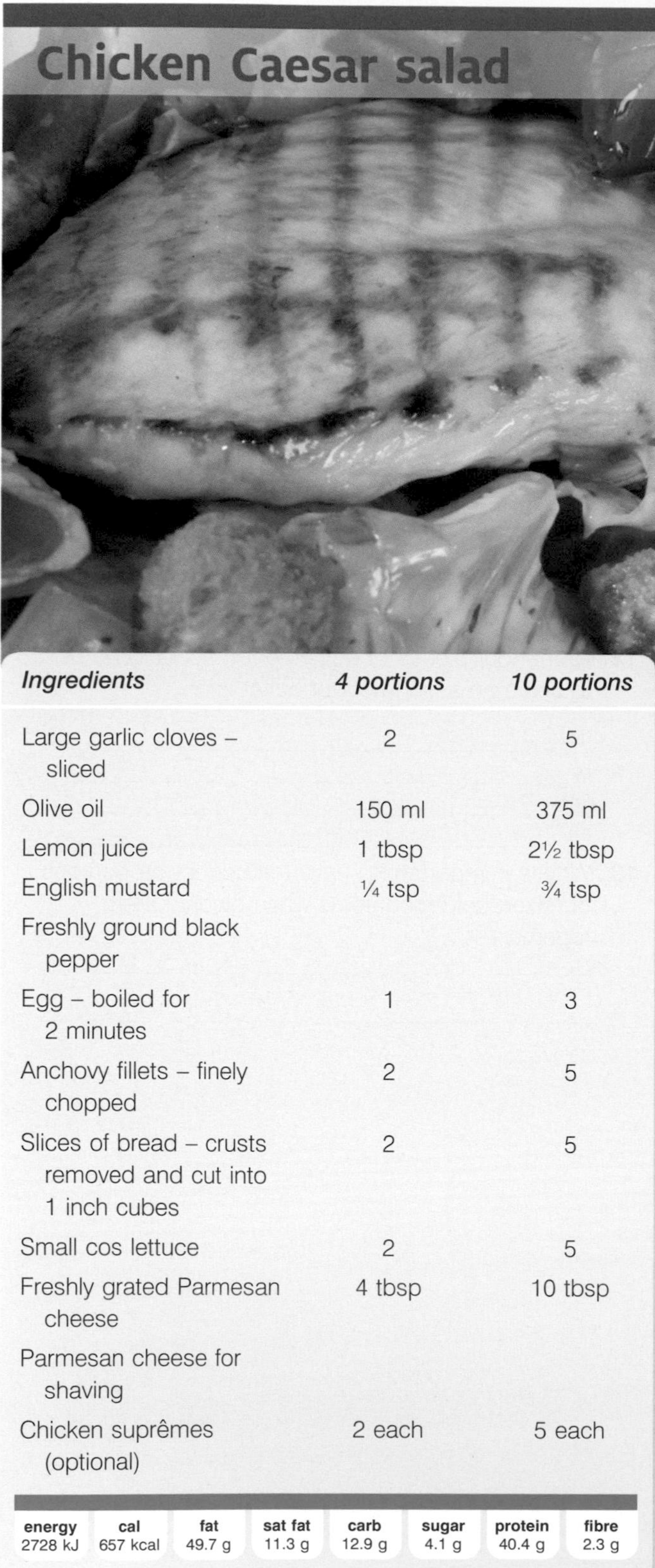

Ingredients	4 portions	10 portions
Large garlic cloves – sliced	2	5
Olive oil	150 ml	375 ml
Lemon juice	1 tbsp	2½ tbsp
English mustard	¼ tsp	¾ tsp
Freshly ground black pepper		
Egg – boiled for 2 minutes	1	3
Anchovy fillets – finely chopped	2	5
Slices of bread – crusts removed and cut into 1 inch cubes	2	5
Small cos lettuce	2	5
Freshly grated Parmesan cheese	4 tbsp	10 tbsp
Parmesan cheese for shaving		
Chicken suprêmes (optional)	2 each	5 each

energy	cal	fat	sat fat	carb	sugar	protein	fibre
2728 kJ	657 kcal	49.7 g	11.3 g	12.9 g	4.1 g	40.4 g	2.3 g

METHOD OF WORK

1. Remove the best leaves (whole) from the cos lettuce carefully and wash. Drain and carefully place in a tray and chill. Keep the lettuce, if storing, in a moist but cool environment.
2. Mix the garlic with the oil and leave to marinade for 20 minutes.
3. Strain off ¾ of the oil to make the dressing and add it to the lemon juice, mustard, pepper and egg. Whisk well and add the finely chopped anchovies and grated Parmesan cheese. Check and adjust the seasoning as required.
4. Pour the remaining oil into a frying pan, with the garlic, and heat slowly. When the garlic slices begin to sizzle, remove them with a perforated spoon. Add the bread cubes and fry, turning frequently with a slice or perforated spoon until the croutons are crisp and brown.
5. Using a perforated spoon, lift out the croutons and drain on absorbent paper.
6. Toss the lettuce in the dressing. Sprinkle over the croutons and serve in a bowl with fresh Parmesan shavings.

Note: 'Chicken' Caesar salad has become a popular choice throughout the world.

This includes the addition of a chicken breast, which has usually been grilled or griddled.

Poached salmon with cucumber salad

Ingredients	*4 portions*	*10 portions*
Pin-boned supremes of salmon (150 g)	4	10
Court bouillon (poaching liquid)	1 litre	2.5 litres
Small cucumber	1	2
Vinaigrette	20 ml	50 ml
Mayonnaise (optional)	250 ml	700 ml
Water	1 litre	2.5 litres
White wine vinegar	50 ml	125 ml
Sliced carrots	25 g	65 g
Sliced onions	50 g	125 g
A few parsley stalks		
A few sprigs of thyme		
Bay leaf	1	3
Peppercorns	8	20

energy	cal	fat	sat fat	carb	sugar	protein	fibre
3482 kJ	841 kcal	74.8 g	11.6 g	6.2 g	4.0 g	35.9 g	2.2 g

METHOD OF WORK

1. Bring the court bouillon to a gentle simmer in a wide flat saucepan (e.g. sauteuse).
2. Carefully place the salmon supremes into the liquid and poach gently for 3 to 4 minutes.
3. Remove from the heat, leaving the salmon in the court bouillon until cold.
4. Once cold, remove from the pan and place on a tray. Carefully cover with cling film and chill.
5. To present, place neatly onto a plate and serve with cold mayonnaise (optional), cucumber salad (page 212) and a wedge of lemon.

Mayonnaise

Ingredients	4 portions	10 portions
Fresh egg yolk	1 yolk	3 yolks
Vinegar or vinaigrette	¾ tsp	2 tsp
Salt and ground white pepper (to season)		
Mustard (e.g. English, Dijon, whole-grain)	¼ tsp	½ tsp
Olive or other good quality oil	100 ml	250 ml
Boiled water (just below boiling point)	1 tsp	1 tsp

energy	cal	fat	sat fat	carb	sugar	protein	fibre
988 kJ	240 kcal	26.3 g	4.0 g	0.1 g	0.0 g	0.7 g	0.0 g

METHOD OF WORK

1. Place yolks, vinegar and seasoning in a bowl and whisk well.
2. Gradually pour on the oil very slowly, whisking continuously.
3. Add the boiling water whisking well.
4. Correct the seasoning and consistency (i.e. if too thick, a little vinegar or water may be added).

Mayonnaise has a variety of uses, for example, in hors d'œuvres, in sandwiches or even as a dip.

VIDEO CLIP Making mayonnaise. 

Note: Mayonnaise will curdle/split due to the following:

- The oil is added too quickly.
- The oil is cold.
- The sauce is insufficiently whisked during production.
- The yolks are stale.

The method of re-thickening a curdled/split mayonnaise is as follows:

- Take a clean bowl, add a teaspoon of boiling water and gradually whisk in the curdled sauce.
- Take a fresh yolk thinned slightly with half a teaspoon of cold water. Whisk well before gradually whisking in the curdled sauce.

Tartare sauce

Ingredients	4 portions	10 portions
Mayonnaise	125 ml	300 ml
Capers – chopped	12 g	30 g
Gherkins – chopped; parsley – chopped	25 g	60 g

energy	cal	fat	sat fat	carb	sugar	protein	fibre
897 kJ	218 kcal	23.7 g	3.6 g	0.9 g	0.6 g	0.5 g	0.2 g

METHOD OF WORK

1. Mix all the above ingredients together to form a blended sauce.

Coleslaw

Ingredients	*4 portions*	*10 portions*
Mayonnaise	125 ml	300 ml
White cabbage – finely shredded (chiffonade)	200 g	500 g
Carrot – julienne or finely grated	50 g	125 g
Onion – finely sliced	50 g	125 g

energy	cal	fat	sat fat	carb	sugar	protein	fibre
982 kJ	238 kcal	23.9 g	3.6 g	4.6 g	4.0 g	1.4 g	1.7 g

METHOD OF WORK

1. To shred the cabbage, first remove the outside leaves.
2. Cut the cabbage into quarters through the stalk.
3. Remove the centre stalk from each quarter at an angle and wash the remaining leaves.
4. Taking a manageable batch of leaves at a time, shred finely using a rocking motion with the knife.
5. Mix with the julienne or grated carrot and finely sliced onion.
6. Bind with mayonnaise and season with salt and pepper.
7. Serve chilled in an appropriate bowl.

VIDEO CLIP Making coleslaw.

Pesto sauce

Ingredients	*4 portions*	*12 portions*
Pine nuts	50 g	150 g
Olive oil	150 ml	450 ml
Garlic cloves	2	6
Large bunch of basil	1	3
Parmesan cheese	50 g	150 g
Salt and freshly ground black pepper		

energy	cal	fat	sat fat	carb	sugar	protein	fibre
2006 kJ	487 kcal	50.0 g	8.5 g	2.2 g	0.7 g	7.2 g	0.7 g

METHOD OF WORK

1. Lightly brown the nuts under the grill or through the oven, then allow to cool.
2. Take the garlic cloves and basil and grind to a paste.
3. Add the Parmesan cheese, toasted nuts and oil and blend to a puree by placing in a blender or, more authentically (traditionally), using a pestle and mortar.
4. Season with salt and freshly ground white pepper and place in a jar for up to 2 to 3 days in the fridge.

Tuna Nicoise salad

Ingredients	*4 portions*	*10 portions*
Grilled supreme of tuna	4 x 125 g	supremes
	10 x 125 g	supremes
Medium tomatoes	8	20
Hard-boiled eggs	8	20
Cooked anchovy fillets or tinned anchovies	8 fillets or 350 g (tinned)	20 fillets or 700 g (tinned)
Cucumber	1	2
Green peppers	2	5
Spring onions	4	10
Small broad beans or haricots verts	200 g	500 g
Garlic clove – peeled and cut in half	1	3
Black olives	100 g	100 g
Olive oil	4 tbsp	10 tbsp
Basil leaves	4	10
Salt, pepper		

energy	cal	fat	sat fat	carb	sugar	protein	fibre
2395 kJ	575 kcal	38.0 g	7.1 g	19.7 g	13.1 g	40.4 g	9.3 g

METHOD OF WORK

1. Blanch, peel and quarter the tomatoes.
2. Salt them slightly on the chopping board.
3. Quarter or slice the hard-boiled eggs.
4. Cut each anchovy fillet into three or four pieces.
5. Peel the cucumber and slice finely.
6. Cut the peppers, onions and broad beans (or haricots verts) into very thin slices.
7. Rub a large salad bowl thoroughly with the two halves of the clove of garlic and put in all the above ingredients.
8. Make a dressing with the olive oil, the finely chopped basil, pepper and salt.
9. Toss the salad ingredients lightly with the vinaigrette.
10. Arrange the salad ingredients neatly in a bowl for presentation.
11. Serve immediately topped with a freshly grilled supreme of tuna (as demonstrated on page 139).

Horseradish sauce

Ingredients	*8 portions*
Horseradish	25 g
Vinegar or lemon juice	1 tbsp
Salt, pepper	
Cream or crème fraiche – lightly whipped	125 ml

energy	cal	fat	sat fat	carb	sugar	protein	fibre
254 kJ	62 kcal	6.3 g	4.2 g	0.8 g	0.6 g	0.5 g	0.1 g

METHOD OF WORK

1. Wash, peel and re-wash the horseradish.
2. Grate finely.
3. Mix all the ingredients together.

Potato and chive salad

Ingredients	*4 portions*	*10 portions*
Cooked potatoes or new potatoes (chilled)	200 g	500 g
Vinaigrette	1 tbsp	2½ tbsp
Chives	25 g	70 g
Mayonnaise	50 ml	125 ml
Salt and freshly ground pepper		

energy	cal	fat	sat fat	carb	sugar	protein	fibre
789 kJ	191 kcal	16.1 g	2.4 g	10.5 g	0.7 g	1.2 g	1.2 g

METHOD OF WORK

1. Cut the potatoes in-to ½ inch dice and lightly coat with the vinaigrette (new potatoes can be left whole or cut in half).
2. Thin the mayonnaise slightly with a tiny drop of water and correct the seasoning, if required.
3. Finely chop the chives and mix into the mayonnaise, reserving some for decoration.
4. Mix the mayonnaise with the potatoes. The mayonnaise should bind the potatoes, rather than provide a sauce!
5. Sprinkle with the remaining chopped chives.
6. Serve in an appropriate bowl or dish.

Vinaigrette

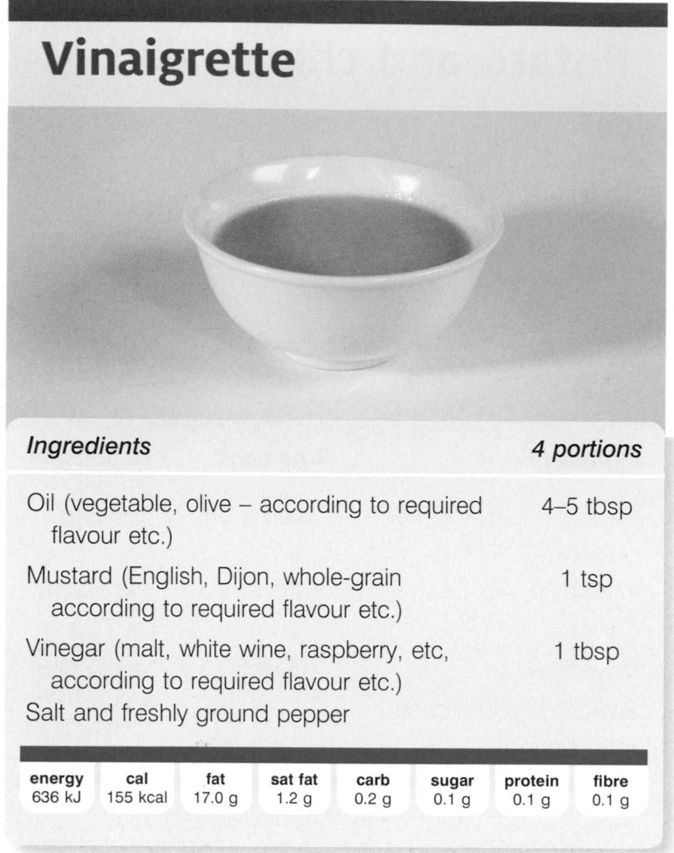

Ingredients	4 portions
Oil (vegetable, olive – according to required flavour etc.)	4–5 tbsp
Mustard (English, Dijon, whole-grain according to required flavour etc.)	1 tsp
Vinegar (malt, white wine, raspberry, etc, according to required flavour etc.)	1 tbsp
Salt and freshly ground pepper	

energy	cal	fat	sat fat	carb	sugar	protein	fibre
636 kJ	155 kcal	17.0 g	1.2 g	0.2 g	0.1 g	0.1 g	0.1 g

Note: When making vinaigrette, the ratios of ingredients remain the same – e.g. between 4 to 6 parts oil to 1 part vinegar according to taste.

METHOD OF WORK

1 Place the vinegar in a mixing bowl, add the mustard and seasoning and mix well.
2 Using a whisk, gradually add the oil whisking vigorously until the oil emulsifies with the vinegar.
3 The dressing will thicken slightly as the oil is added.
4 Finally check for taste, particularly the sharpness from the vinegar and adjust the seasoning, if necessary.
5 Serve as required.

Tomato, feta and red onion salad

Ingredients	4 portions	10 portions
Baby plum tomatoes	200 g	500 g
Feta cheese – cubed and marinated in olive oil with fresh herbs (e.g. basil, tarragon, thyme, etc.)	200 g	500 g
Red onion – finely shredded	200 g	500 g
Fresh pesto		
Freshly torn basil leaves		

energy	cal	fat	sat fat	carb	sugar	protein	fibre
1211 kJ	292 kcal	25.1 g	9.2 g	7.4 g	5.4 g	9.6 g	1.5 g

METHOD OF WORK

1 Mix the tomatoes, feta cheese and sliced red onions in a bowl.
2 Coat with the dressing (pesto) and check for seasoning.
3 Place in a suitable bowl and sprinkle with freshly torn basil leaves.

Vegetable salad/Russian salad

Ingredients	4 portions	10 portions
Shelled peas	100 g	250 g
Green beans	100 g	250 g
Cauliflower florets	6	15
Potatoes	2	5
Carrots	2	5
Small gherkins – drained and diced	3	8
Cooked beetroot – diced	1	3
Mayonnaise to bind		

energy	cal	fat	sat fat	carb	sugar	protein	fibre
1111 kJ	267 kcal	12.6 g	2.2 g	30.4 g	8.1 g	9.3 g	6.7 g

METHOD OF WORK

1 Cook the peas, beans, caulilower, potatoes and carrots in separate pans of boiling water until al dente. Drain well and chop into fairly small dice (other than the peas).

2 Put all the vegetables in a salad bowl with the gherkins, beetroot.

3 Bind with the vinaigrette (or mayonnaise). Check and adjust the seasoning.

4 Chill in the refrigerator for at least 1 hour.

5 Serve in an appropriate dish or bowl. Some neatly diced blanched tomatoes (concasser) and sliced spring onions can be used to garnish and complement the salad (optional).

Mint sauce

Ingredients	8 portions
Mint (fresh or dried)	2-3 tbsp
Caster sugar	1 tsp
Vinegar	125 ml

energy	cal	fat	sat fat	carb	sugar	protein	fibre
38 kJ	9 kcal	0.0 g	0.0 g	1.5 g	0.8 g	0.2 g	0.4 g

METHOD OF WORK

1 Chop the washed, picked mint and mix with the sugar.

2 Place in a bowl and add the vinegar.

3 If the taste is too sharp, dilute it with a little water.

Fresh fruit salad

Ingredients	*4 portions*	*10 portions*
Orange	1	2-3
Dessert apple	1	2-3
Dessert pear	1	2-3
Kiwi	1	2-3
Grapes	25 g	100 g
Mango	1	2
Plum	2	5
Peach	1	2
Banana	1	2-3
Soft fruits (e.g. strawberries, raspberries, blueberries)	40 g	100 g
Stock syrup		
Caster sugar	50 g	125 g
Water	125 ml	375 ml
Lemon, juice of	½	1

energy	cal	fat	sat fat	carb	sugar	protein	fibre
926 kJ	218 kcal	0.7 g	0.1 g	54.2 g	51.7 g	2.4 g	5.7 g

METHOD OF WORK

1. For the syrup, boil the sugar with the water and place in a bowl.
2. Allow to cool, add the lemon juice.
3. Peel and cut the orange into segments.
4. Quarter the apple and pear, remove the core, peel and cut each quarter into two or three slices, place in the bowl and mix with the orange.
5. Stone the peach and plums, cut in half and then into slices
6. Cut slices, lengthways through the mango, cut the flesh into squares by making slices into the flesh one way and then another. Invert and then cut the cubes from the skin.
7. Cut the grapes in half, peel if required, and remove the pips.
8. Wash and hull strawberries and cut in half if large.
9. Mix carefully and place in a glass bowl in the refrigerator to chill.
10. Just before serving, peel and slice the banana and mix in.

Rice salad

Ingredients	4 portions	8 portions
Tomatoes	100 g	250 g
Long grain rice – cooked	100 g	250 g
Peas – cooked	25 g	60 g
Haricot verts (cooked and finely sliced)	25 g	60 g
Mixed peppers (de-seeded and cut into fine dice)	25 g	60 g
Vinaigrette	1 tbsp	2 ½ tbsp
Salt		

energy	cal	fat	sat fat	carb	sugar	protein	fibre
442 kJ	107 kcal	6.9 g	1.0 g	9.2 g	1.0 g	1.7 g	1.2 g

METHOD OF WORK

1. Cut the tomatoes into quarters, remove the seeds and cut in ½ cm dice.
2. Mix the tomatoes with the rice, peas, haricots verts, mixed peppers and vinaigrette.
3. Taste and correct the seasoning.

Green vegetable salad

Ingredients	4 portions	10 portions
Green beans – cooked	200 g	500 g
Vinaigrette	1 tbsp	2.5 tbsp
Onion – chopped and blanched if required	15 g	40 g
Chives – chopped into snippets	To garnish	To garnish
Spring onion	2	5
Green pepper – cut into small dice	1	2
Gherkin – sliced (optional)	2	5
Celery – peeled and sliced	0.5	1

energy	cal	fat	sat fat	carb	sugar	protein	fibre
424 kJ	102 kcal	7.2 g	1.0 g	7.6 g	5.8 g	2.4 g	3.7 g

METHOD OF WORK

1. Combine all ingredients.
2. Bind with the vinaigrette
3. Taste and season with salt and freshly ground pepper.

Couscous salad

Ingredients	*4 portions*	*8 portions*
Couscous	100 g	400
Boiling water or stock	To cover	To cover
Vegetable oil	3 tbsp	7 tbsp
Onion – chopped	50 g	125 g
Garlic cloves – crushed	2	5
Courgettes – diced	2	5
Red pepper – deseeded and diced	1	2 ½
Cumin – ground	1 tsp	2 ½ tsp
Paprika	1 tsp	2 ½ tsp
Ginger – ground	½ tsp	1 ¼ tsp
Allspice	½ tsp	1 ¼ tsp
Fresh coriander	2 tbsp	5 tbsp
Blanched tomato	1	2

energy	cal	fat	sat fat	carb	sugar	protein	fibre
1064 kJ	256 kcal	17.1 g	1.4 g	21.2 g	7.4 g	5.5 g	3.5 g

METHOD OF WORK

1. Heat the oil in a pan and gently fry the onion and garlic until soft and golden brown.
2. Add the courgettes and red pepper, and gently fry, stirring occasionally.
3. Add the spices and cook for 1 minute.
4. Place the couscous in a sauce pan and just cover with the water or stock. Leave for 3 to 4 minutes and then separate the grains and fluff up the couscous.
5. Mix the vegetables with the couscous.
6. Cut the tomato into neat dice and sprinkle over the salad.
7. Sprinkle with freshly chopped coriander.
8. Season with a suitable dressing – e.g. vinaigrette, olive oil or a mixture of sesame oil and soya sauce if a more oriental taste is desired.

Cucumber salad

Ingredients	*4 portions*	*10 portions*
Cucumber	0.5	1
Dill – chopped	10 g	25 g
Vinaigrette	1 tbsp	2.5 tbsp

energy	cal	fat	sat fat	carb	sugar	protein	fibre
270 kJ	66 kcal	6.7 g	1.0 g	1.0 g	0.7 g	0.5 g	0.4 g

METHOD OF WORK

1. Peel the cucumber and slice finely. Alternatively, cut the cucumber into small dice (as shown in the picture above).
2. Bind with the vinaigrette and mix in the chopped dill.
3. Chill and serve.

Salsa

Ingredients	4 portions	10 portions
Blanched tomatoes – diced	2	5
Onion – finely chopped	1	2.5
Chilli – finely chopped	1	2
Peppers – cut into dice	1	2.5
Vinaigrette	1 tbsp	2.5 tbsp

energy	cal	fat	sat fat	carb	sugar	protein	fibre
372 kJ	90 kcal	6.9 g	1.0 g	6.1 g	4.8 g	1.2 g	2.0 g

METHOD OF WORK

1 Mix all prepared ingredients together.

Note: This is a raw salsa as opposed to one that is cooked and more like a sauce. A raw salsa makes a very fresh accompaniment to grilled or barbecued meat and fish.

Iced Amaretto

Ingredients	8 portions
Double cream	350 ml
Egg yolks	4 yolks
Sugar	100 g
Amaretto	75 g
Leaf of gelatine	1 leaf
Victoria plums	8
Plum syrup	
Water	300 ml
Suger	300 g
Star anise	1 star anise
Cinnamon stick	½ stick
Split vanilla pod	1 pod
Clove	1 clove

METHOD OF WORK

1 Whisk the double cream until holding but not too firm, reserve.

2 Put the yolks into a mixing bowl and slowly whisk, cook the sugar to 121°C.

3 Pour the sugar onto the yolks and mix, dissolve the pre-soaked gelatine in the warmed Amaretto, pass into the mixture and continue whisking until cold.

4 Gently fold the whipped cream into the egg/sugar mixture until incorporated.

5 Mould and freeze until required.

For the plums

1 Split the plums in half and remove the stone.

2 Make a syrup with the remaining ingredients in table.

3 Add the plums to the boiling syrup, bring back to the boil and then leave to cool.

To Serve

De-mould the parfait and place on the plate, decorate with a little crème Anglaise and some reduced plum syrup. Garnish with a biscuit (brandy snap or cigarette) sprinkled with finely chopped pistachio nuts.

APPENDIX 1: AREAS WHERE HAZARDS MIGHT OCCUR

STEP	HAZARD	CONTROL
Purchasing	• Contaminated high risk foods • Damaged goods • Growth of pathogens during delivery	• There must be sufficient storage facilities • Purchase only from approved suppliers • Deliveries to be delivered under suitable conditions. Chilled food at 8°C or below Frozen food at –18°C or below
Receipt of goods	• Contaminated high risk foods • Damaged or decomposed goods • Incorrect specifications • Growth of pathogens between the time of receipt and storage	• All deliveries checked • Appropriate labelling • Prompt and correct storage
Storage	• Contamination of high risk foods • Contamination through poor handling • Contamination by pests • Spoilage of food by decomposition	• Correct usage of refrigeration regimes • Foods suitably stored in the correct packaging or receptacles • Materials that are in direct contact with food must be of food-grade quality • A contract for a pest control service must be in place • Correct stock rotation • Out of date and unfit foodstuffs removed from the premises
Preparation	• Contamination of high risk foods • Contamination through poor handling • Growth of pathogens and toxins	• Keep raw and cooked foods separate • Use pasteurised eggs for raw and lightly cooked egg dishes • All food contact surfaces must be fit for purpose • Food handlers trained in hygienic food handling techniques • Keep the exposure of fresh foods at ambient temperatures to a minimum • Label all food that is to be used more than one day in advance of production with its description and use by date
Cooking	• Survival of pathogens and spores	• Cook all foods to the minimum recommended temperature
Chilling	• Growth of pathogens, spores = Toxin production • Contamination	• Cool foods as quickly as possible, to 8°C in 90 minutes • Keep food that is chilling loosely covered • Use only clean equipment
Hot hold	• Growth of pathogens and toxin production • Contamination by staff and customers especially in self service operations	• Maintain food at 63°C and discard after two hours • Keep containers covered when not in service • Use sneeze screens • Supervise self service
Cold hold	• Growth of pathogens and toxin production • Contamination by staff and customers especially in self service operations	• Keep food at 5°C and discard after four hours • Keep containers covered when not in service • Use sneeze screens • Supervise self service
Cold takeaway	• If the food is kept at ambient temperature there can be increased growth of pathogens and toxin production while in the possession of the customer	• Keep food refrigerated at 5°C until being sold • Meals to be given out no longer than four hours prior to the time of consumption • Use insulated containers and freezer pack
Hot serve	• Growth of pathogens, spores = Toxin production • Contamination	• Serve immediately on removal from holding equipment • Keep food covered when service is not in progress

APPENDIX 2: BEEF CUTS CHECKLIST

Timings vary according to the thickness of the meat and the degree of cooking preferred.
Timings given are approximate each side.

	GRILLING	FRYING/ GRIDDLING/ DRY FRYING	STIR FRYING	ROASTING	CASSEROLE STEW POT ROAST BRAISING
Beef Steaks					
Sandwich 1–2mm (1/8")	1–2 mins each side	45 secs–1min each side	Not recommended	Not recommended	Not recommended
Thin cut sirloin steaks 1.5cm (5/8")	2–4 mins each side	2–4 mins each side	Cut into strips: 2–4 mins+2 mins with veg	Not recommended	Not recommended
Sirloin, rump, rib eye 2cm (¾")	Rare: 2½ mins Med: 4 mins Well: 6 mins Each side	Rare: 2½ mins Med: 4 mins Well: 6 mins each side	Cut into strips: 2-4 mins+2 mins with veg	Not recommended	Not recommended
Fillet, T-bone, frying, medallions 2–3cm (¾–1¼")	Rare: 3–4 mins Med: 4–5 mins Well: 6–7 mins each side	Rare: 3–4 mins Med: 4–5 mins Well: 6–7 mins each side	Not recommended	Not recommended	Not recommended
Stewing steak (chuck, blade)	Not recommended	Not recommended	Not recommended	Not recommended	Oven temp: gas mark 3, 170°C, 325°F Stew 2–3 hours
Braising steak (shin, leg, neck)	Not recommended	Not recommended	Not recommended	Not recommended	Braise 1½–2½ hours
Beef Joints					
Sirloin, topside, top rump, silverside, rib, brisket	——	—— Do not use these methods for joints	——	Sirloin, topside, top rump, silverside, rib: Oven temp: gas mark 4–5, 180°C, 350°F **Rare** 20 mins per 450g/½kg(lb) + 20 mins **Medium** 25 mins per 450g/½kg(lb) + 25 mins **Well done** 30 mins per 450g/½kg(lb) + 30 mins	Silverside, rib and brisket: Oven temp: gas mark 4–5, 180°C, 350°F **Pot roast** 30–40 mins per 450g/½kg(lb) + 30–40 mins

Glossary

Abrasions scratches.
Accommodation somewhere to stay e.g. a room in a hotel.
Additives and preservatives additional ingredients, sometimes chemically based, to enhance flavours and extend the life span of the product.
Alloy mixture of two or more metals (used to make knives).
Ambient temperature the surrounding air temperature.
Antibacterial gel gel that sterilizes and prevents contamination.
Anti perspirant prevents sweating.
Appetizing appealing, tasty and attractive.
Aromatic ingredients ingredients that create an aroma or fragrance to the dish – e.g. herbs.
Artisan producer someone highly skilled in their vocation or profession – e.g. an artisan baker.
Assessment measurement or review of skills and/or knowledge.
Bain-marie large container of hot water, usually attached to the kitchen range, in which foods (e.g. soups, sauces, mashed potatoes) can be kept hot without burning.
Baste to spoon the cooking fat or liquid over food (e.g. roast joints of meat and poultry) during cooking to keep it moist and succulent.
Beat to mix fat and sugar rapidly until the mixture is light, aerated and almost white. This is a method used when making many pastry products. 'Beat' is also used sometimes when whipping egg whites to incorporate air, e.g. when making meringues. Also referred to as whisking.
Blanch and refresh food items, such as vegetables or fruit, are cooked briefly in boiling water then cooled rapidly in iced or running cold water to stop cooking. The food items are reheated before serving. Tomatoes, for example, can be skinned more easily if they are scored before placing in boiling water for ten seconds and then refreshed in iced water.
Blend to take various ingredients and gently mix (blend) them, e.g. rubbing fat into flour when making pastry, selecting and mixing spices for a savoury dish. Also the mixing (blending) of food (e.g. a soup or sauce) to produce a smooth texture.
Bodily functions the various work the body performs e.g. walking, talking, listening, repairing injuries, etc.
Bouquet garni a small bunch of herbs (e.g. parsley stalks, thyme and bay leaf) tied with string in-between two pieces of leek and/or celery or wrapped in a piece of muslin. It isused to give extra flavour to certain dishes, e.g. soups, sauces, stews.
Brunoise cut of small dice, usually vegetables.
Buffet selection of foods (hot and/or cold) on display, which customers may help themselves to or be served, e.g. cold meats, salads, pastry items, hot food and accompaniments.
Carcass the skeleton of an animal (after removing the meat).
Career progression changing from one job or role to another, usually as a promotion or to advance a career.
Cell structure the way our cells in our bodies are organized.
Chinois conical strainer used for straining foods in small quantities (as opposed to a colander, which is used for larger quantities). The mesh may be fine or coarse. Coarse chinois are also used for passing soups and sauces.
Circumstances situations or times when a situation occurs.
Compensation a payment made for damages (to health, property, reputation, etc.).
Concassé coarsely chopped e.g. peeled and deseeded tomatoes.
Consolidated combined, brought together.
Consumption the intake/eating of certain foods.
Contribution the input individuals make towards a goal/ target.
Cook out to carefully cook the flour in a roux, sauce, soup or stew.
Correcting seasoning and consistency adjusting the seasoning and consistency to improve a sauce before eating.
Corrosion something (material) that is subject to decay.
Creativity originality, imagination, vision, inventiveness.
Criticisms people stating their disapproval or disagreement.
Cuisine the style of food produced and offered by a restaurant.
Deodorant conceals (covers up) undesired smells.
Dietician a person qualified to regulate the amounts and kinds of foods eaten.
Digestion food/nutrients being absorbed/processed by the body.
Dimension another level (additional) of flavour.
Disposable towels towels that are thrown away after use.
Domestic used at home rather than in a commercial (working) environment (situation).
Drain to place food (e.g. cooked vegetables) in a colander to allow the water to drain away.
Economical the cheapest or providing the best value.
Economy the relationship between money, industry and employment in a country.
Egg wash beaten egg with a little milk added.

Emergency Services Police, Fire Brigade, Ambulance.
Enhanced improved by the addition (e.g. of herbs).
Escalope a thin slice of meat, e.g. pork, turkey.
Excreta waste discharged from the body – faeces, urine.
Exposure being in contact or in the direct environment e.g. exposure to loud noises could cause hearing problems.
Fire detection equipment equipment that detects smoke and/or heat and raises the alarm, e.g. smoke alarms.
Flammable substances materials/liquids that will ignite.
Flan an open pastry tart with a filling that can be sweet (e.g. lemon, fruit) or savoury (e.g. quiche).
Hazardous substances materials/liquids that could cause injury or damage to health.
Hors d'oeuvre an appetizing cold or hot first course dish (starter) or a small selection of dishes, e.g. vegetable salad, crab salad, meat salad.
Garam masala a combination of spices that includes black cardamoms, cinnamon, black cumin, cloves, nutmeg and black peppercorns. The mixture should be used sparingly and is usually put into foods towards the end of their cooking period. It can also be used as a final light sprinkle over cooked foods, e.g. cooked meats, vegetables, soups. It is used predominantly in Indian cuisine.
Garnish the final trimming or addition to a plate or dish of food, e.g. glazed vegetables, chopped herbs.
Grate to use a food grater to shred foods (e.g. carrot, cheese) into fine pieces.
Graze to nibble or use as a snack/a light bite.
Humidity the amount of moisture in the air.
Immune system the body's natural resistance to disease. This protects the body and promotes recovery.
Induction a period of induction and initial training in the workplace/organization.
Inferior of a lower standard.
Infused items immersed/soaked in a liquid to extract their flavours.
Ingestion eating.
Innovation new ideas and styles.
Insulated containers lined to prevent temperature change, protected.
Intense method deep, severe and powerful.
Intensify flavour to make stronger.
Interpersonal relationships the way people get along/the relationship (working) between people.
Jardinière vegetables cut into batons
Julienne vegetables cut into fine strips.
Jus-lié a gravy thickened with arrowroot diluted in water, used for many dishes, e.g. chicken casserole.
Knead technique when making strong doughs (e.g. for bread, buns). When the dough is first mixed it is sticky. It has to be worked and manipulated in a strong way (kneaded) until it is smooth.
Labour costs the costs of employing staff.
Lardons small pieces of streaky bacon. These are usually shallow fried to a golden brown colour and used as a garnish in many dishes and salads.
Legislation law that has been passed by an official body (government).
Liaison combination e.g. of cream and egg yolks.
Licensed sector pubs, bars and clubs.
Liquidize to make various foods (e.g. soups, sauces, smoothies) into smooth mixtures using a food processor.
Lubricate to make fluid and allow movement.
Manufacturer the producer of the product (e.g. food).
Marinade mixture used to flavour and tenderize food. There are two types of marinade.

- A wet marinade is a rich, spicy, pickling liquid (usually made of red wine, oil and vinegar, herbs and spices). Meats (e.g. beef) are soaked in the mixture to give them flavour and to tenderize.
- A dry marinade is a mixture of herbs and spices that can be sprinkled onto meat.

Marinate to flavour food with a marinade.
Marketing potential the opportunity for positive advertising and promotion.
Menu list of all the dishes available and their prices.
Mirepoix mixture of roughly cut onions, carrots, leeks and celery.
Mise-en-place the basic preparations that need to be done before the service begins.
Misinterpretation misunderstanding/misreading a form of communication.
Mixing ingredients (e.g. for soups, salads, cakes) to produce the correct consistency, texture, blend and finish.
Moist environment wet/humid atmosphere/surroundings.
Monitoring food checking and observing the food throughout the cookery process.
Muscular structure the composition (arrangement) of muscles (i.e. in a piece of meat).
Muslin delicate cotton fabric used in cookery for its infusion and straining properties.
Nausea feeling sick/sickness.
Nutrient imbalance disproportion – uneven and unsuitable range of nutrients consumed.
Nutritional deficiency shortage of certain nutrients in the diet.
Nutritional requirements the nutrients (types of food) the body requires to function properly and efficiently.
Obesity overweight/carrying a higher level of fat than is considered to be healthy.
Obligatory compulsory, absolutely necessary.
Offal the edible innards of an animal, e.g. liver, kidneys, heart, etc.
Organism life form.
Origin of food where the food comes from (its source).
Oven chamber the oven compartment.
Particularly absorbed (e.g. water) is partially soaked up (e.g. when cooking pasta).
Pathogen bacteria that can cause disease.
Pané food (e.g. chicken meat, fish) that has been coated with flour, egg wash and breadcrumbs before frying.
Passing forcing a liquid (e.g. sauce) through a conical strainer (chinois).
Penetrate to go through, e.g. for heat to penetrate food.
Portable appliances small pieces of electrical equipment which can be moved from one location to another.
Portion control the number of portions expected from an item of food, e.g. a roast chicken to serve four people.
Premises building, property.
Preserve to protect and sustain the life of foods.
Productivity the output from staff – how much work is produced in a period of time.

Programmed controlled by an automated system e.g. computerized.

Prohibited forbidden, illegal, not allowed.

Proportion of ingredients the balance of ingredients or ratio.

Prove term applied when making yeast dough products. After the dough has been mixed it is covered and left in a warm place to double in size (to prove).

Pulses dried peas and beans

Ragout stew, usually applied to a beef stew.

Reduce to reduce the quantity of a stock by gentle simmering. This concentrates the flavour (makes it stronger).

Refresh to place hot food under cold running water, e.g. meats and bones should be refreshed after they have been blanched.

Roux a basic mixture of fat or oil and flour that is cooked and used for thickening a variety of sauces, e.g. béchamel, velouté, espagnole.

Salamander a grill that heats from above.

Sanitization very clean and hygienic.

Sauté to toss in fat, a form of shallow frying, e.g. sauté potatoes, chicken sauté. Literally means 'to jump'.

Scalding a burn caused by water vapour or hot liquid.

Score to cut lightly through the fat or the skin (e.g. best-end of lamb/loin of pork) with a small sharp knife before cooking.

Seasoning salt and usually pepper to a dish to enhance flavour. White pepper should be added to light-coloured sauces and fresh black pepper to dark sauces. Seasoning should be added carefully in stages, tasting each time a little more is added.

Sector a part/division of the whole (industry), e.g. restaurants are one sector of the hospitality and catering industry.

Septic an injury that has become infected.

Servicing equipment checked/examined by professional people to ensure that it is safe and in good working order.

Shred to slice vegetables into very fine strips. The opposite of 'chopping'. For example, to shred an onion:

1. Peel it and cut it in half.
2. Remove the root.
3. With the root pointing away from you, slice the onion into very fine slices.

Simmer bringing a liquid to the boil and then lowering the heat so that it is gently bubbling to avoid damage or break-up.

Skim to remove any fat or scum (which may contain impurities) from the surface of a simmering liquid (e.g. stock). If you do not skim frequently, some of the fat or scum may boil into the liquid and spoil its flavour.

Smoked foods foods that have been cured or cooked by placing in a smoke-filled environment (e.g. from cindering oak chips) to impart flavour, e.g. smoked salmon, smoked duck breast, smoked garlic, etc.

Specification of a dish the conditions expected or desired in a dish, e.g. quality checks – size, appearance, taste, etc.

Spores a resistant form taken by some bacteria and fungi in response to adverse conditions.

Straining as for passing.

Stock rotation ensuring that stock is used in the correct order to minimize waste and/or deterioration.

Submerged placed under/flooded by, e.g. water or oil.

Sweat to cook vegetables (e.g. cut vegetables for a soup) with a little fat in a covered pan without colouring. This is an important process that, if carried out correctly, improves the quality and flavour of the dish.

Tainted (by fumes) spoilt by the flavour imparted by the fumes.

Thermostatic control a device that senses and controls temperature.

Transfer of heat heat moving from one location to another – i.e. from the heat source into the pan, then from the pan into the oil and finally from the oil into the food (in shallow frying).

Transferable shelf a shelf that can be moved to various areas, e.g. of a grill or oven.

Velouté a French term associated with sauces and soups. It reflects the velvet-like texture that should be present in a veloute sauce or soup.

Ventilation circulation of clean/fresh air.

Versatility flexible and very useful.

Visually clear apparent by sight, e.g. a surface could be extremely hot but this may not clear by its appearance.

Vulnerable groups people that are at a higher risk than normal.

Whisk mix thoroughly to blend two ingredients e.g. mayonnaise; beat to incorporate air and increase volume e.g. egg whites or meringues and cream. A whisk is also the piece of equipment that can be used to do the whisking.

Working in isolation working alone – by themselves.

Working methodically working in a well-organized, systematic and thoughtful way.

Working practices the systems/approaches to work.

Index